The Future of the
Multinational Company

The Future of the Multinational Company

Edited by:
Julian Birkinshaw
Sumantra Ghoshal
Constantinos Markides
John Stopford
George Yip

London Business School

WILEY

Other Wiley Editorial Offices

John Wiley & Sons Inc., 111 River Street,
Hoboken, NJ 07030, USA

Jossey-Bass, 989 Market Street, San Francisco,
CA 94103-1741, USA

Wiley-VCH Verlag GmbH, Boschstr. 12,
D-69469 Weinheim, Germany

John Wiley & Sons Australia Ltd, 33 Park Road,
Milton, Queensland 4064, Australia

John Wiley & Sons (Asia) Pte Ltd, 2 Clementi Loop #02-01,
Jin Xing Distripark, Singapore 129809

John Wiley & Sons Canada Ltd, 22 Worcester Road,
Etobicoke, Ontario, Canada M9W 1L1

Wiley also publishes its books in a variety of electronic formats. Some content that appears in print
may not be available in electronic books.

Library of Congress Cataloging-in-Publication Data
Future of the multinational company/edited by Julian Birkinshaw . . . [et al.].
        p. cm.
    Includes bibliographical references and index.
    ISBN 0–470–85065–5 (cloth: alk. paper)
    1. International business enterprises.   I. Birkinshaw, Julian M.
    HD2755.5.F865 2003
    658′.049–dc21   2003007457

British Library Cataloguing in Publication Data
A catalogue record for this book is available from the British Library

ISBN: 0–470–85065–5

Typeset in 10/12pt Garamond by Florence Production Ltd, Stoodleigh, Devon.
Printed and bound in Great Britain by TJ International Ltd., Padstow, Cornwall
This book is printed on acid-free paper responsibly manufactured from sustainable forestry
in which at least two trees are planted for each one used for paper production.

Contents

Introduction

This book has its origins in a *festschrift* for John Stopford – a celebration of his ideas and achievements as an academic – held at the London Business School (LBS) in June 2002. John was nearing his formal retirement from the LBS, though anyone who knows John is fully aware how little difference that will make to his work or to his intellectual curiosity. But this event, we realized, was an excellent opportunity to bring together a group of scholars with whom John had interacted over his 30-year career, both to honour his contribution to the fields of international business and strategy, and also to engage in a dialogue around the contemporary challenges facing multinational enterprises.

The conference brought together four generations of academics from around the world, from John's classmates at Harvard Business School in the late 1960s through to the current crop of PhD students at the London Business School today. Over two glorious summer days, we discussed a wide-ranging set of issues from the moral imperatives of capitalism through to the logic of open-source software development. The common thread was essentially John's academic career – the broad set of issues that occupied his attention as a researcher, writer, teacher and consultant, and in particular his three most influential books – *Managing the Multinational Enterprise* (co-authored with Lou Wells), *Rival States: Rival Firms* (with Susan Strange), and *Rejuvenating the Mature Business* (with Charles Baden-Fuller). We invited leading academics to prepare papers on each of these topic areas, and the papers were then brought together and edited to create this book. The net result is a collection of observations, new ideas and research findings from 19 of the most well-respected thinkers in the fields of strategy and international business.

Overview

There are four sections to the book. Each of the first three is focused around the theme of one of John Stopford's major books, with between four and eight papers looking at different aspects of that theme. The final section consists of a retrospective paper by John himself, pulling together some of the common threads from his 30 years of academic work.

Section One: Rival States, Rival Firms[1]

The first section builds on John's book with the late Susan Strange written in 1992. This book quickly became an important contribution to the field of International Political Economy, and more specifically to the debate surrounding the relationship between the nation state and the multinational enterprise (MNE). Stopford and Strange showed how global structural changes often compelled governments to seek the help and cooperation of managers of multinational enterprises. Growing interdependence meant that the rivalry among states and the rivalry among firms had become fiercer. The four chapters in this first section all relate to how continuing globalization is affecting the behaviour of firms, partly in how they relate to governments. Interestingly, the relatively low emphasis on the roles of governments reflects the continuing shift of relative power between states and firms in the 1990s. As firms have globalized more their dependence on national governments has become less.

Chapter 1 by Louis Turner (*The (A)political Multinational: State–Firm Rivalry Revisited*) deals the most directly with state–firm rivalry. He briefly surveys the shifting balance of power between the two, from the era of multinational ascendancy in the 1960s and 1970s, through the more balanced period of trade liberalization and (generally) harmonious relationships between firms and nation states, to the current backlash against multinationals in the form of the 'anti-globalization' movement. Turner develops a series of eight propositions. These suggest, in broad terms, that most firm–state relationships are now handled in a routinized manner, but there will continue to be a number of important and contentious issues to be resolved, particularly in terms of how firms interact with smaller and less-developed countries.

Chapter 2 by John Dunning (*The Moral Response to Capitalism: Can We Learn from the Victorians?*) deals with the broader issue of the moral basis of capitalism, something of relevance in justifying MNE activity with governments and their electorates. He surveys the moral bases of capitalism over the past two centuries, focusing on the Victorian era. He argues that there are second-order virtues from the operation of capitalism within the framework of the rule of law, such as honesty, trust, hard work, thrift, etc. In the 20th century domestic governments took on a much larger role for such virtues, and extended their role into the international sphere. Dunning advocates for today a soft form of global corporatism: co-operation as a covenant among governments, international organizations, non-governmental organizations (NGOs), and business, in terms of legislation, but also perhaps in terms of legislating morality for the higher virtues.

In Chapter 3, Örjan Sölvell examines *The Multi-home-based Multinational: Combining Global Competitiveness and Local Innovativeness*. He demonstrates how multinational companies no longer depend on their home countries for their

---

1 This discussion draws on comments made by Razeen Sally (London School of Economics) and Neil Hood (University of Strathclyde) during the Symposium in honour of John Stopford.

primary base. Indeed his theme is that many MNEs now have multiple bases from which they derive competitive and other advantages. MNEs need to locate different activities in different geographical 'clusters', the latter being cities or regions that are the centres of innovation for particular industries or parts of the value chain. Successful MNEs will operate in several of these clusters.

Chapter 4 is by Alan Rugman and Alain Verbeke, entitled *Regional Multinationals: The Location-bound Drivers of Global Strategy*. This chapter extends and greatly strengthens their long stream of work on how MNEs operate essentially regional (i.e. multi-country) strategies rather than national or global strategies. At the same time, they focus exclusively on the location of sales as the criterion for globality or regionality. But the competitive advantage of MNEs clearly depends on all the activities in their value chains. So while many MNEs may concentrate their sales within specific major regions such as North America, Europe or Asia, many also operate across regions for other activities such as sourcing and knowledge access and transfer.

Sölvell's and Rugman and Verbeke's chapters also start to show us that MNEs are moving away from dependence on their home bases and hence home governments. So a new evolution of the rivalry between states and firms may become that between rooted states and rootless firms.

Section Two: Managing the Multinational Enterprise[2]

The second section of the book consists of eight papers, all concerned with the strategy and structure of the multinational company. These papers all trace their heritage back to the 'Stopford and Wells' model, which John Stopford proposed in his doctoral thesis, and was later published in *Managing the Multinational Enterprise* (the book essentially brought together Stopford's work on strategy and structure with Wells' work on joint ventures and host government relationships).

The Stopford and Wells model incorporated two important insights. First, it took the logic of environment–strategy–structure fit (Chandler, 1962) into the international domain, by showing how a firm's choice of strategy and structure was predicated on an understanding of the drivers of globalization in its industry. Second, it provided detailed evidence regarding the evolutionary development of organization structure, from the international division to either the global product or area division, through to some form of global matrix (though, to be fair, Stopford placed a question mark after 'global matrix' because there was limited evidence of its emergence at that point).

The first three chapters in this section are concerned primarily with the link between strategy, structure and performance.

Chapter 5, by José de la Torre, José Paulo Esperança and Jon Martínez, is entitled *The Evolving Multinational: Strategy and Structure in Latin American Operations, 1990–2000*. It provides a new angle on an old question. The authors describe their recent empirical study of the structural changes in a sample of multinational firms

2 This discussion draws on comments made by Michael Goold (Ashridge Strategic Management Centre) and Paul Verdin (Solvay Business School) during the Symposium in honour of John Stopford.

operating in Latin America between 1990 and 2000. They found, as expected, that firms were adopting significantly more integrated strategies at the end of the 1990s than at the beginning. They also found an interesting performance link, namely that those firms who most effectively matched their level of integration to the economic drivers were the highest performers. Those firms, in contrast, who adopted excessively or weakly integrated structures were relatively poor performers.

In Chapter 6, Don Lessard describes a fascinating study of the relationship between *Risk and the Dynamics of Globalization*. Lessard uses a longitudinal study of the electric power industry to show how an explicit understanding of the nature of risk, and how firms respond to it, helps to explain the level of globalization in the industry. The electric power industry, it turns out, is highly global in terms of the strategies of companies such as GE, Siemens, and Enron, yet there are few advantages to be gained through cost economies. Instead, the advantages of multinationality emerge from the ability to hedge, diversify, transfer knowledge, and access financial markets, all of which are risk-related factors.

Chapter 7 by Anthony Leung and George Yip is entitled *The Global OEM: The Transformation of Asian Supplier Companies*. This chapter looks at the global strategies of a new category of firms they call Global OEMs (original equipment manufacturers). These firms began as suppliers to large multinationals, but some are now sufficiently large and diverse that they qualify as significant multinationals in their own right. The key difference is that their products are not branded – they are typically sold under their customers' brand names. Leung and Yip describe the key differences between the strategies of Global OEMs and traditional multinationals, in terms of their configuration of activities, market orientation and approach to foreign investment.

The second group of papers in Section 2 are focused predominantly on the evolution of organization structure in the multinational firm.

In Chapter 8, Larry Franko examines the impact of capital market pressures on the strategies and structures of large multinational firms (*Designing Multinational Organizations: Is It All Over Now?*). Franko worked alongside John Stopford in the Harvard Multinational Enterprise project during the 1970s, and he was also an early adherent of the idea that matrix structures would become the dominant way of supporting large multi-country, multi-business firms. But as he shows, the reality turned out rather different. Many of these firms became unduly complex, and under pressure from smaller and more flexible competitors many opted to break themselves up or refocus around a smaller number of businesses. The invisible hand of the market, in other words, won out over the visible hand of management, though as Franko observes this victory was not absolute.

Chapter 9 (*The Customer-focused Multinational: Revisiting the Stopford and Wells Model in an Era of Global Customers*) is by Julian Birkinshaw and Siri Terjesen. It also takes the complexity of the modern multinational as its starting point, and it acknowledges many of the restructuring and refocusing efforts that Franko describes. But the authors then move on to argue that the key structural challenge facing multinationals today is how they manage the interface with their global customers. They show how many multinationals are creating global account management and front-end/back-end structures to deal with the increasing demands from their customers, and they describe the challenges of making these structures work.

In Chapter 10, Eleanor Westney focuses on the role of *Geography as a Design Variable* in the multinational firm. The Stopford and Wells model identified the area (or country) structure as one of the primary structural forms of the multinational, but gradually its importance diminished, and it was superseded by both global business structures and by a variety of process-based organizations. Westney argues why this shift in emphasis occurred, and then shows how the role of geography is beginning to make a comeback. These shifting patterns are described using a detailed analysis of ABB's structural changes during the 1990s.

Chapter 11 by Paul Verdin, Venkat Subramanian, Alice de Koning and Eline Van Poeck is called *Regional Organizations: Beware of the Pitfalls*. Here, the authors evaluate the pros and cons of regional organization structures in multinational companies. Like Eleanor Westney in the previous chapter, they suggest that the shift towards global business unit structures has perhaps gone too far, and that many multinationals are now looking for ways of becoming more responsive to local needs, without losing the benefits of global scale. An attractive solution, they argue, is to create a regional organization structure. Such a structure provides a healthy balance between global and local imperatives, it helps to build critical mass in certain competency areas, and it often serves a 'political' purpose to build buy-in for change. However, the regional organization also has a number of potential pitfalls that need careful attention.

The final chapter of this section, Chapter 12, is by Yves Doz, Jose Santos and Peter Williamson, and is entitled *The Metanational: The Next Step in the Evolution of the Multinational Enterprise*. While it certainly addresses issues of strategy, structure and performance, it represents a significant departure from the previous chapters in one key sense. As the authors explain, a key assumption in the entire multinational management literature is that the firm has a home base, out of which firm-specific and country-specific advantages flow. Their model of the metanational, in contrast, avoids such a restrictive assumption, and shows how it is possible for a firm to seek out, meld and leverage knowledge on a worldwide basis. This chapter builds on their recent book, *From Global to Metanational*.

Section Three: Rejuvenating the Mature Business

The third section, *Rejuvenating the Mature Business,* builds on John Stopford's book with Charles Baden-Fuller. This book was a notable contribution to the literature on organization change, but it also broke new ground in its analysis of such issues as corporate entrepreneurship and renewal. In particular, the 'crescendo' model of rejuvenation proposed by Stopford and Baden-Fuller foreshadowed a great deal of the current thinking on how to effectively manage a large-scale change process.

The first two chapters in this section build explicitly on the ideas in Baden-Fuller and Stopford's book, by offering alternative interpretations of the ultimate drivers of rejuvenation in the specific companies they studied. The next two papers focus on approaches to strategic innovation, as one possible model of rejuvenation. And the final paper takes a tangential approach to the challenge of rejuvenation in large firms by questioning whether such firms are needed in the first place.

It should be noted that while the firms discussed in these five chapters are all multinationals, the emphasis is no longer on the difficulties of managing the relationship with the host country or coordinating across multiple business units in multiple countries. Instead, the emphasis shifts towards the challenges of growth and rejuvenation in a fast-changing business environment; critical issues, to be sure, and in many ways complementary to those discussed in the previous sections.

In Chapter 13, John Stopford and Charles Baden-Fuller re-evaluate and extend the ideas in their 1994 book (*The Critical Role of Sense-making in* Rejuvenating the Mature Business). They first describe the 'crescendo' model of change at the core of the book, and then they focus in on the role of sense-making as a key driver of renewal. Their argument is that a process of collective sense-making among top managers helps to shape the initial framing of their situation, and also motivates the team's subsequent actions. While these themes were present in the original book, eight years of reflection makes it clear to the authors that they underplayed this vital link between strategic analysis and implementation.

In Chapter 14 (*The Invisible Underpinnings of Corporate Rejuvenation: Purposeful Action Taking by Individuals*), Sumantra Ghoshal and Heike Bruch begin at the same point as Stopford and Baden-Fuller: they look back at the four success stories in *Rejuvenating the Mature Business* and they ask themselves, what lay behind these transformations? Their answer is purposive individual action taking. Building on additional case-study data on the four companies in Stopford and Baden-Fuller's book, as well as their own research on Lufthansa, they show how purposive action taking is the engine behind most successful transformations. They then move on to discuss the drivers of purposive action, and the practical steps managers can take to engage those drivers.

The next two chapters by Peter Williamson and Costas Markides are both about *strategic innovation* – how firms create new sources of competitive advantage for themselves, rather than relying on squeezing more out of a decaying or outdated business model. For them, strategic innovation is a powerful form of rejuvenation; it is by no means the only form, because rejuvenation can also be achieved by re-thinking and turning around an existing business model, but it is certainly an important one in today's fast-paced business environment.

Williamson's approach to strategic innovation in Chapter 15 (*Rejuvenation Revisited: Identifying and Managing Strategy Decay and Innovation*) is to invest in real options – in a portfolio of ideas, experiments and ventures all directed towards potentially important capabilities and future customer needs. By actively managing the pipeline of options, and by recognizing when these options should be exercised (or killed), a company is likely to be far better placed to capture new sources of competitive advantage and avoid the worst perils of strategy decay.

Markides' approach to strategic innovation in Chapter 16 (*Racing to be Second: Innovation Through Imitation*) is paradoxically to argue that large firms should not bother with coming up with strategic innovations. He shows how the inherent conflicts between strategic innovations and the firm's established lines of business make such innovations unattractive and almost impossible to manage effectively. Instead, he argues, large firms should focus their attention on responding to the innovations that are bound sooner or later to invade their markets. He then goes on to describe three different ways of responding: focus on the original game to make it more attractive, disrupt the disruptive innovation, and embrace the disruption but scale it up.

Chapter 17, the final paper in this section, is by Rob Grant, Andrea Lipparini, Gianni Lorenzoni, and Elaine Romanelli (*Who Needs Multinationals? Lessons from Open-source Software*). They tackle a rather different initial question: why should the firm be seen as an optimally efficient institution for producing and distributing goods and services across national borders compared with more decentralized modes of ownership and control? So rather than assume that large firms are needed, it may be more useful to examine other possible modes of coordination that do not suffer the typical ailments of inertia, strategy decay and bureaucracy that we find in most large firms.

Grant and his colleagues examine the curious case of Open Source Software (OSS) communities such as Linux that have begun to challenge industry leaders such as Microsoft and IBM, despite being made up of thousands of loosely networked individuals. They ultimately conclude, however, that coordination in OSS communities 'occurs through the same kinds of structures and processes present in conventional business firms'. Whether such communities also end up becoming inertia-ridden and bureaucratic – and in need of rejuvenation – remains to be seen.

Audience

The primary audience for this book is executives working for or advising large multi-national corporations. We have kept the tone informal, avoided academic referencing, and tried to focus on practical insights to managers or policymakers. At the same time, we hope to see a strong uptake among fellow academics and advanced students (MBA or PhD) who are looking for new ideas and themes in the worlds of strategy and international business. This book addresses the 'state of the art' in terms of policies and practices in multinational corporations, so it is important reading for any serious student of the field.

Acknowledgements

The number of authors on the book's cover is a clear sign of the collaborative effort that was required for the whole project to take shape. We would like to acknowledge first of all the contributions from the 17 chapter authors, who made both the conference and the book possible. At the conference there were also valuable commentaries from Razeen Sally, Neil Hood, and Michael Goold, which unfortunately could not be included in this book for space reasons.

Second, there were many people working behind the scenes at the London Business School who put in long hours to help make the book a success. Special thanks to our PhD students – Susan Hill, Mats Lingblad, Susan Lynch, Michelle Rogan, Siri Terjesen, Peter van Overstraeten, Bala Vissa, and Tiemen Wang – for helping with the editing – and to Jo Lakey, Ann-Maree Bolton and Jon Ashton for excellent administrative assistance. We also owe a big debt of gratitude to George Bickerstaffe for his help with creating a consistence style of writing throughout the book.

Finally, we would like to thank Diane Taylor, Susan Williams, Cedric Crocker, and Lorna Skinner at John Wiley, who provided much of the initial impetus behind the conference as well as financial support. They also skilfully maintained the pressure in the months following the conference to ensure that the book came out within 12 months of the original event – no mean feat if our prior experiences are anything to go by.

Julian Birkinshaw
Sumantra Ghoshal
Constantinos Markides
John Stopford
George Yip

Section 1

RIVAL STATES, RIVAL FIRMS

The (A)political Multinational: State–Firm Rivalry Revisited

Louis Turner

Asia-Pacific Technology Network

As a young academic in the mid-1960s I started my career researching the alleged evils of multinational companies. John Stopford first alerted me to the existence of Jean-Jacques Servan-Schreiber's *Le Defi Americain*, the world best seller that triggered a *tsunami* of polemical attacks on that apparently new phenomenon, the multinational corporation (MNC).

We all wrote our books, good and bad but with resounding titles such as *Sovereignty at Bay*, *Silent Surrender*, *Invisible Empires*, and *The Sovereign State*. Then, gradually, through the 1970s, the heat left the debate. Partly this was because the Europeans started to realize that an American 'challenge' built round corporate basket cases such as Chrysler might be somewhat overstated. More importantly, the OPEC revolution of the 1970s led to a systematic 'third world' onslaught on all the old unequal bargains of the colonial era. As nationalizations in developing countries peaked in 1975, so it became much harder to argue that the multinationals ruled the world. If the 'seven sisters' (the oil giants) couldn't look after themselves, why should we worry about other lesser MNCs?

To some European amusement, there was a brief flurry of polemics in the 1980s as aggrieved American authors attacked the Japanese for much the same list of crimes that Servan-Schreiber had aimed at US MNCs some 15 years earlier.

Then, for about a decade, the analysis of corporate power was left to the academics and it was during this period that Stopford wrote his book *Rival States, Rival Firms* with Susan Strange. This was an impressive piece of scholarship, focusing on MNC relations with a trio of developing countries – Malaysia, Brazil, and Kenya. Interesting as it was, I felt that they had chosen the wrong kinds of country, in that the most important developments within the MNC debate were taking place within the industrialized world not within relatively marginal developing economies.

Over the last decade, the polemicists have returned to the fray, primarily coming from an anti-globalization and/or developmental background. Some of them (*Silent Takeover*) take me back to my youth, though the splendidly titled *Jihad vs McWorld* show that there were some new issues in play. However, most of the issues raised are little different from those in the literature of the late 1960s. What is new is the emphasis on 'corporate social responsibility', which has taken some of the themes identified earlier to a much higher level of sophistication.

However, despite the numbers published, I still have not come across one over-arching book that comes close to providing a convincing, balanced overview of the power relations between companies and states. So here I will try to look at the broad range of issues that any such analysis might cover. Some of the issues are of interest to technocrats, others to the radical political scientist. Either way, a balanced view of state–firm relations has to cover both extremes. Since space is limited, I use a series of propositions to stimulate debate.

Underlying Forces

A comprehensive analysis has to range across:

- recent history, looking at trends;
- companies, both big and small;
- industries, be they commodities, manufacturing, or services;
- countries, big, small, industrialized, emerging, resource-rich, resource-poor;
- the different varieties of corporate involvement from out-and-out skullduggery to lobbying on technical regulatory issues;
- the technological infrastructure underpinning MNC activities.

In particular, a comprehensive review has to start with a sense of some of the underlying forces that have changed the state–company relationship over the recent decades. Four key forces can be identified as follows.

First, there has been the communications revolution, which has both increased the power of MNCs by making them more mobile but, simultaneously, decreased their influence by encouraging the rise of well-informed and organized countervailing international non-governmental organizations (INGOs).

Second, there has been the casting-off of dependent mind-sets within the developing world. The breakthrough of the oil states in the early 1970s was a key factor.

Third, there has been the steady march of democracy. This has both increased the legitimacy of regimes in host economies and the transparency within which companies now have to operate.

Finally, there has been the triumph of the market (the neoliberal, or Thatcher/Reagan revolutions). Particularly within the industrialized world, this has brought into power politicians who believe in competition, whatever its nationality.

Proposition 1: The Era of High-profile MNC Skullduggery Did Exist but Came to an End in the 1970s

It is important to accept that, historically, some companies felt that they had the right to select, overthrow, or corrupt national leaders. It did not happen on a huge scale. But companies such as United Fruit in Central America, the oil industry in Iran,

Union Miniere in the Congo, ITT in Chile, and arms companies (Lockheed and Northrop to the fore) all operated on the assumption that local governments could be treated as dispensable. To be fair, as you get closer to the evidence of what actually went on it becomes clear that these companies were often just one of a set of actors. However, the picture of amoral and ruthless executives caring little for democratic niceties is a fair one.

The era when such behaviour would go largely unchallenged came to an end in the early 1970s. First, the resolve of developing world leaders to bring MNCs under control was strengthened by the success of the OPEC powers in clawing back control over oil production. In addition, there was the global outrage, channelled through the United Nations, triggered by the allegations that ITT had been willing to interfere in the Chilean democratic process that ultimately led to the election of President Allende.

Quite simply, developing country governments, which had generally been timid about tackling the colonial-era excesses of MNCs, now realized that parent governments would no longer send in the marines, gunboats, or the CIA to defend their multinationals.

Second, in the post-Watergate era, US legislators produced the Foreign Corrupt Practices Act, which signalled that the overt bribery by American MNCs that had been exposed in the post-1970 period would no longer be tolerated.

Finally, the global storm of anti-ITT protests triggered by the disclosure of its anti-Allende activity ultimately led to its destruction as an independent company. This was an early sign that companies now had to live within an increasingly transparent world. After ITT, there were global protests against Union Carbide for its role in the Bhopal disaster and Exxon for the *Exxon Valdez* oil spill in Alaska. Initially, these protests were uncoordinated but by the 1990s the emergence of INGOs such as Greenpeace meant that corporate transgressions would be punished heavily in the court of world public opinion.

In short, there was both a significant toughening of the attitude of developing world governments and a realization by mainstream MNC managements that there were new limits to their political freedom.

Proposition 2: This Does Not Mean That All Problems to Do with Corruption Have Gone Away

Away from the Anglo-American business world, it becomes clear that the corporate corruption of politicians (sometimes vice versa) is far from being eradicated. Just as the Watergate affair of the early 1970s forced Washington politicians to tighten up political funding from corporations, so the end of the Cold War in the early 1990s allowed investigative judges and journalists to start unravelling the murky funding of anti-communist political parties, which had been tacitly ignored while communism seemed a real threat.

In countries such as Italy, Japan, Germany, and France high-level politicians fell (and were occasionally jailed) for raising funds from corporate (sometimes, as in Italy, from blatantly criminal) sources. In most cases, the politicians were dealing with purely local companies. But there were cases such as ENI in France where corporate funds were being channelled with official support not only through former colonies but also to friendly neighbouring politicians such as Chancellor Kohl in Germany.

During the 1990s the spread of democracy into previously totalitarian states produced other cases of the exposure of the corrupt interplay between national companies and former political elites.

Russia threw up a different kind of problem. In its first post-communist decade, its politicians were effectively creating a democratic society from scratch. Inevitably, there were challenges to the new political structures from a variety of sources, which included the first wave of successful entrepreneurs (the 'oligarchs', which included individuals like Berezovsky) and powerful former state-owned enterprises such as Gazprom. This had monopoly control of the world's largest supplies of natural gas, created at least one prime minister and was influential in Yeltsin's re-election, refused to pay taxes, and generally behaved as a state within a state. At the time of writing, Gazprom is being brought under political control but no history of Russian politics during the 1990s will be complete without an analysis of the interplay between Gazprom, the oligarchs, and the emerging new Russian political elite.

Proposition 3: There Will Continue to Be Contentious Cases Where Companies Are Caught in the Middle of Disputes Not of Their Making

Today, there are a number of cases in which multinationals are involved in politically unpleasant or complicated parts of the world. One thinks of Shell and the hanging of Saro-Wiwa in Nigeria, Talisman Energy in the Sudan, Premier Oil in Burma, and the relationship of De Beers with the 'blood diamonds' that have fuelled civil wars in Central Africa.

At their worst, allegations are made that companies are actively giving support to unpleasant, murderous regimes and that there is blood on their profits.

Significantly, a high proportion of these cases involves resource-based companies. This is a reminder that there are still industries where companies do not have much choice about where they locate their investments. If significant oil reserves happen to be in territory fought over in a vicious civil war, then oil companies are faced with the kind of dilemma that Gulf Oil had during the war for Angolan independence during the 1970s. It will be tempted to do deals with local paramilitary forces on either side simply to protect its operations. Sometimes that means companies will end up giving succour (however tacit) to some less-than-savoury people.

The issue for any company is to know when it should walk away from a particular investment because the human rights implications are so appalling. The trouble is that there always seems to be smaller, more desperate, companies willing to step into any investment vacuum. The temptation therefore will always be for companies to stay put, particularly when the potential reserves are significant (as is the case for Colombia and Nigeria). However even-handed and ethically pure companies may try to be, there will inevitably be cases where world opinion finds it extremely hard to unravel the precise role that particular multinationals have (or should have) played.

Finally, in situations such as civil wars and coups, one should be aware of the sometimes critical importance of company airstrips (whose troops can use them?) and, even, private jets. Even quite small companies will have assets (in the military sense) that can be of significance to one or other side of a dispute. In an era of fragile or failed states, even quite a small company can provide assets that can significantly affect a particular political situation.

Proposition 4: Within the OECD World, the Treatment of MNCs Has Become Increasingly Routine. This Will Also Happen in the Developing World

The contemporary relationship between mainstream MNCs and their host economies is becoming pretty routine. Companies accept the legitimacy of the states within which they invest. They may not enjoy taxation but they accept that states do have the right to tax their operations. They accept that states provide a legal infrastructure within which companies must work and that states also provide educational and security systems.

In this sense, MNCs do not challenge the legitimacy of states and, in a narrow sense, claims that footloose multinationals are going to lead to some kind of stateless world are clearly over-blown.

On the other hand, when one looks at what policies states can practically use to control MNCs, then one sees there are serious constraints on their freedom of action. In fact, what the world has seen in the 40 or so years since *Le Defi Americain* has been an increasingly formal acceptance that MNCs should be given 'national treatment' – treated no differently from locally owned companies.

This shows most obviously in the steady decline in the perceived legitimacy of policies based on 'national champions' or devices like 'screening institutions' such as Canada's FERA, which tried to ensure that foreign investments made a proper contribution to the host economy. In the 1960s and 1970s such policies were accepted as legitimate counters to the power of US companies. Today, they have lost that legitimacy.

Naturally, there are still areas of resistance to MNC investment. Mergers and acquisitions involving foreign companies are still a contentious area. Hostile bids by foreigners are still difficult in most countries bar the US and UK. Change is coming but it is slow. Germany, for example, is still extremely uneasy about Vodafone's acquisition of Mannesmann. Japan has been impressed with Renault's turnaround of Nissan but the relationship between the two companies is still more of an alliance than a formal acquisition.

Given those few examples, why has there been such a substantive change over recent decades? How much has been the result of corporate power? And how much the result of enlightened self-interest?

First, there was pressure from leading economies clearly interested in furthering the interests of their nationally based MNCs. The concept of national treatment was codified by the OECD in the late 1970s and has occasionally been used aggressively. The US, for example, pressured Canada not to designate its Arctic territories as a preserve for the Canadian national oil champion. Similarly, the rapid increase in the number of bilateral investment treaties has meant that a steady stream of new host countries has also been forced to accept this concept.

On the other hand, the Thatcher–Reagan neoliberal revolution of the early 1980s meant that the two leading MNC parent economies were run by political leaders who genuinely believed that competition was good, wherever it came from. By the early 1990s, for example, the UK had, with minimal controversy, let foreigners take control of its consumer electronics, computing, automotive, and financial service industries – a massive retreat from the concept of national champions. This policy has continued. At the time of writing, the UK government is proposing to abolish most of the serious constraints on foreigners buying into the national media – a sector where most countries are still sensitive to foreign ownership.

So far, the MNCs have played a minor role in bringing about this change in political attitudes. Competition for incoming Japanese investment meant that relatively xenophobic countries such as France slowly became aware that they were failing to attract blue-chip Japanese investments, which were going across the Channel to the UK. Inevitably they started to compete with the British in terms of the generosity of their packages for inward investors. And what happened in France was happening elsewhere in the industrialized world. Outside of a few sensitive sectors (the media, aerospace, and telecoms) host governments started to encourage inward investment, and that meant competing with neighbouring countries since most investors had the option to locate a new plant in at least three countries.

However, we should not overstate the power shift towards MNCs that came from their ability to play off one country against another. Corporate taxation has been easing downwards but it has not collapsed.

At the same time, the relocation of established corporate activities is becoming a significant phenomenon that is starting to worry host governments. Within Europe, the relocation of manufacturing to Eastern Europe, with its low labour costs, and the equivalent relocation at a global level to China, is forcing host governments to step up campaigns to reinforce the competitiveness and flexibility of their economies. The Stopford–Strange world in which governments, increasingly concerned with stimulating economic growth, have to compete more ruthlessly for incoming FDI (foreign direct investment) is becoming more convincing.

At the same time, the industrial powers still have considerable coercive power. We are, for example, in the later stages of a concerted attack on the freedoms of tax havens (in itself, this attack is the culmination of a campaign against banking secrecy that started a couple of decades ago). Most of these havens are committed to tightening their regulatory regimes in return for being allowed continued freedom to interact with the world's financial centres.

In turn this points to the ultimate power that the core industrialized powers have over new less-regulated competitors. The dominant capital and merchandise markets are still to be found within the US, Europe, and Japan, which means that new competitors, wanting access to such markets, have to play by their rules. Within the core economies there is competition for MNC investment but mechanisms are in place to avoid such competition becoming self-destructive.

Proposition 5: MNCs Are Increasingly Active in Setting Agendas

If mainstream multinational transactions have become increasingly routine, there are still areas of corporate activity that are of considerable diplomatic interest. In particular, leading MNCs are becoming increasingly active in helping set the global agenda in areas of key concern to them, particularly in trade diplomacy.

US MNCs and their industry lobbies have won the right to sit as advisers to US trade negotiators at WTO rounds. Going back into recent history, one can point to the way that American Express was active in getting financial services put onto the trade agenda. Hollywood was equally active in getting cultural goods into the debate, much to the chagrin of countries such as France, which feel that cultural goods should not be treated as just another commodity.

The culmination of this sector-specific lobbying was the WTO's initiatives in the field of financial services, telecommunications, and information technology. Under these, the bulk of world players (including countries like China) were dragooned into agreeing precise timetables for opening up these markets to foreign trade and investment. These are very significant initiatives given that they involve the countries responsible for at least 80 % of the relevant global transactions. Of course, these are sectors in which US companies are particularly strong and therefore have an interest in seeing investment liberalized as quickly as possible. Sectors in which US companies are more on the defensive (steel, agriculture, autos, and even airlines) have not been targeted for such special treatment.

A second interesting area of corporate diplomacy surrounds the creation of global standards. Sometimes this simply involves companies manoeuvring against each other – Matsushita/JVC's victory over Sony and Philips in video-recorders and the Windows operating system for computers are good examples.

In other areas such as mobile communications, states and companies may work together. Europe, for example, won a stunning success in second-generation mobile communications with its GSM standard, which virtually became the world standard. It gave European companies such as Nokia and Ericsson some golden years in which to build very strong position in global markets (Nokia being the more successful of the two).

In contrast to the close collaboration between European industry and governments in such standard-setting, the US authorities stood back to let the market determine ultimate standards and, in an industry where the size of networks matters, paid the price as consumers held back, uncertain about which standard would win.

As far as GSM's third-generation successor is concerned, the diplomats are firmly back in the fray, trying to ensure that swing countries like Japan, South Korea, and China adopt the American or European-favoured standard. (To show its technological independence, China has developed its own standard.)

In other areas such as memory devices and the operating systems for mobile phones, companies throughout the lead economies are forming shifting alliances to produce the eventual winning standard. In the case of memory devices, there has been an extremely interesting split between the movie makers (paranoid about the pirating of movies) and the computer makers, whose interest is to have memory devices that are as easy to use as is possible.

Sometimes, though, companies are faced with an international community determined to create new rules or regulations for their particular sector. With the rise of INGOs, companies find they sometimes lose control over the international agenda, as the chemical companies did over CFCs and as the energy-production and energy-consumption industries have done with the diplomacy around the Kyoto protocols.

On the CFC front, the chemical companies ultimately chose to work constructively with the new regime. On climate change some of the oil giants such as BP and Shell have similarly chosen a cooperative approach while others like Exxon have taken a hostile stance and are credited (though Exxon denies it was this important) with keeping the US out of the new climate-change regime.

It depends on how apocalyptic one's views on global warming are, but one could argue that the political consequences of Exxon's refusal to accept the general consensus on the scientific evidence could have consequences that will far outweigh the damage stemming from any previous decision by a leading MNC.

Proposition 6: It Is Legitimate to Raise Questions About the Cultural Impact of MNCs

Ted Levitt's arguments about cultural homogenization and the concept of 'Coca-Colonialization' seemed to make sense in a world where global brands were extending their reach, strengthened by internationalization and the emergence of global media empires such as AOL TimeWarner, News Corporation, and Walt Disney. US 'soft power' appeared to be increasing at a time when American 'hard power' seemed close to unstoppable.

In practice, the picture is much more complicated. For those who worry about an American-dominated century (and some do), one only has to look at the globalization of sport. Soccer – dominated by Europeans and Latin Americans – is by far the dominant world sport. US-dominated sports such as baseball, basketball, and American football have failed to find a global standing to rival even such sports as cricket and rugby union, which went international on the back of the British Empire. If media ownership were so important, US-dominated sports should be doing far better in the global market place.

To make sense of arguments about cultural dominance, one has to distinguish between two phenomena.

The first is the ability of Anglo-American companies, taking advantage of the English language and their ability to put global M&A strategies in place, to create global business empires in areas such as the media and branded goods. This seems to be an observable fact and the logic would seem to be that their success will lead to cultural homogenization.

Second, the technology that has broken down hierarchical corporate structures means that we have moved from a world of 'broadcasting' to one of 'narrowcasting' in which programming and brands are aimed at ever-narrower groups of consumers.

Somewhere along the line, Levitt's model of cultural homogenization has become obsolete.

To illustrate, one only has to look at MTV and STAR Television (News Corporation's satellite broadcasting operation in Asia). MTV started with a model of pushing English-language popular music round the globe. But wherever it has gone it has found indigenous reservoirs of pop, which has meant it has had to segment its channels and feature indigenous strands of popular music (J-pop, Hindi-pop, and so on).

Similarly, STAR was created by Hong Kong entrepreneur Richard Li as an English-language satellite channel targeted at Asia's elite. Under Rupert Murdoch's ownership, however, it has indigenized much of its output and is now producing separate programming for south Asia, north Asia, China, and so on.

However, even if one rejects the arguments that global business empires will lead to cultural convergence, one can make the more subtle point that they are still producing ideological convergence towards a consumption-oriented, market-based outlook on life. Broadcasters may not be using English as their chosen language but they are bringing formats (the sit-com, the annual pop music awards, the quiz shows) from the industrialized world. Whatever the language spoken, the underlying attitudes are consumerist and must reinforce wider shifts towards more market-oriented dispositions.

It is no accident that STAR TV began broadcasting into India in the early 1990s just as the country started to liberalize its economy. It is no coincidence that the Chinese authorities are letting STAR into China (with some controls) at the same time as the country is joining the World Trade Organization. The global media empires give implicit ideological support to market-oriented regimes.

One can in fact argue that Rupert Murdoch, having been a crucially important supporter of the Thatcher revolution in the UK, is now, through News Corporation's satellite broadcasting activities in the world's two largest countries, India and China, helping to lock the majority of the world into the market-oriented revolution that Thatcher was so important in launching in the early 1980s.

On a much narrower front, all companies tend to take their dominant managerial cultures with them as they go overseas. In the 1970s and 1980s, the leading examples were the Japanese companies that took the lean manufacturing and quality revolutions with them into Europe and North America. Today, it is Anglo-American investment banks, accounting companies, ratings agencies, and vulture funds that are exporting the Anglo-American business culture into the fledgling capitalist cultures of the former Soviet Union and the communitarian capitalist cultures of continental Europe and Asia.

In the countries of the former Soviet Union, accounting companies and consultancies have been heavily involved in creating the basic legal and regulatory structures needed as they move from command to market economies. The slow reorganizations favoured by communitarian economies are being challenged by the occasional hostile M&A (Vodafone for Mannesmann), the long pursuit of 'zombie' companies – still technically alive but on all objective measurements bankrupt (GM for Daewoo Motors) – successful foreign turnarounds of floundering companies (Renault of Nissan), and hard analysis that exposes the wishful thinking of bureaucrats and executives who want to deny the depth of the problems they face (the ratings agencies and Japan).

Proposition 7: Micro States and Failed States Will Continue to Have Some Problems

At the extremes of the MNC community there are companies that have no real concept of enlightened corporate citizenship. As BCCI showed, legitimate companies can be captured by crooks. As surveys have shown, companies emerging into the international arena from 'crony capitalist' economies are prone to using bribery as a management tool.

This means that there will be inevitable cases of countries being 'captured' by ruthless managements. This may involve a company persuading a state to write its financial legislation in a way that gives the company almost total tax-free independence. It may involve regimes ignoring environmental degradation. At the extreme, it may involve regimes being so heavily bribed or intimidated that they will accept any kind of economic activity on their territory – be it legal or criminal.

Proposition 8: On Balance, Large, Technologically Sophisticated Economies Should Have Little Problem in Keeping Multinationals under Control

The picture that emerges from this analysis is that MNCs have considerable lobbying power that allows them to look after their interests on the world stage. Governments are finding it increasingly difficult to control them. The concept of national champions is close to extinction in the industrialized world, while the idea that governments can protect infant industries is coming under strong attack in the developing world. Footloose industries such as shipping, gambling, financial services, and film production have all developed strategies to minimize their tax obligations on a worldwide basis.

All of this suggests that the balance of power between company and state has swung irrevocably in favour of the former.

However, the picture is far more complex than that.

Basically, the relationship between company and state is like a poker game in which each player – state or firm – has cards whose strengths may well vary over time.

The bargaining power of a particular country will be affected by:

- its population (China has greater power than Fiji);
- its per-capita income (Belgium over Rwanda);
- its mineral resources (Saudi Arabia and Russia over Japan);
- its human resources (East Asia over Latin America on education);
- the competence and coherence of its political elite (East Asia over the average African state);
- its general level of competitiveness (Japan of the 1980s versus Japan of today).

Companies' bargaining power can vary in similar ways in relation to:

- their size (General Motors over a one-person consultancy);
- their technological strengths (Microsoft and Intel over the cement industry – though technology can become obsolete);
- their footlooseness (a shipping company has more bargaining options than a mining or pipeline company; a company has more options when choosing an initial investment site than when the plant is established);
- the power of the parent government (an American over a Taiwanese company).

Viewed in this framework, the advanced industrial countries have rather more power than some pessimists would argue. For example, despite the apparent attractions of tax havens, the authorities in leading financial centres like New York and London have been able to maintain tough reporting requirements because most companies need access to the pools of capital such centres control. Similarly, most companies need access to the richest and most dynamic markets for tradable physical goods.

It is, though, still essential that national authorities consciously work together to counter their tendency to over-compete for new investment. In many areas, such collaboration is working well both within and between NAFTA and the EU. Europe has the problem of overly heavy subsidies under control. The concerted drive against tax havens is putting some kind of floor to the secrecy they can offer.

On the other hand, there are areas of competition between states that are not yet under control. There is, for example, as yet no consensus within the industrialized world about what an ideal level of taxation and social welfare provision should be. So, within a band with the US at one end and the Scandinavian welfare states at the other, companies do have some freedom to relocate within the industrialized world towards the most favorable tax regimes. This suggests that Rhineland capitalism will come under increasing pressure to move taxation rates towards Anglo-American levels.

So, for the mainstream industrial economies, we end with a picture in which companies are active lobbyists, focusing on their particular interests. They do not challenge the legitimacy of the nation state, but they will bargain toughly where they can and they will continually seek the most attractive investment climates on offer that still allow them effective access to markets, supplies of capital, and high-quality employees.

The technical sovereignty of the state is not at issue. However, the explicit and implicit bargaining power of corporations sets limits to the policies that governments can actually impose. Sovereignty is not precisely at bay, but it is being somewhat bruised around the edges.

2 The Moral Response to Capitalism: Can We Learn from the Victorians?

John H. Dunning

University of Reading and Rutgers University

In this chapter we argue that any capitalist system, if it is adequately to fulfil its economic and social objectives, needs the underpinning of a moral ecology that promotes the appropriate values and behavioural patterns in its constituent institutions. A secondary contention is that since the nature and content of any capitalist system depend on its context – and particularly how that changes over time and space – so, in part (but *not* in whole), will the content of that moral ecology.

First, we offer some observations and propositions that, taken as a whole, make up an analytical framework to allow us to evaluate the interaction between the moral health of a nation and the successes and failures of its economic system.

Second, in considering the various concerns expressed about the present state of Western-style capitalism and what might be done about them, we look at the way the Victorians in the UK reacted to the moral challenges and opportunities presented by the emergence of industrial capitalism in the early 19th century. What we find is that although there were many similarities between the two eras of capitalism and their moral imperatives, global capitalism, as it is emerging today, requires its own unique reconfiguration and reprioritization of its ethical foundations.

The Model

The Changing Features of Capitalism

There are six components to the framework we can use in comparing and contrasting present-day capitalism with its Victorian counterpart. Figure 2.1 identifies four of the main features of Western capitalism and how the contents and form of these have changed over three main stages of economic history (our main interest is in comparing the second and third stages). The features identified are: the main sources of wealth creation; how such wealth creation is organized; the spatial radius of the institutions of capitalism; and some of the leading values or virtues that made up the moral ecology of the capitalism of its time.

	17th to Early 19th Century	**19th Century to Later 20th Century**	**Late 20th Century Onwards**
Primary source of wealth and form of activity	Land Based: Agriculture and Forestry. Some local and international merchant commerce	Machine/Finance Based: Manufacturing	Finance/Knowledge Based: Producer and Consumer Services
Spatial dimension	Local/Regional	Regional/National	Regional/Global: but with some national or sub-national clusters
Principal organizational form	Traditional Economy: Mixture of Feudal and Entrepreneurial: Nation state only in its infancy	Managerial/Hierarchical: Generally adversarial economic relationships: Elements of a command economy	More market-oriented: Alliance/Heterarchical: More cooperative economic relationships
Moral virtues	Obedience, externally imposed discipline and enforced trust. Some familial and community spirit of cooperation	Hard work, civic responsibility, social justice, entrepreneurship, individualism	Personal responsibility, creativity, spontaneous sociability, trust, reciprocity and compassion

Figure 2.1—Features of three stages of market-based capitalism (a Western model).

The contents of Figure 2.1 are largely self-explanatory. The important point to stress is that the substance and importance of the features identified have significantly changed over the years as has the 'required' moral capital for their sustenance. More importantly, the values and behavioural mores necessary to uphold a globalizing, knowledge-intensive, and alliance-based capitalist system are different in kind and degree from those that lubricated the smooth functioning of the machine-based, hierarchical, and quasi-international system of the 19th century.

The Institution of Capitalism

Figure 2.2 sets out our view of the four main institutions of the contemporary capitalist system: *the market* (comprising all kinds of buyers and sellers in product, labour, and asset markets); *governments* (at regional, national, or sub-national level); *civil society* (non-profit, cultural, and non-government organizations (NGO); and *supranational entities*.

The role played by each of these institutions is likely to vary according to the particular brand or variety of capitalism being practised, which, as we have said, is context specific. Some of the so-called liberal market economies rely principally on market forces to achieve their objectives. In others, for example coordinated market economies, governments and civil society play a more important role.

Capitalism, then, is a concept much wider than the market. It is best viewed as the system within which the market (and its facilitating and regulatory institutions) is fashioned, embedded, and regulated.

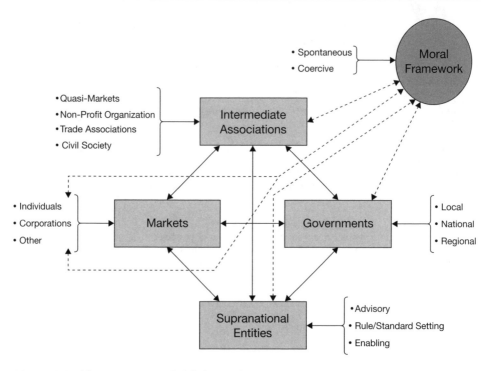

Figure 2.2—The institutions of global capitalism.

Global capitalism embraces all the different brands of capitalism throughout the world and the interactions between them. It is neutral with respect to the goals of its participants, except it does assume that each behaves in a rational and consistent fashion. For the moment, however, there is no such entity as global capitalism as, for example, there is the global firm with a centralized command system. What we have (at best) is a partial integration of the capitalist systems of a large number of countries (including those of a Christian, Judaic, Islamic, or non-religious tradition) in the world economy.

At any given time, each of the four institutions – and the system of which they are part – possesses its own particular stock of moral capital. However, this may change as a result of an upgrading, downgrading, or reconfiguration of moral values both within the system and also outside it (what one might refer to as extra-capitalistic moral values).

Tasks of Capitalism

What is the function of capitalism and its institutions? Figure 2.3 identifies three of its primary goals: to determine how many and which kind of goods and services should be produced; to determine how, by whom, and where these are produced,

---

- How many, what kind and what quality of goods and services should be produced?
  - Tangible and intangible assets
  - Intermediate products, final products
- How, by whom, and where these are produced, using the scarce resources and capabilities available
- The distribution of
  - The means of production
  - The benefits arising from the wealth creating process

Figure 2.3—The tasks of capitalism are to determine these factors.

using the scarce resources and capabilities available; and to determine the distribution of both the means of production and the benefits of the wealth created.

The first goal may be influenced by values of society that are *exogenous* to capitalism *per se*. However, the accumulated experience of its constituents, the role of advertising, government incentives, and enforcement mechanisms may create their own *endogenous* demands. These values can and do change according to income, which particular products are available, and what consumers regard as important to their quality of life. In other words, the provision of final goods and services depends heavily on the context and is influenced by many things including religious ideologies and cultural perceptions. Note, too, that some goals of capitalism may also incorporate the reduction of 'bads' in society (for example drugs, crime, and pollution) and a variety of non-economic objectives such as the protection or promotion of sovereignty, cultural identity, and environmental protection.

The successful achievement of the second goal involves the optimization of economic and organizational efficiency. But it also takes account of the preference of consumers between investment and consumption of goods, of quality of work issues, of the downsides associated with uncertainty and volatility, and of the implications of any concentration of the ownership and management of scarce resources.

The third goal includes the distribution of the ownership and/or control of assets because we are concerned with the allocation of both the costs and benefits of capitalism. These include the ability to create further wealth together with the distribution of the fruits of existing wealth. As capitalism widens its geographical radius, so inter-country distributional issues become more important.

While these are the primary goals sought by all economic systems, there is one other over-arching objective that straddles each. Put in question form, it is: 'For whose benefit is the capitalist system organized?' Is the goal, for example, 'the greatest happiness of the greatest number of people'? Or does it in some way try to distribute the potential benefits according to some measure of deservedness, or between current and future generations? The inter-generational aspects of production and distribution have come to the fore in the last half-century or so.

Two things are certain. The first is that the answer to these questions and the role played by the respective institutions in meeting these goals is strongly contextual. The second is that the moral capital available to and generated by these institutions is a critical ingredient of their success.

Failures of Capitalism

But how can we judge whether or not capitalism is performing these tasks in an optimal way? For the purposes of this chapter, we will focus on ways of improving the existing system rather than to consider any radical alternative to it, though we accept that a pluralism of capitalist systems may be preferable to any dominant (for example US-based) system. To do so, let's consider what are the sub-optimal characteristics of the contemporary state of capitalism and how these might be upgraded without losing benefits elsewhere in the system. (Though this presumes we can identify what is 'optimal' – itself a moving target.)

Figure 2.4 classifies some of the actual or perceived inabilities of capitalism – and particularly global capitalism – to achieve the objectives set out in Figure 2.3 into three main categories: market failure; extra-market institutional failure (for example of civil society, governments, and supranational agencies); and moral (value systems)

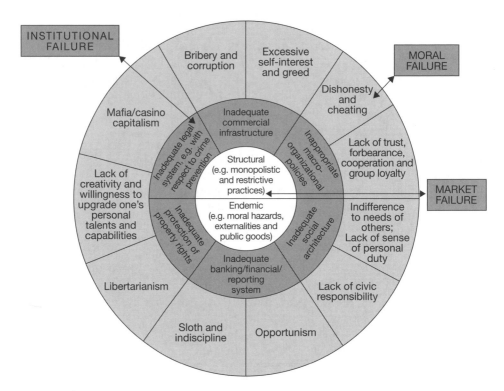

Figure 2.4—Illustrations of three perceived ways in which global capitalism might fail.

failure. Illustrations of each of these – some of which are primarily technical-cum-economic, others of which are social-cum-cultural – are given in the figure.

Until recently, economists – and particularly those steeped in the neoclassical tradition – paid most attention to market failure. But earlier classicists, notably Adam Smith, fully recognized the role of extra-market institutions in setting the framework for and monitoring market transactions and in the direct provision of public goods. For most of 19th and 20th centuries, it was left to sociologists such as Emile Durkheim, political economists such as Karl Marx, and institutionalists such as Thorstein Veblen and John Commons to look into institutional failure. Since the 1980s, the work of Douglass North and latterly that of the World Bank, George Soros, and Lester Thurow has acknowledged the responsibility of non-market institutions in affecting the content of global capitalism and in advancing economic welfare.

But for the most part scholars of all disciplinary persuasions have shied away from the concept of moral failure – or at least that part that is exogenous to the 'proper' working of markets and extra-market institutions. However, over the last 30 years or so, organizational, marketing, and management scholars – and to a certain extent economists – have begun to embrace the concept of culture in their writings.[1]

The Pyramid of Morals

So what is moral failure or a depletion of moral capital? Moreover, assuming these terms can be adequately defined, can we identify an ethos or moral ecology that could command global agreement? In the case of market failure and even many kinds of institutional failure, it is possible (though not easy) to produce a number of objective measures (related primarily to different kinds of inefficiency). In the case of moral failure – at least that part exogenous to market or extra-market failure – this is much more difficult. Moreover, while immorality is generally regarded as a 'bad thing', there is little consensus over what constitutes immorality.

Historically, there have been two extreme approaches to evaluating the role of morality or immorality. One is typified by the statement: 'Do in Rome as the Romans do'. This suggests a strongly relativist and reactive approach to morality; it also implies that any attempt to establish a global ethic is bound to be fruitless.

The other approach is a 'do as you would be done by' philosophy, which assumes that, to some extent at least, human beings have the same feelings, desires, and aspirations. It is, I think, best summed up in the Dalai Lama's belief that 'happiness' and the 'avoidance of suffering' are mankind's two most commonly shared goals.

In the context of commercial transactions and international business, Tom Donaldson takes a 'half-way house' approach. He believes there are some near-universal, basic, or fundamental moral virtues that the great majority of cultures (corporate and country) accept, even though their exact interpretation may differ, while there are others that are specific in space and time.

---

1 See e.g. the interdisciplinary approach taken by various authors in a recently edited volume entitled *Culture Matters* (Harrison and Huntingdon, 2000).

Figure 2.5 presents a pyramid of moral values. Starting at the top are those that come closest to being universally accepted (or are likely to be so). These include those identified by the UN in its *Global Compact,* by Hans Kung in his concept of a *Global Ethic*, and by Donaldson himself. Among the specific core values are respect for life and human dignity, reciprocity, minimum labour standards, truthfulness, and justice.

Further down the pyramid are values such as honesty, solidarity, trust, and forbearance, which are essential to the efficient working of a capitalistic system but which may be subject to subtle differences in interpretation by different cultures. At the bottom of the pyramid are a host of largely contextual 'lesser' virtues (indeed some cultures may not consider them to be virtues at all) such as temperance, reliability, diligence, benevolence, thrift, and self-discipline that may play an important role in influencing economic behaviour.

Each country is likely to generate its own particular pyramid of virtues as, indeed, might the same country over time. Pyramids will vary both according to degree of flatness and content. Certainly, those of countries that are fully involved in a global knowledge-based economy are likely to be different from those of a poorer developing country, whose wealth is largely based on its agricultural sector and which engages in little trade or foreign investment. Similarly, the pyramids of the proponents of Islam are likely to be different from those of their Christian and Jewish counterparts; while, more generally, the balance between upgrading (apparently) conflicting virtues, such as compassion compared to justice and individual freedom compared to social responsibility, may be difficult to achieve.[2]

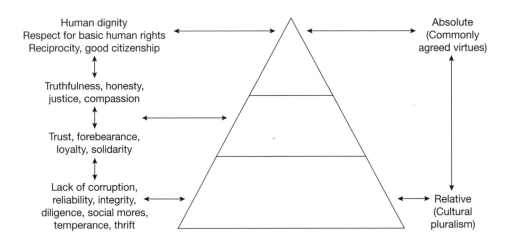

Figure 2.5—The pyramid of moral virtues.

2 In his writings, Isaiah Berlin explored the conjugate principle in some depth. In doing so, he saw fewer conflicts in societal attempts to reduce immorality (i.e. negative virtues) than to promote morality (i.e. positive virtues) (Berlin, 1991).

Upgrading Moral Values

Finally, how can moral values be upgraded in such a way as to reduce the failures of capitalism? We suggest a multi-pronged and interactive approach. In particular, we distinguish between two specific approaches: the 'bottom-up' and 'top-down' approaches. The former is largely proactive, spontaneous, and endogenous. Its stimulus to improving a community's moral ethos comes from individuals, families, and NGOs upwards towards influencing markets, governments, and supranational agencies. The latter largely comprises the regulations, incentives, and moral persuasion by supranational entities and governments (but sometimes, too, by particular interest groups) and how they influence the behaviour of subsidiary institutions and individuals.

The second distinction is between the 'direct' and 'indirect' moral virtues. The former are those that are largely (but not wholly) specific to capitalistic-related transactions, for example honesty, reliability, reciprocity, trust, and so on. The latter are those that comprise the more general moral armoury of society but which, nevertheless, may influence the moral ecology of commercial intercourse.

Figure 2.6 sets out the interaction of these determinants in the form of a 2x2 matrix. On the bottom right-hand side are general legislation, policy initiatives, and moral persuasion by governments to combat social misbehaviour or dysfunction. On the left-hand side are the spontaneous actions by the participants in global capitalism to abide by and/or upgrade the moral underpinnings of the system (for example, avoidance of unethical business practices, intimidatory tactics on the part of special interest groups, minimizing moral hazard by international agencies, and so on).

Again, the relative significance of the role of each of the four boxes (which, incidentally, are not independent of each other, certainly over time) is likely to be contextual and the contents and significance of the 21st century matrix contains both similarities to, and differences from, its 19th century counterpart.

DIRECT (SPECIFIC)	Formation of consumer and investor groups to promote more ethically acceptable behaviour on part of firms, governments, supranational agencies	Codes, legislation/policies/moral suasion of governments and supranational agencies to reducing 'bads' in society, e.g. crime, drugs, anti-social behaviour
INDIRECT (GENERAL)	Recognition of need by individuals, interest groups and firms to upgrade such virtues as truthfulness, honesty, commitment, trust and a sense of social responsibility in their commercial transactions	Promotion (via education, moral suasion *et al.* means) of a more tolerant non-racial and open society

Figure 2.6—Upgrading moral virtues.

The Challenges of Capitalism: Then and Now

Earlier, we looked at some perceived failures of capitalism, though emphasizing that judged in the light of the overall achievement of any capitalist system such failures may be an acceptable price to pay and, in some cases, could not be disentangled from the benefits. At the same time, one implication of this statement is that the winners should be able and willing to compensate the losers; and this, perhaps, is the most daunting challenge of global capitalism.

In considering some of the specific concerns about global capitalism, we will concentrate on those features that, *prima facie* at least, seem to be common to both contemporary and early Victorian capitalism. The basic proposition is that global and knowledge-based capitalism is at a similar stage of development now as was industrial capitalism in the first half of the 19th century.

At that time, the consequences of the Industrial Revolution were first welcomed with open arms then with concern as the downside became apparent. This was then followed, over a long period of time, by the introduction of a range of responses (of both a 'bottom-up' and 'top-down' character), including those designed to encourage a moral ecology better suited to the new industrial age.

Our contemporary stage of capitalism began in the late 1980s with the advent of a new generation of far-reaching technological and communication advances, the Thatcher and Reagan eras, the break-up of Communism in Eastern and Central Europe, and the emergence of a market-based economy in China.

For the first five or so years after the fall of the Berlin Wall, all was sweetness and light. Then a reaction set in and between the mid-1990s and the end of the century a plethora of books and tracts appeared identifying the less desirable effects of global capitalism (as perceived by the commentators). Most recently (partly, perhaps, as a result of the events of September 11th 2001 and their aftermath) came the emergence of a new realism and consensus. If global capitalism is to become more socially acceptable, more attention needs to be addressed both to promoting its benefits and to minimizing its costs; and also to the ways in which every participant in the system can contribute to its success in a democratic way.

Returning to Figure 2.4, let's look at some of the moral or value-laden components of the 19th and 21st centuries in so far as they interact with those of the economic (and other) actions taken by the main participants in global capitalism. In particular, we will consider how these may (and should?) impact on the three main functions of capitalism set out in Figure 2.3 – what to produce, how and where to produce, and how to distribute the fruits of production.

What to Produce?

Can one identify an over-arching goal of capitalism? Let me define this as 'advancing the quality of life for its participants and those affected by it by an appropriate use and upgrading of society's scarce resources and capabilities'. By taking this broad definition we can include not just goods and services transacted in the market place but all those plus the conditions of sale and purchase attached to them, which together make up a person's quality of life. I would include in these all public goods as well as a person's living conditions and leisure pursuits.

Now, clearly, any quality-of-life interpretation is likely to be highly contextual – that of a poor Muslim man in Pakistan is likely to be very different from a rich non-religious woman in Canada. However, one of the beauties of capitalism is that it can accommodate different preferences in a wide range of consumers. At the same time, there is a possible drawback in that. Unless its institutions are properly motivated and/or regulated, there is a danger that, first, too much attention is paid to certain aspects of the quality of life (most noticeably that of advancing material welfare) and, second, that through various means, including advertising, a dominant view of the 'optimum' standard of living may be imposed on those who do not share it.

It is here that the moral values underpinning and fashioning capitalism come into the picture. It is here, too, that the *awareness* of individuals both of their own and other people's interpretation of the quality of life has to be considered; and also their concern about the failure of governments and supranational entities to properly incorporate quality-of-life issues into their indices of economic welfare. For example, a dollar allocated to reducing such 'bads' as AIDS, mental illness, drugs-related crime, or international terrorism is counted as the same as that spent on housing, food, and clothing. At the same time, there are some goods and services that cannot easily be accommodated in any (current) measure of income or gross domestic product. These include safety, reputation, status, sovereignty, freedom, and justice. And it is precisely these that are forming an increasingly important component of the quality of life of ordinary men and women throughout the world in the 21st century.

So where does the moral ecology of a society enter into the picture in determining or fashioning the goals of capitalism? Figure 2.7 offers some comparisons between the situation in the early 19th and 21st centuries. While the figure largely speaks for itself, there are five observations worth making.

- In the 19th century the choice of what to produce was still quite constrained, although less so than in previous centuries. At the same time, there were fewer public and social goods underpinning, or arising from, those generated by private markets. This, indeed, was a major cause for dissatisfaction for many people. Today, there is more recognition of the importance of public goods, including international public goods, but, as contemporary events in the UK are demonstrating, there still remains a good deal of concern. This concern is expressed both by consumers (for example over the quality of health and education) and by producers (for example with respect to the transport and communications infrastructure).

- Compared to the 19th century, the 21st century places a higher value on the sustainability and protection of the environment, on health, education, and safety, and on the reduction of some kinds of social dysfunction such as crime, terrorism, and drugs.

- In our present age, advertising and credit play a more important role in influencing consumer choice than they did in the 19th century. Expectations of consumers tend to be higher as incomes rise. The extent and depth of the moral responsibility of those influencing consumer tastes and expenditure are considerably more than in the Victorian era.

- In the 21st century, the 'radius' of self-interest has widened both in scope and geography. Through travel and television there is more awareness of 'how the other half lives'. The role of both internationally oriented NGOs and governments in fashioning consumer expenditure is more important; and with it has come an enhanced 'moral' responsibility to the less fortunate members of society.
- Regarding indirect moral virtues, the present age (in Western society), like the early Victorian era, emphasizes the freedom of the individual and self-expression. In the 19th century, in spite of religious revival sparked off by John Wesley and other clerics, the influence of the Enlightment continued to affect the morality and behaviour of individuals and institutions and the fashioning of the goals of capitalism. In contemporary society, the level and pattern of consumer expenditure, especially with respect to luxury goods and services, strongly reflect the moral ethos of society. So, indeed, does the production of public goods including those designed to minimize the 'bads' of society.[3]

How and Where to Produce: The Ownership of Production

The moral ecology of Victorian and contemporary capitalism is perhaps most clearly shown in the conditions of production. Figure 2.8 shows that there are direct comparisons between the concerns of the two periods.

19th Century	21st Century
• Restricted options of what to produce	• Wider choice of goods and services
• Relatively little attention paid to public goods	• Public goods more important component of qualify of life
• Few concerns over environment	• More attention on environment
• Little advertising; limited credit facilities	• Role of advertising and credit more powerful
• Radius of self-interest and 'awareness' factor limited	• Travel, the Internet and television have added to 'awareness' factor
• Less public awareness of 'bads' of society	• Greater recognition of 'bads' of society
• Limited expectations about product improvement/innovation	• High expectation about product improvements/innovation

Figure 2.7—Value and attitudes to goals of individuals and society.

---

3 Some of which may be specific to capitalism, others of which may have more to do with the religious or ideological underpinning of society.

The first relates to the 'dark satanic mills' of the UK in the 19th century. These have their contemporary counterparts in the sweatshops of today's poorest countries. Globalization and technological advances have not only helped create such questionable working conditions in the 21st century but have added to the awareness of individuals and institutions of them. In doing so they have touched their moral consciousness – as occurred two centuries earlier.

The second concern relates to the adulteration of food and drink products. In the Victorian era, unscrupulous producers were not afraid to add ingredients to food processing that were harmful to the consumer or replace nutritious substances with relatively useless ones.[4] There are parallel concerns (albeit at a rather more sophisticated level) today about the action of some agricultural producers and food and drink firms – most noticeably in the field of genetically modified foods.

In the 19th century there were many examples of fraud and sharp practice in business dealings, of environmental degradation, of dishonesty and corruption, and of exploiting gullible consumers and/or investors. There was immoral speculation and the securing of shareholders' funds to an extent that it 'was allegedly threatening the integrity of public life'. Several Victorian novelists, notably Dickens, Smiles, Trollope, Thackeray, and Kingsley, give examples of imprudent, dishonest, and greedy behaviour; and drew attention to the financial swindles of the 1830s and 1840s, the malpractices of some of the railway companies of the late 1840s, and several banking collapses of the 1850s.

Each of these has its counterpart in several unsavoury features of contemporary capitalism. These range from the corporate scandals in the US and elsewhere backwards to the East Asian crisis of the mid-1990s and the corruption of large segments of the Russian economy since the collapse of the Soviet empire. Referring back to Figure 2.2, we see that most of the concerns – not to mention distaste – about the workings of the capitalist system are directed not to the failure of markets *per se* but to the inadequacy of the moral ecology of individuals and institutions.

19th Century	21st Century
• Dark satanic mills	• Sweatshops in poorer developing countries
• Adulteration of food and drink products	• Unacceptable additives in food; genetically modified foods
• Environmental degradation	• More awareness of such degradation
• Immoral speculation, financial impropriety, greedy behaviour	• Corruption, e.g. in segments of Russian economy; the corporate scandals in US and elsewhere

Figure 2.8—The moral ecology of production, 19th and 21st century concerns.

---

4 According to one analysis of food and drink products carried out in the 1850s, 'scarcely a single item of common consumption was not widely adulterated' (Searle, 1998, p. 91).

One other production-related failure of the early 19th century was the weakness of the public sector in providing the necessary support services for the private sector, particularly those the latter found it unprofitable to supply. Examples include the early transportation network but more obviously, in so far as they affected the quality of life of the growing number of urban dwellers, housing, public utilities, and sanitation. Part of the reason for the indifference of successive governments was ignorance and not knowing how best to deal with the problems of industrialization, part was lethargy, and part was lack of compassion for the least fortunate members of society. In turn, this reflected an ineffective civil society (later to be remedied) and the absence of parliamentary democracy. (It was not until the Reform Act of 1832 that the right to vote became commonly available – and then only to men.)

In our own age, there is no less concern among some countries and various interest groups about the alleged undemocratic nature of some supranational entities and, indeed, of some national governments. Such a state of affairs is perceived to be an unacceptable and serious flaw in the current state of global capitalism. It is also one to which such entities as the World Trade Organization (WTO), the World Bank, and the IMF are giving increasing attention.

Viewing at least some of these anxieties from a global perspective (rather than that of the UK) it has to be admitted that there is little consensus about their relevance or seriousness, either from an ethical standpoint or from that of global capitalism *in toto*. Thus, turning to Figure 2.5, while some patterns of behaviour, for example those to do with the worst abuses of sweatshops, offend fundamental principles, others to do with greed, bribery, corruption, sex or racial discrimination, and lack of democracy are condemned heartily by some cultures but not by others.

At the same time, looking at indirect moral values – for example those concerned with the accumulation of wealth, the role of women in society, duty and responsibility (each of which may affect the quality of decisions taken by individuals and the institutions comprising capitalism) – there are very considerable differences in the approaches of various religions, especially that of Islam as compared with Judaism or Christianity.

Distribution

The proponents of market-based capitalism have never pretended that the system results in an 'equitable' distribution of income or, indeed, of wealth-creating resources and capabilities. Even so, apart from market fundamentalists, they would accept that extra-market institutions have an important role to play in setting the rules and enforcement mechanisms that ensure that the market operates in as fair a way as possible and taking action to alter the distribution of income determined by the market whenever this is perceived to be socially desirable.

In Victorian times, until quite late in the 19th century, successive UK governments were less concerned with tampering with income distribution than with minimizing the level of poverty and ameliorating the worst effects of industrial and financial capitalism. As we shall see in the following section, it was not until 1909 that governments seriously concerned themselves with income distribution.[5] Until the introduction of a national insurance system in 1911, it was largely left to socially responsible employers and civil society to provide a safety net for those who, through no fault of their own, were disadvantaged by the consequences of market forces.

Today, income distribution is high on the political agenda. There are two main reasons for this. First, the principle of social justice has been upgraded from a lesser to a core moral virtue in many societies. Second, there is a much greater awareness of the huge differences in the economic well-being of people both within, but more especially between, countries. The issue of poverty and how the wealthier nations may help the poorest to climb up the development ladder is now accepted as an ethical responsibility and priority by both international agencies and governments of wealthier countries.[6] At the same time, within wealthier countries, compared with two centuries ago, there is a much greater acceptance of the need for safety nets.

What of the indirect and more general moral values that might affect the attitudes and actions of individuals and institutions towards sharing the benefits of a capitalist economy? My interpretation is that, compared with that of the early 19th century, the moral virtue of compassion, and the radius of its application, is more widely accepted and practised now, notwithstanding the breakdown of traditional family relationships and the waning influence of formalized religion. This, I think, is partly the result of a lessening of the social stigma (or personal shame) attached to poverty and partly to a growing acceptance that change inevitably brings with it losers as well as winners and that winners, or the society of which they are part, have some responsibility for the losers.

At the same time, it is also true to say that until very recently, the mode of compassion in post-19th century capitalism has gradually become institutionalized, with governments taking on the responsibility previously borne spontaneously by individuals and/or civil society. However, in the last decade or more, the concept of 'subsidiarity' in welfare provision has become more widely accepted, particularly in the more liberal market economies.

The Solution: 19th and 21st Century Reactions

The Victorian Solutions

The actions taken by Victorian society to combat or ameliorate the moral downsides of early industrial capitalism can be compared with those that are being taken or might be taken to upgrade the moral ethos of contemporary capitalism.

Figure 2.9 lists some of the more important comparisons. It also categorizes the moral response of the various institutions of capitalism according to whether it was, and is, 'top-down' or 'bottom-up' and whether it was, and is, directly or indirectly related to the three main goals of capitalism. Basically these reveal a combination of (complementary) 'top-down' or 'bottom-up' approaches.

---

5 It was this Budget that introduced the old age pension and the first National Insurance System and unemployment benefits were introduced.

6 See, for example, World Bank (1999), HMSO (2000), HM Treasury (2002) and Brown (2003).

In the 19th century, the 'top-down' response mainly consisted of actions by the UK government, though it was the vision and initiative of particular reformers, commentators, and politicians such as William Wilberforce, Elizabeth Fry, Charles Dickens, John Howard, Arthur Hassall, and Thomas Carlyle, that, through their actions and writings, persuaded parliament to enact appropriate legislation and provide the right infrastructure and enforcement mechanisms for individuals and institutions to behave in a (more) morally acceptable way.

Thus, for example, starting with the Factory Act of 1833, successive UK governments introduced a variety of laws and regulations to limit the hours of work and improve working conditions and major reforms relating to health, sanitation, and housing. They passed legislation to reduce the adulteration of food (and drink) and to lessen the likelihood of financial impropriety. They widened the franchise of the electorate and pioneered free compulsory education. The introduction of limited liability and improved legislation to protect property rights followed. They initiated various moral reforms to reduce prostitution, control gambling, and encourage temperance. Both local and central governments helped to finance and, sometimes, provide public works and new means of transport, for example canals and railways.

Successive administrations, not to mention Queen Victoria herself, did much to support a moral framework for Victorian society[7] by stressing the importance of family life, self-discipline, self-respect, thrift, and social responsibility. New legislation was also enacted to reduce the high levels of crime and social unrest of the early 19th century.

Top Down	Bottom Up
(a) Direct	(a) Direct
• Legislation – Poor Law – Factory Acts – Property rights protection – Limited liability	• Family values • Churches (religious beliefs) • Education • Socially responsible firms • Civil society (philanthropic agencies, friendly societies)
• Moral suasion: influence of clerics, commentators, writers etc. on individual/ corporate behaviour • Socialism • State intervention – Transport – Public utilities	• Influence of writers, commentators, politicians on actions of governments (b) Indirect • Family values • Role of churches • Education • Moral suasion/example
(b) Indirect • Reform Act 1932 • Education • Legislation/policies towards crime, social dysfunction • Moral suasion	

Figure 2.9—Victorian responses to downsides of industrial capitalism.

The second 'top-down' approach was more revolutionary and it occurred more abruptly on the European continent. This was to replace, partly or wholly, the burgeoning capitalist system by socialism or social democracy. The argument was that however much capitalism may have pushed out the boundaries of wealth, it had failed to ensure the social well-being of the majority of people. It was *de facto* an exclusive economic system and governments were either unable or unwilling to intervene in the workings of the market to foster more inclusiveness. Those espousing socialism believed it to be a morally superior economic system since it was based on the philosophy of 'to each according to his needs, from each according to his ability'.

These ideals were applauded by some clergymen at the time, notably Frank Maurice and Thomas Carlyle. Others, led by Thomas Chalmers and Harriet Martineau, were urging that the downsides of capitalism should be counteracted by fostering more acceptable patterns of behaviour by its constituents. In this they echoed the sentiments of Edmund Burke that civil liberty can only flourish if individuals put moral chains on their appetites. In any event, the socialist challenge was held at bay in the UK (and the US), until the inter-war depression of the 1930s, when the writings of the economists Keynes and Beveridge began to take root.

The 'bottom-up' response essentially took two forms. First, the 19th century saw a spectacular rise in the role of civil society in the guise of religious organizations, friendly societies, philanthropic agencies, and privately supported schools. (In 1861, it was estimated that 69 % of the £13 million spent on public education in the UK was contributed by private subscription and only 31 % by the government.)

These early non-profit organizations took upon themselves the task of ameliorating the worst social effects of the new industrial age and in certain cases also pressurizing governments to do the same. There was a strong humanitarian impetus behind this movement – which was as prominent in the US as in the UK.

Second, and interacting with the previous response, there was a concerted and vigorous effort by Victorian religious and other organizations to instil patterns of morally responsible behaviour in both individuals and institutions. Examples include the preaching of the Protestant ethic by such clerics as Joseph Tucker, Thomas Carlyle, and Richard Whately; the proselytizing of such philosophers and commentators as Herbert Spencer, Hannah More, and Hippolyte Taine; and the writings of such popular authors as Dickens, Trollope, and Thackeray.[8] Each of these, by helping to inculcate large swathes of the population with such virtues as honesty, thrift, self-discipline, duty, and character, not only spawned a new culture of social responsibility but also strengthened the hand of capitalism *per se*. Prominent examples include the emergence of a clutch of charitable enterprises and of socially responsible firms such as Titus Salt, Rowntree, and Cadbury, and of philanthropic, civic, and educational institutions.

---

7 Victorian moralists believed in a strictly limited view of the State. T.H. Green (1882), for example, was opposed to paternal government. He wrote: 'The State should promote morality by strengthening the moral disposition of the individual, not by subjecting the individual to any kind of moral tutelage' (Green, 1941, quoted in Himmelfarb, 1995, p. 262). Wise words, and highly relevant to today's debate!

8 The published works of these authors were the main way in which the general populace got to know about contemporary life in Victorian England. Today television and the Internet are the main sources of information about some of the effects (perceived or otherwise) of global capitalism.

Lessons for Tackling the Moral Downsides of Global Capitalism

So what of the contemporary stage of capitalism? Well, like its predecessor, it is heralding a new phase of economic organization. Also like its predecessor, it is being fuelled by a succession of new ideas, dramatic technological breakthroughs, and a widening and deepening of cross-border commerce. Such events are challenging established economic structures, life-styles, and ideologies by their speed, scope, and intensity and in so doing are creating a host of social and moral challenges. But they are also occurring at a time when the cult of individualism is reaching new heights and the value or legitimacy of such concepts as solidarity and community is being severely questioned.

At the same time, there are some unique features of contemporary capitalism that offer their own particular challenges. Some of these are set out in Figure 2.10. First, and most obvious, the geographical radius of capitalism, via commerce, travel, and the Internet, is now embracing institutions from more diverse ideologies, social structures, and cultural mores than ever before.

Second, the critical engine of wealth in today's global economy is human capital. Such an asset is not only the main source of innovation, entrepreneurship, and the upgrading of managerial and organizational expertise but of ideals and moral values as well.[9] *Inter alia*, this demands that both public and private employers should accord more respect and attention to the aspirations, behaviour, and participation of their work force in the wealth-creating process than had previously been the case. It has also deepened and accelerated the process of change. In addition, the new uncertainties and instabilities engendered by it, together with the increasing volatility of the international financial markets, are further testing the moral fabric of capitalism.

Third, the present age of capitalism has to embrace a gamut of ethically related issues not known, or little cared about, by the Victorians. These include environmental protection, the (possible) abuses of advertising, credit card fraud, international drug smuggling, and terrorism. Fourth, as evidence of the emergence of alliance capitalism, we see a huge explosion of all forms of inter-firm coalitions and inter-government agreements.

And, fifthly, we live at a time when apart from some notable exceptions, for example China, democratic governments reign. This is in total contrast to the situation in the early 19th century, even in most Western economies. At the same time, the power and influence of large firms and some supranational entities have increased considerably and, according to some observers, in an undemocratic way.

These five aspects of contemporary global society pose their particular challenges to, and opportunities for, the institutions of capitalism. On one hand, we have far more awareness, knowledge, and experience than we had in the past of how to deal with the market place and there are far more extra-market organizations seeking solutions to these challenges and imperfections than ever before. On the other hand,

---

9 To quote from Michael Navak: 'Human capital includes moral labels, such as hard work, cooperativeness, social trust, alertness, honest and social habits such as respect for the rule of law' (Novak, 1999).

some of the options open to Victorian society in dealing with the less welcome affects of capitalism are not as readily available or as appropriate today. In particular, organized religion (and especially the Christian religion) is not as strong or pervasive a mentor to moral behaviour as it once was.

Living in a more multi-religious, multi-cultural society poses new moral challenges, particularly with respect to accommodating differences in the interpretation of the virtues at the bottom of the moral pyramid. Also, the present generation has much higher expectations of capitalism as an economic system than did its predecessors. And with a growing freedom of expression has come a much sharper sense of criticism.

Conclusions

Can we, then, provide a prescription for upgrading the moral ecology of 21st century capitalism? There are five points to make.

Top Down	Bottom Up
(a) Direct	(a) Direct
• Supranational entities	• Consumer capitalism
• Global compact (UN)	• Shareholder capitalism
• Global civil society	• Social responsibility of business
• International NGOs	• Resurgent role of NGOs
• Transnational religious groups	• More intra- and inter-firm cooperation
• Reducing moral hazard	(raising importance of virtues, e.g.
• National governments	trust and forbearance)
• Debt relief	
• Incentives to stimulate the upgrading of human capital and entrepreneurship	
• Anti-monopoly policy	
• Compensatory systems for the disadvantaged	
(b) Indirect	(b) Indirect
• Coordinated cross-border institutional action to curb production of, and trade in, 'bads'	• A new sense of communitarianism/ solidarity: a recognition that self-related goals can be better achieved by cooperation with others
• Legislation/policies towards anti-social (including anti-racial) behaviour	
• Education and training	
• Increased responsibility to less fortunate members of society	

Figure 2.10—Twenty-first century responses towards making global capitalism more responsible.

- The moral pendulum needs to swing back to take on some of the ideas and principles of the Victorian age but these need to be adapted to the specific needs of the 21st century and particularly those of a multicultural society. In particular, whereas individual 'freedom' is most certainly one of the central (if not key) virtues of contemporary capitalism, the need for enhanced social responsibility (not so much at a societal but at an individual level) requires to be placed higher on the agenda.

- The reconfiguration of the moral underpinnings of commercial traditions should be brought about by a combination of 'bottom-up' and 'top-down' approaches. Particular attention should be paid to the kind of moral values necessary for upgrading the economic efficiency and social acceptability of globalizing, knowledge-intensive, and alliance-based capitalism.

- Each of the four main institutions has a critical role to play in promoting the right moral ecology for sustainable capitalism. While there are virtues directly related to the functions of capitalism that need to be upgraded, it is no less important to encourage the upgrading of more general virtues. This is best served by a 'bottom-up' approach but with governments and/or supranational entities providing the right incentives and regulations to persuade or enforce individuals and interest groups to behave in a morally acceptable manner.

- The particular feature of 21st-century capitalism is that it extends the spatial radius of moral responsibility. How far, by whom, and in what manner is still very much up for debate. But by such direct means as debt relief, indirect ones such as the exploration of a global ethic, and/or a global compact between firms and societies, some progress is being made. If, however, it is accepted that the moral capital and ecology of capitalist societies are an important ingredient of their success, is there not a case for establishing regular 'summit meetings' among leaders of the main religious and other traditions (rather like the Group of Eight in the economic domain)? There is far more consensus among the main religious traditions (which themselves are global entities) about appropriate moral codes and behaviour than there are differences, particularly at the top of the moral pyramid.[10]

- The problems and challenges outlined in this chapter need to be addressed both from a short-term and long-term perspective. The first leads to a 'top-down' approach by governments and supranational entities in minimizing (by legislation, moral persuasion, and other means) the most identifiable and unacceptable behaviour of individuals, interest groups, and firms. In the medium term, the most productive results are likely to emerge from improving the moral infrastructure of the four main institutions of capitalism by a combination of exogenously generated pressures (both 'bottom-up' and 'top-down') and by endogenous self-improvement.[11] Examples include a reconfiguration of the WTO

---

10 As demonstrated, for example, by several chapters authored by religious leaders in Dunning, 2003.

11 Some commentators (e.g. Hayek, 1998, Lal, 2003) believe that endogenous upgrading of institutional performance (whether by 'moral' or other means) is the only valid way of making capitalism work.

and IMF and a more responsible attitude on the part of the corporate sector to the values and goals of each of its stakeholders, and to those of society as a whole.

In the long run, I see no other way to increase the social acceptability and sustenance of global capitalism than by the inculcation of the appropriate values into the attitudes and behaviour of individuals. This will come by their upbringing, education, peer pressure, and a more pronounced sense of self-respect than is evident at present. It is here particularly that the Victorians have much to teach us. But it is in our hands and it is our responsibility to find a way in which we can best integrate their principles and values with the benefits of economic freedom, self-fulfilment, and democratic capitalism that more of us at least hold so dear.

The Multi-home-based Multinational: Combining Global Competitiveness and Local Innovativeness

Örjan Sölvell

Institute of International Business, Stockholm School of Economics and
Institute for Strategy and Competitiveness, Harvard Business School

Cross-border economic activity seems to increase at an accelerating rate with the establishment of global markets for many goods, services, and factors of production including capital, technology, and people. These flows are to a large extent managed through multinational corporations (MNC) with global networks of subsidiaries and alliance partners.

With increased globalization we have also witnessed a parallel process leading to an increasingly strategic role for particular local environments, such as Hollywood, the world's leading feature film, TV, and entertainment cluster. In a world of globalization it seems as if such 'Hollywoods', in both old and new industries, increase their attraction for mobile resources such as talented people, technologies, venture capital and other finance, and direct investments by MNCs from around the world.

The more resources and capabilities move around the globe the more specialized and differentiated the world will become. Well-established trade theory also suggests that with open trade nations will specialize where they have 'comparative advantage' and the world will tend to become more differentiated.

However, in predicting in what areas a specific region or nation will specialize trade theory is predominantly occupied with endowed factors. In Michael Porter's seminal work *The Competitive Advantage of Nations* (Porter, 1990) the focus is on created factors and the endogenous processes leading to upgrading of factors and increased specialization.

Take a recent example. People, firms, and technologies linked to the pharmaceutical and biotech industries are constantly looking for the most attractive regions with excellent universities and the R&D operations of leading MNCs. Today, three countries constitute the home bases of 13 of the top 15 companies in the world: the US, Switzerland, and the UK. In the global filtering process now taking place the US seems to out-compete much of the world. And within the US, New Jersey, and the San Diego and Boston areas seem to out-compete most other potential locations.

In the spring of 2002, Swiss pharmaceuticals group Novartis announced that it would move its global R&D headquarters to Boston. And long before the Second World War, other Swiss pharmaceutical firms began investing in R&D operations in New Jersey.

When large MNCs make these kinds of strategic choices there is a trickle-down effect that attracts students, researchers, entrepreneurs, inventors, and other skilled people. Hence, the increased mobility not only of goods and services but also of all kinds of factors of production is creating a world based on a 'new geography'. Somewhat paradoxically, in this new geography increased globalization goes hand in hand with increased localization.

Corporate executives now face critical strategic and organizational choices in this world of increased globalization and localization. MNCs typically benefit from globalization, selling their products worldwide and tapping world markets for factors of production and input goods and services to enhance their overall efficiency. Localization forces, on the other hand, seem to be more challenging to corporate management. Local markets have, of course, outplayed their role for most goods and services. But dynamic local clusters of inter-related industries and specialized institutions are playing increasingly important roles as centres for corporate innovation. They constitute 'home bases' for continuous upgrading of competitive advantage.

So, should we develop home bases or spread out core functions to maximize global coverage? Should we move our home base to a more dynamic cluster? Can we tap capabilities from afar or should we invest to become insiders in relevant 'Hollywoods'? Should we link different core subsidiaries/home bases or should they play roles that are more independent?

These are some of the fundamental strategic and organizational challenges facing MNC executives today. We would argue that they have less to do with globalization and operational efficiency, or *competitiveness*. Instead, these concerns have to do with the need for continuous upgrading of products, process technologies, and all sorts of critical capabilities inside a firm – or what we label *innovativeness* – which in turn is intimately linked to the forces of localization. One of the main strategic challenges facing top management in today's MNCs is therefore to configure and coordinate international activities in such a way that the efficiency of global markets is combined with innovativeness emanating from world-leading clusters.

Here we will outline a simple model of how MNCs can build competitive advantage through a combination of innovativeness and competitiveness, taking into consideration the forces of globalization and localization. We begin with a discussion of the new geography – combining globalization and localization forces – move on to issues of innovativeness and competitiveness of MNCs, and end with a discussion of a model combining the two dimensions. Three main strategies for MNCs are outlined, of which one – the multi-home-based multinational – is argued to hold the most promise in the emerging new geography. (The concept of the multi-home-based multinational was first presented in a book, *Advantage Sweden* (Stockholm: Norstedts, 1991), written jointly by the author with Michael E Porter and Ivo Zander.)

The New Geography: Globalization and Localization

Rather than a 'new economy', where demand and supply curves are turned on their heads and scale economies are rendered obsolete, we have a new geography. This new geography must be taken seriously by MNC executives. They should be asking what the forces of globalization and localization mean for their strategy and operations. In this section, we will touch only briefly on the issues of globalization and its meaning for MNCs, since this is well understood, and instead turn to localization.

In most industries today, global markets offer a road to enhanced efficiency through improved economies of scale in varying parts of the value chain such as R&D, sourcing of materials, components, or systems, manufacturing, and marketing and sales. Depending on the homogeneity of demand and technology, trade restrictions, and transportation costs, global sales can involve more or less local adaptation and design and more or less dispersion of packaging, assembly, testing, and full production.

The more a firm faces one homogenous market, with little or no trade barriers, and the lower the transportation costs, the more one global source for development and production can be used. However, in many industries today some fragmenting forces still prevail, forcing MNCs to run dispersed operations, often reducing some of the potential advantages of global scale.

In addition to enhanced economies of scale, global markets can be utilized to gain maximum access to pools of labour, for export platforms in emerging markets, codified technology, financial capital, and other tradable resources. Through trade shows, travel and local scanning operations, the global market can be selectively tapped.

It has been argued that MNCs have the ability to tap any resource or capability in any location. However, as we will see below, MNCs using global markets for innovation purposes typically face an insider/outsider dilemma. The more critical technologies and skills are often not traded globally for competitive reasons, and cannot be easily tapped from afar because they are usually embedded in companies or cultures and are often tacit in nature. To overcome these problems MNCs can build insider positions in clusters through long-term investment and acquisitions. However, such a policy increases the 'insiderization' of a particular subsidiary unit, allowing it to control strategic and often unique resources and capabilities within the MNC and in effect making sister units within the MNC 'outsiders'. In organizational terms this often translates into formal regional or world mandates referred to as centres of excellence.

Clusters

Tendencies for clusters to form around cities or smaller regions have long been evident in traditional industries, for example car manufacturing around Detroit and in southern Germany, pulp and paper in parts of Sweden and Finland, and clothing and shoes in northern Italy. In earlier times, natural factors such as climate and soil, location of raw materials, and endowments in terms of energy (forests, waterfalls, and so on), and transportation routes (rivers, natural ports) played an important role in the location of industries and whole clusters.

Pure entrepreneurship has also come into play, such as in the much-cited case of carpet manufacturing in Dalton, Georgia. Access to specialized skills and advanced markets has been decisive for patterns of economic agglomeration in service industries such as financial services in London and on Wall Street, fashion in Paris, auction houses in London, and advertising offices on Madison Avenue. Agglomeration of economic activity on a global scale, such as in Hollywood, is perhaps most pronounced in technology-intensive industries such as pharmaceuticals, biotech, telecommunications, consumer electronics, computers, and IT.

But why are local clusters so critical to innovation? We think there are three crucial arguments as to why innovation processes tend to be highly localized:

- the need for incremental reduction of technical and economic uncertainty;
- the need for repeated and continuous interaction between related firms and specialized institutions (including research and education);
- the need for face-to-face contacts in the exchange and creation of new knowledge.

The first characteristic derives from the fact that innovative processes are fundamentally uncertain in terms of technical feasibility and market acceptance. Few projects turn out to be commercial successes. Even if the level of uncertainty varies with industry and type of innovation, technical aspects are commonly worked out by means of trial and error, testing, and modification. Such incrementalism and trial-and-error problem solving in turn lead to a need for continuous interaction, both in informal networks and formal cooperation.

The two other arguments build on the notion that proximity within clusters adds tremendously to continuity and face-to-face interaction in personal networks that are vital to the transfer of tacit skills (facilitated by common language and training). Finally, innovative sources are often found outside the firm where again near-by customers, competitors, and various institutions play important roles.

In summary, dynamic clusters are characterized by the following.

- Intense local rivalry (in addition to global competition) stimulating continuous upgrading and change and creating a foundation for a more advanced and diverse supplier base.
- Dynamic competition emanating from the entry of new firms, including spin-offs from larger incumbents.
- Intense cooperation organized through various institutions for collaboration such as professional organizations, chambers of commerce, and the like. Clusters also exhibit intense informal interaction typically based on personal networks.
- Access to increasingly specialized and advanced factors of production (human and financial capital) as well as to research via universities and public or private research institutes.
- Linkages to technologically related industries that share pools of talent and new technological achievements.
- Closeness to sophisticated and demanding buyers, both business buyers and consumers.

Successful clusters are not primarily characterized by advantages of scale but rather by a capacity for perpetual innovation and upgrading of goods, services, human capital, and other factors plus a process of increasing specialization. They are also characterized by an 'upward spiral' where incumbent firms gain from, and add to, local spillovers. However, one must not forget that spillover effects have to be created; they do not just arise automatically because industries are co-located. The degree to which interaction resulting in spillovers takes place depends on the legacy of a region, social capital, and policy choices.

Firms inside clusters have access to specialized and advanced factors of production. The process of factor upgrading is in fact endogenously driven by competition and sophisticated demand inside the cluster. In addition to these local conditions, free and substantial mobility between the cluster and the surrounding world is vitally important if the local environment is to avoid stagnation. To achieve vitality in the long term, local clusters need to be able to attract companies, venture capital, skills, and other resources from all over the world, what we have termed the 'Greta Garbo effect'.

Cluster firms must also have good access to world markets to be able to sustain efficiency and competitiveness. Thus, a dynamic cluster exhibits three distinct processes: local dynamism, global attractiveness, and global reach. Since leading clusters are typified by high costs (wages, land, and so on) they run contrary to competitiveness but are critical for sustained innovativeness among firms, which we turn to next.

Competitiveness and Innovativeness

In traditional economics the concept of competitiveness is static and based on cost advantages. Firms are competitive when they face relatively lower input costs (land, energy, taxes, wages, and so on) compared to competitors in other nations. As a result, government subsidies, natural endowments, and currency devaluations, which fortunately are less of a tool today, make indigenous firms more competitive. However, lower costs create the potential to compete on the basis of lower prices for a limited period of time, until the emergence of an even lower cost competitor in the global marketplace.

However, increased competitiveness has little to do with the fundamentals of sustainable competitive advantage but more with the ability to innovate around products and processes and the ability to upgrade resources and the capabilities of the firm. In fact, advantageous cost positions tend to work in the opposite direction, slowing down the speed of modernization and change and undermining the innovativeness of a firm.

In a world of increased competitive pressures MNCs need not only to improve their operational efficiencies but also to sustain and enhance their innovativeness. Whereas strategies focusing on global efficiency are easily copied, insider positions in a certain cluster are more firm specific and idiosyncratic and therefore more sustainable.

Four Strategy Elements Facing the MNC

Combining the two dimensions outlined above results in a four-box matrix (see Figure 3.1), each box representing a critical strategy element. The upper left-hand corner puts emphasis on the innovativeness emanating from a lead cluster – a 'Hollywood'. The upper right-hand corner focuses on innovation as a global process, often referred to as transnational solutions, combining resources and capabilities in several locations. The lower left-hand corner covers strategies of cost efficiency with emphasis on the home market (often true for MNCs with large home markets), and the lower right-hand corner global efficiency, or global cost leadership.

MNCs tend to combine different elements of the matrix and we will point to three important models each combining two elements. Two of these are found in mainstream literature on MNCs and the third is identified as a future growth model.

Multi-domestic MNCs

Leading MNCs from small home countries have been very successful in achieving high levels of competitiveness in global markets. By selling their products and systems across internationally important markets they have been able to exploit advantages of scale comparable to firms from larger markets. Gradually, MNCs from smaller countries have managed to achieve further gains in cost-effectiveness by establishing assembly and production units close to large markets where conditions for particular types of production are better or because of protectionism or government demands. Instead of carrying one flag these MNCs have many flags and have many 'homes'.

The strategy has been characterized as multi-domestic, with the MNC seeking to combine the efficiencies of both global and local markets. In manufacturing industries, core components and sub-systems are often produced on a global scale

	Localization	Globalization
Innovativeness	Cluster insider	Transnational innovation
Competitiveness	Protected market	Global efficiency

Figure 3.1—Four strategy elements.

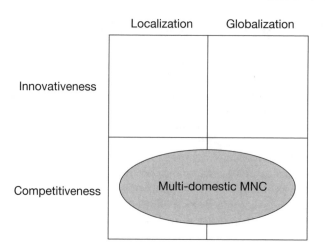

Figure 3.2—The multi-domestic MNC.

while assembly and local adaptation are carried out on a country-by-country basis. Global outsourcing has also been central to multi-domestic MNCs.

Cost efficiency is not enough to guarantee long-term profitability and market survival, however. Long-term competitive advantages are based primarily on innovativeness, that is, the capacity to benefit customers by continuously innovating and upgrading the content, quality, and delivery of products.

Transnational MNCs

The model of transnational MNCs, first proposed by Chris Bartlett and Sumantra Ghoshal, was a response to increased globalization and the development of more sophisticated MNCs with highly dispersed networks of subsidiaries. A central feature of the model is that it not only involves global efficiency-seeking but also global innovation.

Under this model the primary concern of strategy is how to foster the development and integration of internationally dispersed capabilities on a worldwide basis. Exactly how MNCs should go about learning and creating new practices on a global scale was mainly theoretically derived, underpinned by a few case studies. Only recently have a number of empirical projects tried to illuminate the issues of cross-border learning and transfer of skills on a broader basis, though this has exposed some of the weaknesses of the model. Innovation and creation of new knowledge in cross-border settings tend to be expensive and lead to delays in time-to-market.

In spite of its intuitive attractiveness, we argue that transnational strategies have proven problematic. Company attempts to create new solutions through innovation projects involving global teams have often turned out to be miscalculations because of high costs and major delays. To learn and share across the globe is appealing but it involves high costs and organizational barriers.

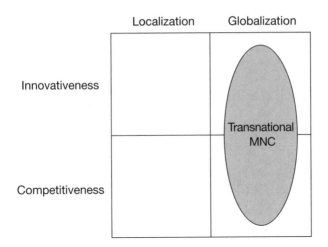

Figure 3.3—The transnational MNC.

Multi-home-based MNCs

Success in the new geography means both ensuring innovativeness by building insider positions in one or more leading local clusters and competitiveness via a global strategy for production, sourcing, and sales. As most MNCs are diversified to a certain degree, each line of business needs to find its home base. Depending on the need to link different businesses, these home bases become more or less independent centres, developing their own strategies and organizational models. The home base unit (business headquarters, R&D, design, and, where appropriate, core manufacturing operations) plays a global role. In addition, organizational

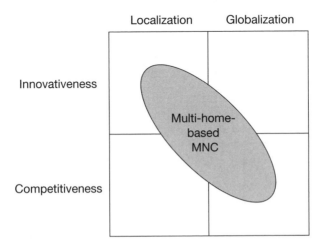

Figure 3.4—The multi-home-based MNC.

resources (typically sales subsidiaries and local partners involved in market penetration) are spread around the world to ensure maximum competitiveness through
global efficiency and scale.

Organization of the Multi-home-based MNC

Multi-home-based MNCs have something in common with federal structures where
global headquarters is more of a parent 'set up' by children for their own benefit
than a parent in tight control of its offspring. Corporate headquarters should
be separated from the business units (as in the recent case of Boeing moving its
corporate headquarters out of Seattle) and have its own location, preferably in a
headquarters city such as London. Corporate headquarters plays a role in coordinating financial and legal matters, brand protection, and setting overall portfolio
strategy. Business unit headquarters, on the other hand, should be co-located with
strategic functions in appropriate 'Hollywoods'. We do not believe that the MNC
should be geographically split up in terms of core functions, with the exception of
corporate world headquarters (and in rare instances corporate R&D), but kept
together in units of critical mass in world-leading clusters.

The multi-home-based MNC needs some form of monitoring in regions where
it lacks insider positions. To ensure effective long-range tapping, resources and
activities (travelling executives and experts, scanning units, and so on) should be

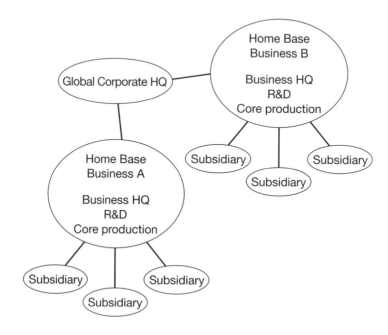

Figure 3.5—Organization of the multi-home-based MNC.

dedicated to transmitting new technologies and ideas back to the home base and should not be allowed to develop them locally. For example, Boston and Cambridge, Massachusetts are full of such scanning units surrounding MIT and Harvard.

The multi-home-based MNC is a distinct model implying a certain set of strategic and organizational choices. It is different from the multi-domestic model in that it emphasizes the role of innovation. It is also different from the traditional home-country MNC since it allows for different home bases (not necessarily the original home country). It is also different from the transnational model in that it downplays globally linked innovation projects and intense skill transfers.

Instead of building increasingly complex organizational forms to integrate complicated processes of innovation around the world, the multi-home-based model puts emphasis on simple organizational structures. There is a clear home base for each line of business and a strict hierarchy between strategic activities critical to innovativeness (home base) and other activities critical for enhanced efficiency and competitiveness (for example, sales subsidiaries). If there is a need for interaction between home bases, we suggest that the corporation be organized in such a way that dependencies between home bases are sequential with each base having a clear mandate for a part of the value chain. It is important that simple interfaces are created to ensure efficient hand-over of the baton between them.

How about moving the home base? Following long-term investment and major mergers or acquisitions, MNCs tend to add new home bases. A common result of M&A is a duplication of home bases. Over time, duplication seems to erode when certain units, often due to internal competition, become stronger and others weaker. Not surprisingly, the units that tend to become centres of excellence are those located in the more dynamic clusters. We have seen cases of smaller MNCs that grew up in a cluster that subsequently went into decline actually move all their core resources to a new cluster. However, this is a highly complex process. Often a better long-term strategy is to make sure that the home base strategy also covers strengthening the overall home cluster

We would argue that a number of traditionally under-emphasized factors should be considered when assessing the degree to which global innovation may become a major force in the future multinational.

First, the introduction of internationally integrated innovation projects requires incentive systems that reward involvement in projects that are temporary and fall in between national organizations. These systems are hard to set up and most managers testify that involvement in temporary projects without an organizational home does not help individual careers.

Second, the cross-border context adds complexity because dispersed units tend to have their own identity and understanding of what constitutes an effective development process. Unless projects that cut across different national units are carried out on a regular basis, these differences will continue to have a negative effect on inter-unit collaboration and the effectiveness of cross-border innovation.

Third, recent findings suggest that information processing in the established multinational is not necessarily based on objective data. The difficulties involved in agreeing what skills reside where, and lack of willingness to share skills among subsidiaries, will hamper any attempts at global innovation.

Finally, we remind readers of the insider–outsider dilemma that emerges with the expansion and deepening of involvement in foreign clusters. In essence, the process of increasing insiderization – essential in getting access to local cluster spillovers and the most advanced and specialized human capital – appears to evolve together with processes that build independence and distance between units in the multinational network. Thus, by becoming more of an insider in a local cluster the unit becomes more of an outsider within the MNC. The multi-home-based MNC is an attempt to solve this dilemma. There are of course advantages and disadvantages with such a strategy, but in the new geography facing MNC executives today, we argue that this model has a lot to offer in both ensuring competitiveness and innovativeness.

4 Regional Multinationals: The Location-bound Drivers of Global Strategy

Alan M Rugman[1] and Alain Verbeke[2]

[1]Kelley School of Business, Indiana University and Templeton College, University of Oxford

[2]Haskayne School of Business, University of Calgary and Templeton College, University of Oxford

This chapter analyses the latest available data on the location of MNEs. As earlier research revealed, these are still distributed on a triad basis (the 'triad' being the US, Western Europe, and Japan). The implications for regional (rather than 'global') strategy are discussed below and, not surprisingly, arguments for a 'global' strategy are found to be incompatible with the evidence on choices of regional/triad strategy by MNEs

We also provide empirical evidence that demonstrates that the majority of even the most 'global' MNEs in reality operate on a regional/triad basis. Of the world's 20 MNEs with the most geographically dispersed sales, assets, and employees, few if any appear to have adopted truly global strategies; the remainder are based in their home triads and need regional strategies.

Figure 4.1 distinguishes between global, regional, and national MNE strategies. The vertical axis represents the product characteristics of an MNE at these three levels. The extent to which products are standardized at the global, regional, or national level represents the 'revealed preferences' of MNEs either to institutionalize a particular approach globally or to adapt to the requirements of national/regional markets.

The horizontal axis is more a reflection of 'stated preferences' – the extent to which MNE managers view strategic decision making as a process concentrated in a single home base or dispersed across regions or countries.

More specifically, it represents the location of decision-making power for corporate, business, or functional strategy issues. In other words, are an MNE's key strategic decisions such as choice of product/market niches and competitive strategies taken in a single location or are at least a substantial portion of them taken in several 'home bases' at the national or regional levels?

Figure 4.1 adapts our earlier (1993) framework on 'global' strategies. There we argued that the truly important decisions to be taken by MNEs are related to two parameters. These are, first, the number of home bases with which they function – i.e. the number of locations where important strategic decisions are taken (equivalent to the horizontal axis of Figure 4.1) – and, second, the use of non-location bound versus location bound firm-specific advantages, or FSAs (equivalent to the horizontal axis of Figure 4.1).

The former allows various approaches to standardize an MNE's product offering across borders and to earn the benefits of integration related to scale, scope, and benefits of exploiting national differences. The latter provides the potential to gain the benefits of national responsiveness.

The difference between our earlier resource-based perspective and Figure 4.1 is that we have now explicitly introduced a regional dimension to the analysis. This is needed because our emerging empirical work suggests that 'global' strategies are not appropriate for most MNEs, which actually operate on a regional/triad basis. More specifically, on the horizontal axis this regional dimension implies that a number of strategic decisions are left to regional, rather than national, headquarters.

The vertical axis implies the development of FSAs that are useful at national level within a region. These are regional company strengths – they can contribute to survival, profitability, and growth beyond a single nation but they are still location bound in that they cannot be deployed globally. Indeed, the view that a global company acts on a global scale applies in practice to very few, if any, MNEs. Most MNEs rely largely on sets of location bound and regional FSAs as the basis for their competitiveness.

Figure 4.1 helps identify some of the more important mistakes made by proponents of globalization and a global strategy for MNEs. They view global strategy not as only appropriate in cell 1 but also in cells 2, 3, 4, and 7 (where other strategies than globalization are required). In cells 2 and 3, they focus on the decisions and actions of corporate leaders, typically the CEO, the top management committee, and the MNE's board of directors. Undoubtedly most key financial decisions in MNEs are taken at that level. However, even if all major corporate strategy decisions are taken centrally (left column of Figure 4.1), cells 2 and 3 reflect respectively the existence of substantial regional and national involvement in the product offering.

In other words, MNEs that tailor their product offering to regional and national circumstances do not pursue a simple global strategy as suggested by cell 1. Considerable resources are allocated to allow for the required level of sub-global responsiveness in terms of what is being delivered to the market. In addition, even if an MNE's product offerings were largely global this does not necessarily imply that all important decisions on market penetration, distribution, advertising and so on can be taken centrally. Local constraints are likely to force corporate management to delegate important decisions to regional and national levels, positioning the firm closer to cells 4 and 7.

This point is vitally important since many critics of globalization suffer from a similar misconception. They view MNEs as centrally directed, profit-maximizing

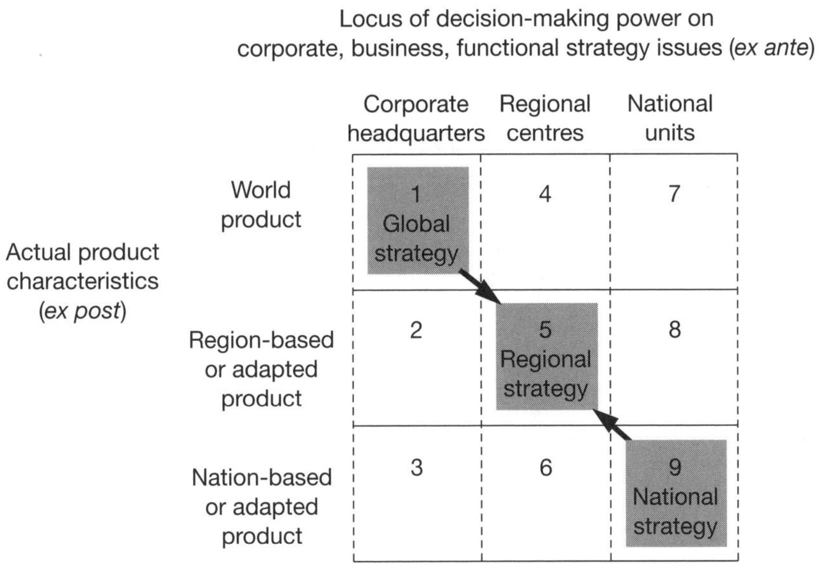

Locus of decision-making power on
corporate, business, functional strategy issues (*ex ante*)

Figure 4.1—A framework for analysing 'globalization'.

entities, eager to sell standardized products around the world. Anti-globalization critics state that MNEs are insensitive to host country and host region demands, especially those of host country governments. In fact, the presence of intense international rivalry and the reality that every MNE is perceived as 'foreign' in regions other than its own forces MNEs to be particularly sensitive to the requirements of host country governments and other important stakeholders.

Of course, this does not imply that MNEs can or should adopt a cell 9 approach, becoming fully polycentric with products carefully tailored to each national market and most strategy decisions left to host country subsidiary managers. Much conceptual and empirical evidence suggests that a 'multi-national' approach leads to overlapping efforts and duplication in innovation, inconsistent national strategies, opportunistic behaviour by subsidiary managers, and more generally a waste of resources and lack of clear strategic direction.

The great strength of an MNE is its ability to overcome market imperfections in national markets and to develop systemic, network-related rather than asset-based FSAs. Even for MNEs with a history of polycentric administration, cells 6 and 8 are likely to be much more relevant than cell 9. In cell 6, attempts are made to achieve decision-making synergies across markets by, for example, developing pan-European or pan-American strategies in particular functional areas. In cell 8, economies of scale and scope are pursued by the national subsidiary managers themselves by standardizing product offering across national markets that have strong similarities in demand. In this case, subsidiary initiative is critical.

The strategy experts have done a good job distinguishing between cells 1 and 9 but issues involving most of the other cells have rarely been addressed. For example, the basic matrix of integration (cell 1) and national responsiveness (cell 9) popularized by Christopher Bartlett and Sumantra Ghoshal in their 1989 book *Managing Across Borders: The Transnational Solution* distinguished between a pure global cell 1 strategy and the 'act local' national responsiveness strategy of cell 9. In addition, the key contribution of their 'transnational solution' framework was the prescription that MNEs should combine strategies in cells 1 and 9 by attempting to develop the capability to implement either a national or a global approach within each separate business, each function within that business, and each task within that function.

The Bartlett and Ghoshal framework can usefully explain cell 3 (centralized, global strategic decision making combined with local product offering) – the act global-think local approach. It also allows the analysis of less common cases in cell 7, where powerful national subsidiaries are responsible for delivering global products but themselves choose which products have the most potential in their national markets and largely take responsibility for delivery – an approach found in many global professional services companies. Yet their framework cannot handle cell 5 – triad-based strategies – very well nor the intermediate cases of cells 2, 4, 6, and 8 – all cases where the regional level is important.

Here we report data that suggest an increasing number of MNEs operate largely at the regional level. As a result, regional issues are becoming increasingly important in many MNEs either in terms of strategic decision making or actual product offering. The empirical evidence provided in the next sections suggests many MNEs are at least partially operating in cell 5 on a triad basis. So any strategy-related analysis of MNEs' operations must first take into account the need to deconstruct their strategic decision-making processes and product offering on global, regional, and national lines, building on a more complex analytical tool than a conventional integration–national responsiveness matrix.

This will allow analysis of the actual extent of triad-based decision-making power and investigation of the rationale for region-based and/or adapted products and services from MNEs. If the theoretical construct of a 'regional solution' (cell 5 in Figure 4.1) is neglected, empirical research on strategy and structure in MNEs cannot portray accurately the present importance and future potential of the regional approach.

The regional approach of cell 5 is an efficient corporate response to several factors. First, internal information-processing requirements are critical. If the 'rules of engagement' are different in each region (different industry structures, different regulatory system, different competitive position of the firm, different product scope, and so on), then intra-regional information processing must equip affiliates to cope effectively with shared external circumstances and develop regionally consistent strategies.

Second, customer requirements may differ greatly across regions depending on the level of economic development, culturally determined preferences, and so on.

Third, regional clusters may impose specific types of behaviour on firms in order for them to be perceived as legitimate. This particularly applies to suppliers, related and supporting industries, the non-business infrastructure, and others. Here, regional flexibility may be critical for firms to function effectively as true insiders in the area.

Finally, political requirements at the regional level are increasingly important. It could be argued that regional cooperation agreements such as the North American Free Trade Agreement (NAFTA) and the European Union's (EU) single market represent the elimination of trade and investment barriers and therefore allow MNEs to reduce the attention they pay to government policy. In fact, however, regional agreements usually imply not merely the elimination of national regulations but a shift of regulatory authority to the regional level, forcing MNEs to allocate resources to monitor and manage relationships at that level.

This is reinforced by the new trade regime of the World Trade Organization (WTO), which has to devote enormous managerial resources to arbitrate triad-based trade disputes. The new protectionism of health, safety, and environmental regulations is preventing an open world market and reinforcing triad markets. NAFTA is being expanded into the Free Trade Agreement of the Americas (FTAA) and 13 countries are in negotiations to join the EU. These political developments reinforce the triads and the need for regional government policies and triad-based firm strategies.

Empirical Evidence on Triad Activity

From an organizational complexity perspective, the analysis of global strategies is particularly interesting when studying firms with a dispersed configuration of activities (rather than merely global exporters). Here, the focus is simply on geographical dispersion of sales, assets, and employees in terms of 'foreign-to-total' (F/T) ratios. UNCTAD reports the F/T ratios for sales, assets, and employees on an annual basis for the world's largest 100 MNEs, ranked by foreign assets. By weighing equally each of these three ratios, UNCTAD constructs an index of transnationality (TNC).

The TNC index for 1999 data is reported in Table 4.1 as the 'internationalization' index. Discussing global strategy only makes sense for companies that have a high share of foreign sales and assets and employees abroad. The others, almost out of necessity, build mainly on domestic practices in strategy formulation and implementation. The index itself, however, is merely a proxy for an MNE's physical level of internationalization and does not provide any information on its global strategy. However, after identifying the set of firms with the highest physical level of internationalization, the interesting question arises of whether these firms, faced with the most complex environmental and internal organization challenges, actually do pursue global strategies or instead rely more on regional and national approaches.

The 20 MNEs in Table 4.1 are mostly from small, open economies such as Canada, Switzerland, or Norway or are members of the EU such as France, the UK, Germany, and Sweden. There are no US MNEs in the top 20 internationalized firms – not all that surprising given the huge size of the domestic US market.

Table 4.1—The world's most 'Internationalized' MNEs, ranked by TNC index, 1996

Rank	Company Name	Country	UNCTAD Foreign as % of Total Sales	UNCTAD TNC Index
1	Seagram Company	Canada	0.9683	0.9734
2	Asea Brown Boveri ABB	Switzerland/Sweden	0.9745	0.9609
3	Nestlé SA	Switzerland	0.9813	0.9531
4	Thomson Corporation	Canada	0.9407	0.949
5	Solvay SA	Belgium	0.956	0.9217
6	Holderbank Financiere	Switzerland	0.8628	0.8978
7	Electrolux AB	Sweden	0.9246	0.8861
8	Unilever	Netherlands/United Kingdom	0.8635	0.871
9	Grand Metropolitan	United Kingdom	0.9046	0.8709
10	Roche Holding AG	Switzerland	0.9817	0.8704
11	Philips Electronics N.V.	Netherlands	0.9511	0.8489
12	Kvaerner ASA	Norway	0.7692	0.8167
13	Northern Telecom	Canada	0.8893	0.8069
14	Bayer AG	Germany	0.822	0.7985
15	Cable and Wireless Plc	United Kingdom	0.7161	0.781
16	Glaxo Wellcome Plc	United Kingdom	0.9211	0.7805
17	Eridania Beghin-Say SA	France	0.7866	0.7634
18	Novartis	Switzerland	0.9795	0.7525
19	LM Ericsson AB	Sweden	0.9325	0.7326
20	Akzo Nobel N.V.	Netherlands	0.7365	0.7308

Source: UNCTAD, *World Investment Report*, 1999. Data in this table are for 1996.

Building on the internationalization levels measured in Table 4.1 allows an additional and more interesting analysis. While these 20 MNEs have the majority of their sales outside their home country, they are still very regional. Their sales are still mainly in their home-triad regional market. This point is demonstrated in Table 4.2, where MNEs are ranked according to their intra-regional sales percentages, that is sales within Europe (and usually within the 15 member states of the EU) for MNEs from those countries and within NAFTA for Canadian and US MNEs. There are no Asia-based MNEs in this list.

The data in Table 4.2 reveal that the majority of the world's most international MNEs are, in fact, operating mainly in their home-triad market. For example, the French MNEs Pernod Ricard (81.7 % intra-regional sales); Eridania Beghin-Say (72.1 %); and Vivendi (68 %) are clearly 'European' MNEs in their sales since over two-thirds of their business is within Europe. They need a Europe-based strategy not a global one. The same is true for several other MNEs with high internationalization levels. These MNEs are operating in their home-base triad for the majority of their sales: Akzo Nobel (63 %); Solvay (61 %); Nortel Networks (54.4 %); ABB (54.0 %);

Table 4.2—Triad-home region sales of the world's most internationalized MNEs

Company	Home Country	2001 % Intra-regional	2001 % Extra-regional	UNCTAD Foreign as % of Total
Vivendi	France	68.0	32.0	NA
Pernod Ricard	France	81.7	18.3	NA
ABB	Switzerland/Sweden	54.0	46.0	97.5
Nestlé	Switzerland	31.6	68.4	98.1
Solvay	Belgium	61.0	39.0	95.6
Thomson Corporation	Canada	84.4	15.6	94.1
Holcim	Switzerland	33.0	67.0	86.3
Electrolux	Sweden	47.0	53.0	92.5
Unilever	Netherlands/United Kingdom	38.7	61.3	86.4
Diageo	United Kingdom	31.8	68.2	NA
Roche	Switzerland	37.0	63.0	98.2
Royal Philips	Netherlands	53.2	46.8	95.1
Kvaerner	Norway	NA	NA	76.9
Nortel Networks	Canada	54.4	45.6	88.9
Bayer	Germany	44.9	55.1	82.2
Cable and Wireless	United Kingdom	NA	NA	71.6
GlaxoSmithKline	United Kingdom	26.5	73.5	92.1
Eridania Beghin-Say	France	72.1	27.9	78.7
Novartis	Switzerland	32.0	68.0	98.0
LM Ericsson	Sweden	46.1	53.9	93.3
Akzo Nobel N.V.	Netherlands	63.0	37.0	73.7

and Philips (53.2 %). There are three other MNEs that are very home triad based: Electrolux (47 %); Ericsson (46.1 %); and Bayer (44.9 %). For two MNEs these data could not be constructed (Kvaerner and Cable and Wireless).

This leaves only seven of the top 20 with widely dispersed activities as potential candidates for a global strategy in terms of strategic decision making and product offering that could be positioned in cell 1 of Figure 4.1. These are:

- Unilever (38.7 % sales in Europe; 26.6 % in North America; 15.4 % in Asia; 12.7 % in Latin America; and 6.6 % in the rest of the world);
- Roche (37 % in Europe; 38 % in North America; and 25 % in the rest of the world);
- Holcim (33 % in Europe; 22 % in North America; 27 % in Latin America; and 18 % in the rest of the world);
- Novartis (32 % in Europe; 43 % in the US; and 25 % in the rest of the world);
- Diageo (31.8 % in Europe and 68.2 % in the rest of the world);

- Nestlé (31.6 % in Europe; 31.4 % in the Americas; and 37 % in the rest of the world);
- GlaxoSmithKline (26.5 % in Europe; 52.5 % in the US; and 21 % in the rest of the world).

Basic strategic knowledge of these firms suggests, however, that few of them pursue a cell 1 strategy. Firms such as Unilever and Nestlé are better known for their regional integration and national responsiveness than for a global approach, both in terms of strategic decision making and product offering. In addition, firms from the pharmaceutical industry such as Roche, Novartis, and GlaxoSmithKline need to adapt their product offering to the various countries and regions in which they operate, depending upon patent laws, idiosyncratic distribution systems, and consumer preferences.

In other words, in this exclusive set of 20 highly internationalized MNEs, two-thirds are really home-triad based in terms of geographical dispersion of activities and therefore are not even candidates for global strategy development; the one-third with widely dispersed activities largely consists of firms with important regional and national elements in strategy development. Most of the other 80 of the top 100 internationalized companies are even less global and are either domestic or home-based MNEs. Location and region appear to be critical parameters in MNE strategy.

In accordance with Bartlett and Ghoshal's transnational solution concept, which acknowledged a diversity of approaches within a single firm, the purpose of Figure 4.1 is not merely to position MNEs in individual cells but rather to show that international strategy does have a regional, often triad-based, dimension. In this context, it should be recognized that different strategic business units (SBU) within an MNE might be faced with different requirements for regional adaptation. While it is difficult to find data on SBU sales by region for the UNCTAD 100 most internationalized companies, some examples are useful to illustrate how, within a single MNE, the presence of substantial international activities may vary strongly across SBUs.

Table 4.3 reports data on the SBUs of Vivendi Universal. Some SBUs, like CANAL+, are 96 % in Europe while others have a larger US presence, such as the Universal Studios Group (57 % US), publishing (35 % US) and music, which is 42 % in the US and 40 % in Europe. Vivendi's water business is part of the environmental services SBU and this is 73 % in Europe.

The large retail organizations are even more triad based than the manufacturing MNEs. Large US retailers like Wal-Mart, Sears, and K-Mart are all North America based. The latter two have no stores outside the US and Canada and Wal-Mart has only 10 % of its stores outside the NAFTA region. Wal-Mart has 4,189 stores of which 3,118 are in the US, 174 in Canada and 499 in Mexico. Only 398 are in international markets. Nonetheless, Wal-Mart is the most international large-scale retailer from the US. In 2001, foreign revenue as a percentage of total revenues was 16.26 % ($35.4 billion of a total of $217.7 billion).

Turning to financial services, the world's largest financial MNE, Citigroup, is also very regional. In Citigroup's consumer banking group, total revenues are 72.7 % in North America. Citigroup has large commercial loans to foreign companies but is not as active in foreign consumer loans, the latter being 65.6 % in the US. Indeed,

Table 4.3—Vivendi Universal 2001 revenues by region (%)

Area	Europe	US	ROW
Music	40	42	18
Publishing	55	35	10
Universal Studios Group	28	57	15
CANAL+ Group & Other	96	2	2
Telecoms	87	–	13
Internet	47	53	–
Total media and communications	62	26	12
Environmental services	73	19	8
Non-core businesses	67	–	33
Total Vivendi Universal	68	22	10

Source: Vivendi Universal Annual Report
Note: Vivendi purchased Seagram in 1999 and the combined operations are reported here

Citibank became even less international in scope after the merger with Travelers as the latter's insurance business was very localized and this offset much of Citibank's banking diversification in South America and Asia.

Implications of Regional Strategies for the 'Rival States, Rival Firms' Framework

John Stopford and Susan Strange's 1991 book *Rival States, Rival Firms: Competition for World Market Shares* represented a landmark study on business–government relations in the international sphere, providing a simultaneous analysis of the increasing cross-border interactions of MNEs and national governments and between the two. In particular, state–business bargaining was viewed as the nexus of international treaties. The increasing power of regions that encompass a number of countries adds an additional layer of complexity to their model, however, as shown in Figure 4.2. We build on the original Stopford and Strange work with an extended model that takes into account the importance of regional power.

The relationships (1), (2), and (3) in Figure 4.2 reflect the conventional cooperative and competitive interactions involving firms and national governments. Of equal interest in a regionalized world are the relationships (4), (5), and (6). Relationship (5) reflects the fact that national governments need to attach as much attention to regional institutions as to conventional state-to-state relationships. In the EU context, the enlargement issue, including the conditions for new states to become member states, is the best example of a dossier that requires permanent monitoring by individual governments. In the NAFTA context, the possible extension of this regional agreement to a free trade agreement of the Americas requires equal attention, especially from Canada, the smallest partner in the present agreement, to carefully assess the expected national costs and benefits of such an extension.

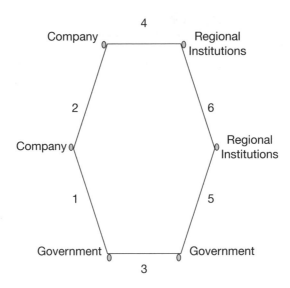

Figure 4.2—Rival states, rival firms, rival regions.

Source: Adapted from Stopford and Strange (1991)

Relationship (6) has been largely neglected so far, as only EU representatives have regularly been given the authority in a variety of international forums to replace national, member state governments. Even there, its standing in multilateral negotiations is not always clear cut and remains the subject of much debate among member states. It can be expected, however, that in the future a deepening of regional integration in various areas of the world will lead to bargaining among regional institutions.

Relationship (4) is the most interesting for our purposes. It implies that MNEs should pay increasing attention to policy making at the regional level, with the EU and NAFTA being again cases in point. At the NAFTA level, firms are interested especially in the functioning of the dispute-settlement mechanisms set up to resolve trade disputes among members.

At the EU level the principle of mutual recognition has been adopted in many sectors, implying that the quality standards accepted in one member state should also be accepted by all others. The advantage of this system has been that unproductive and time-consuming debates among member states, guided by protectionist goals, when searching for common standards have been avoided. However, mutual recognition often imposes additional costs on MNEs compared to a system of EU-wide standards. It allows some firms with lower quality standards to compete on a par with firms that have adopted higher standards and it reduces the incentives to create scope economies by diffusing best practices across the MNE network. It can therefore be expected that a new drive towards common standards will take place in the coming years as a substitute for the principle of mutual recognition. This will require MNEs to devote renewed attention to EU regulatory processes.

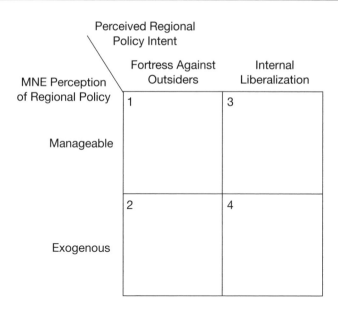

Figure 4.3—Multinationals and regional policy.

In practice, MNEs can adopt four regional bargaining positions, as shown in Figure 4.3. In quadrants 1 and 2 of Figure 4.3, the intent of regional institutions and their policies are perceived by MNEs as protectionist, mainly aimed at creating a fortress against outsiders. There are certainly many examples of regional institutions set up at least partly to increase collective bargaining power and to artificially strengthen insiders. Stopford and Strange have argued that ASEAN has had some success in this area. But in many other cases, this policy approach has failed – for example, the Andean pact signatories' efforts to exercise collective bargaining against MNEs.

In quadrant 2, firms do not attempt to affect regional policy: they view it as either beneficial (if they are insiders) or harmful (if they are outsiders). The interesting effect of this micro-level view is that outsider MNEs may attempt to overcome the perceived fortress wall by becoming 'insiders', as demonstrated by the entry mode choices of many Japanese firms in the EU and North America in response to regional integration efforts. The outcome is thus a regional strategy, as insider status is usually accompanied by substantial product adaptation and delegation of power to regional operations.

In quadrant 1, regional policy is viewed as to some extent manageable by firms. This approach is usually adopted by incumbents, who wish to erect protective walls against outsiders, as demonstrated by the efforts of large European firms to affect the application of EU-administered anti-dumping regulations against non-EU companies. Outside firms are usually less effective in dealing with regional institutions because they are hindered by the liability of foreignness and the lack of institutional competition to attract foreign direct investment found at national and sub-national levels.

Quadrants 3 and 4 represent the MNE perception that regional institutions are there primarily to foster trade and investment liberalization. In quadrant 4, regional policy is viewed as exogenous but, as was the case with quadrant 2, this perception may still affect firm strategies. More specifically, it may lead to substantial efficiency-seeking and asset-seeking foreign direct investment. The former may be needed to respond to the creation of a more open, internal market in which the relative strengths of various firms may be altered by the reduction of trade and investment barriers. The latter may result from the perception that the region has become important but that market expansion can be achieved more efficiently through strategic alliances, mergers, and acquisitions than by greenfield investment.

Finally, quadrant 3 implies the active managing of regional institutions to affect trade and investment liberalization. This may include strategies ranging from attempts to halt regional liberalization to active cooperation in the design of common regional standards.

Given the above analysis, it is clear that Figure 4.3 embodies a wide variety of possible MNE strategies, even within single quadrants. The point is that large MNEs cannot afford to neglect regional policies and regional institutions and that the strategies they adopt crucially depend on their perceptions of regional policy intents and the extent to which they can affect how these are translated into regional policies. In other words, externalities may exist at the regional level, benefiting firms that are aware of their existence and attempt to capitalize on them.

Conclusions

There is abundant empirical support for our proposition that many large MNEs operate on a triad-region basis rather than a global basis. The old-fashioned view of 'global' MNEs, in the sense of firms with a balanced, worldwide dispersion of activities, centralized strategic decision making and standardized products as the predominant form of international business, needs to be replaced. The world's 100 largest MNEs are to a large extent triad-based regional players not global ones. They operate on a regional basis and a relevant framework to analyse MNE strategy needs to recognize this.

Here we have developed a three-stage conceptual framework. First, the importance of regional elements in the strategic decision making and product offering of MNEs must be analysed. We have argued that such regional elements can be found in most MNEs, even those with the strongest dispersion of sales, assets, and employees.

Second, we have argued that Stopford and Strange's model of 'triangular diplomacy' needs to be extended to include the regional level. The interactions between MNEs and regional institutions are especially important in this respect.

Third, MNE strategy towards regional institutions and policies can take various forms, depending on whether these are viewed as attempts to create entry barriers against outsiders or to achieve internal liberalization. In addition, MNE strategies will largely depend on their assessment of the exogenous or manageable nature of regional policies.

Our findings are partially confirmed in work on the triad-based nature of the automobile sector by E. H. Schlie and George Yip in 2000. However, they argue that most MNEs first formulate a global strategy and that some then selectively regionalize; that is, regionalization should be viewed as one possible outcome of a global strategy. We have not observed this. Rather, the triad strategies of MNEs in 2002 are very similar to the nature of triad strategies in 1972 and 1980 when Stopford first identified the importance of triad MNE strategy and structure.

Section 2

MANAGING THE MULTINATIONAL ENTERPRISE

5 The Evolving Multinational: Strategy and Structure in Latin American Operations, 1990–2000

José de la Torre[1], José Paulo Esperança[2] and Jon Martínez[3]

[1]Florida International University, [2]ISCTE, Lisbon and
[3]Universided de Los Andes, Santiago

The degree of market integration has increased dramatically across the world in the past half century. Beginning in the late 1980s the prevailing political winds began to shift throughout Latin America in favour of a liberal market system, following the example first set by the Asian Tigers, then Chile and, later, Mexico – particularly in the areas of trade and competition policy. The resulting decrease in trade barriers, the liberalization of foreign investment regimes, and a general process of privatization and deregulation dramatically changed the relative rewards a multinational corporation (MNC) might reap from operating an integrated network of regional subsidiaries as opposed to a collection of semi-autonomous domestic units.

Local subsidiaries, often under the partial control of different owners and boards of directors, found themselves having to rationalize their efforts or perish (Dasu and de la Torre, 1997). In Perlmutter's (1969) typology, a shift from a polycentric to a geocentric system became mandatory.

This chapter traces the organizational responses of multinational companies originating in Europe and North America to these changed conditions. If our contingency views hold, we should witness a greater degree of integration among MNC subsidiaries in Latin America during the decade, accompanied by the adoption of organizational and managerial practices that support such integration and with positive financial results associated with the 'right' responses.

We discuss first the main arguments for a contingency perspective on MNC structure. Next, we describe the nature and level of change in the prevailing environmental conditions within Latin America during the 1990s. From this, we derive a model relating the two and the resulting expectations regarding corporate performance. Finally, we offer some conclusions as to the applicability of the model and the implications of our findings for MNC management.

Structural and Organizational Responses to Global Integration

The structure-follows-strategy paradigm has a long history in the field of multinational corporate research. Following Alfred Chandler's monumental study of the evolution of US industry, John Stopford, Larry Franko, Dick Rumelt, and others carried out a series of analyses aimed at confirming its validity among multinational firms originating in both North America and Europe.[1]

These studies were followed by an explicit adoption by international business scholars of a contingency model of MNC organization.[2] Prahalad and Doz (1987) argued that firms faced limited choices in terms of structural adaptation to conflicting demands of product diversity and geographical spread and articulated the 'integration–responsiveness' (IR) model of MNC organization. Porter's (1986) classification along two dimensions of coordination and configuration (C&C) echoed this analysis and had similar implications for diversified organizational responses. The specific application of these principles to an analysis of headquarters–subsidiary relations further cemented the link between environmental or industry conditions and the organizational responses deemed most suitable to foster competitive advantage in world markets.[3]

Bartlett and Ghoshal (1989) suggested the adoption of a network structure among multinational company subsidiaries as a way out of the conundrum implied in the IR or C&C frameworks. Such a response, they argued, would facilitate learning in the corporation, assigning roles to different subsidiaries that were particularly suited to their locational and strategic advantages. The need for a network form of organization to deal with the complexity and heterogeneity of MNC strategic tasks had, in fact, been a hallmark of the Swedish school.[4]

A different and earlier stream of work focused instead on the roles that centralization and control systems played in the operations of multinational companies. A number of organizational mechanisms, linked to the firm's chain of command, include the degree of centralization of decision making, formalization of policies, and standardization of procedures, planning, reporting, and control systems. In fact, many students of MNCs refer to these mechanisms as alternative approaches (to pure structural responses) to align the organization with its strategic intent.[5]

More recently, researchers have focused on the role that informal or subtler mechanisms of coordination can play in this regard. Instruments such as lateral

---

1 The key studies were Fouraker and Stopford (1968), Stopford and Wells (1972), Rumelt (1974), and Dyas and Thanheiser (1976). Subsequent research on the link between strategy and structure included Egelhoff (1982, 1988), Daniels et al. (1984), and Davidson and Haspeslagh (1982).

2 Lawrence and Lorsch (1967), Doz and Prahalad (1991).

3 See reviews by Doz and Prahalad (1991) and Egelhoff (1991), and research by Doz and Prahalad (1981); Hedlund (1981); Jarillo and Martínez (1990); White and Poynter (1990); Roth et al. (1991); Birkinshaw et al. (1995); and O'Donnell (2000).

4 See for example Hedlund (1981, 1986).

5 See Dunning (1958), Safarian (1966) and Hedlund (1981).

or cross-departmental teams, task forces, and integrative committees; the use of informal communication processes such as fostering personal contacts among managers, corporate conferences, and annual meetings; policies on cross-national transfers of managers; and socialization processes that may include acculturation seminars, measurement and reward systems, manager rotations, and so on have all been shown to be relevant in fostering particular organizational objectives.

Early research first indicated the importance of these coordination devices.[6] Bartlett and Ghoshal specifically suggested the role such mechanisms play in facilitating the 'transnational' organization, their model for the future, whereas Martínez and Jarillo (1991) tested their importance empirically. From these studies emerges a view that although structure is important as a vehicle to implement strategy – the so-called 'architectural' or 'anatomical' view – there are many processes that are equally if not more important – the 'physiological' and 'psychological' approaches. The issue, therefore, is not one dimensional but multidimensional.

The ensuing complexity of coordination within MNCs is enhanced by the rise in technology diversity and differentiated requirements. As technology intensive MNCs engage in activities for which technologies are embedded in separate units, the resulting complexity requires a collaborative, iterative interaction among the relevant overseas units and headquarters (Medcaf, 2001, p. 1004).

Economic and Political Change in Latin America

For much of the 20th century, the preferred economic philosophy in much of Latin America was that of import-substituting industrialization (ISI). Faced with a rapid decline in primary product prices and the closure of many of Latin America's traditional markets in the aftermath of the 1930s depression, most governments were forced to turn to their internal markets and to a process of industrialization in order to generate domestic employment. This policy had mixed results but was generally successful in the 1950–1970 period, when rapid rates of economic growth prevailed and set the foundation to a gradual modernization and urbanization of society.[7]

The oil shocks and economic crises of the 1970s and early 1980s put an end to this era, culminating in the Mexican financial default of 1982 and a period often characterized as the 'lost decade' during which structural reforms and debt rescheduling led to severe contraction of economic activity and real losses in purchasing power for most citizens of the region. But beginning in the mid-1980s 'a quiet revolution began to shake the traditional foundations of Latin American economic thought. Slowly but steadily the once undisputed popularity of state interventionism, inward-looking development, and protectionism began to erode while the values associated with free markets, liberalization, and privatization started to

---

6 See Wiechmann (1974), Galbraith and Edstrom (1976), and Ouchi and Johnson (1978).

7 For a discussion of these historical trends and their antecedents see Skidmore and Smith (1989) or Clayton and Conniff (1999). Between 1950 and 1980, the region's gross domestic product grew at an annual rate of 5.5 %.

influence the policy dialogue' (Costin and Vanolli, 1998, p. v). This quiet revolution spread from Chile to Mexico, where the government of President de la Madrid began negotiations for Mexico to join the OECD, then to Bolivia and Argentina (under President Menem), eventually reaching Brazil with the introduction of the plan *Real* in 1994.

The elements of this economic reform movement are many.[8] Average tariff and non-tariff protection dropped dramatically from an average regional level of 52 % in 1985, to less than 14 % by 1992.[9] Many countries in the region joined free-trade pacts such as Mercosur in 1991, the 'G3' pact (Mexico, Colombia and Venezuela) in 1993, and the start of negotiations for the Free Trade Agreement of the Americas in 1994. Mexico, for example, led this process by negotiating free trade agreements with Chile (1992); the US, and Canada in the context of NAFTA (1994); Costa Rica, Colombia, Venezuela and Bolivia (1995); Nicaragua (1998); the European Union and Israel (2000); the European Free Trade Association, Guatemala, Honduras, and El Salvador (2001); and a host of pending deals with other countries ranging from South Korea and Japan to Brazil. As a result of these activities, intra-regional trade increased from 10.2 % of total trade in 1990, to 18.7 % in 1999 (27 % if we exclude Mexico, whose trade is overwhelmingly with its NAFTA partners).

Privatization of state-owned enterprises was undertaken with glee, first in Mexico under the Salinas administration and then throughout the region. Income from privatizations averaged about $10 billion annually for 1991–1996 and rose to nearly $30 billion in 1997 and $40 billion in 1998 before dropping in the next two years. Fiscal deficits that exceeded 10 to 15 % of GDP during the heyday of ISI policies were dramatically cut to less than 2–3 % in most countries. Foreign investment restrictions were lifted in most cases, with nearly free access provided to both portfolio and direct investors (with some exceptions, such as petroleum and derivatives in Mexico and Venezuela).

As a result, inward foreign direct investment (FDI) for the seven largest countries in the region rose from an annual average of $6.2 billion in 1985–1990, to $17 billion in 1991–1996, and $59.3 billion in 1997–1999. Cross-border FDI also increased dramatically (from less than $5 billion in 1991 to over $30 billion in 1997) as Latin America-based companies took advantage of the liberalization process and increased liquidity to venture into neighbouring markets.

Many critical reform processes, however, proved to be resistant to change. Labour market rigidities, for example, persisted in many countries and involved high political costs that nascent democracies were unwilling to pay. Civil service and judicial system reform were significantly behind schedule, as were attempts to deal with official corruption and personal insecurity, two large and nearly intractable problems of Latin American society.

Poverty remained difficult to conquer as economic transformation often resulted in higher unemployment; and bureaucracies continued to permeate life and render

8 For two excellent summaries of these developments see Edwards (1995) and Costin and Vanolli (1998).

9 This represents a mathematical average for 14 countries: Argentina, Bolivia, Brazil, Chile, Colombia, Costa Rica, Ecuador, Guatemala, Mexico, Nicaragua, Paraguay, Peru, Uruguay, and Venezuela (Edwards, 1995).

entrepreneurship a test fit only for the most hardy.[10] And as the Mexican (1994), Brazilian (1998), Argentinean (2001), and Venezuelan (2002) crises have proven, much remains to be done to achieve stable growth in the region.

The Challenge to MNCs in the Region

In general, however, it is undeniable that in 2000 the region was more open and exposed to competitive forces than a decade before. The drop in external protection and the phenomenal growth in FDI reported above have driven efficiency considerations to the forefront. MNCs' participation in the region has also increased across all sectors and countries (accounting for 220 of the region's largest 500 companies in 2000, as opposed to 135 in 1995).

Under the 'old regime' foreign investors approached different countries with the expectation that each plant or facility they built would serve primarily its domestic market under conditions approaching monopolistic competition. Since market size, sophistication, and competitive conditions varied greatly in the region, this led to differentiated investment strategies in terms of the scale, technology, and cost structure of local operations. Furthermore, the mandated or implicit preference of local authorities for domestic majority share in the equity of foreign corporations encouraged MNCs to establish joint ventures or licensing agreements with local partners. Thus, many MNC networks in Latin America consisted of largely independent operations, each characterized by different economic structures and ownership arrangements, each operating primarily in its respective domestic markets under highly protected conditions. Figure 5.1(a) illustrates this 'federal' organizational configuration.[11]

As the reform movement took hold in the 1990s, two different factors impacted the strategies of these firms. One was that regional economic prospects must have seemed better than at any time in the recent past. Second, existing operations, which had subsisted side by side in spite of differences in cost performance, quality of output, and product range and which were under the control of different owners and boards of directors, now found themselves in potential competition with each other and needing to rationalize their efforts. Subsidiaries that were hitherto independent of one another had to be integrated into a tight network capable of acting as a unit, such as that illustrated in Figure 5.1(b).[12]

Whether this was in fact so and whether MNCs operating in the region undertook to increase their control over local subsidiaries, integrating their network into a more coherent whole, is the fundamental question we address in this chapter. We

---

10 Nonetheless, the share of population in poverty (defined as earning less than $2 per day) declined from 48 % to 42 % during the decade. According to a study by Harvard University (Djankov et al., 2000) starting a business in several countries of Latin America required over 15 steps and 91 days (on average), whereas the same could be accomplished in the United States or Canada in 2–4 steps and in two days or less.

11 See earlier studies by de la Torre (1997a, 1997b).

12 For more details on such a process see Dasu and de la Torre (1997).

(a)

(b)

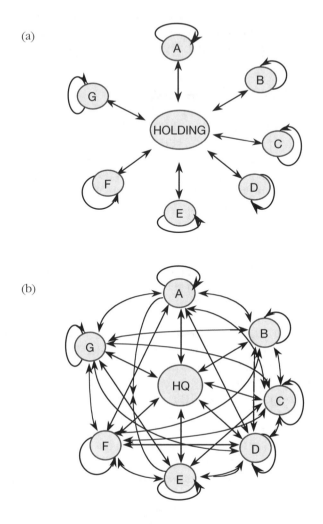

Figure 5.1—(a) Federal structure of independent and semi-autonomous subsidiaries. (b) Integrated network of highly coordinated subsidiaries.

turn now to an analysis of what these expectations would be in the context of our theoretical framework.

Conceptual Model and Expectations

Following the standard interpretation of contingency theory, our initial model states that environmental change (increased requirements for global integration for corporations operating within Latin America) will alter industry economics, which in turn will cause companies to modify their strategies accordingly and thus adapt their organizations in order to implement their modified strategies. Companies that make these strategic and organizational adjustments in a manner consistent with the environmental changes are expected to perform better than others which do not follow suit or which are late in their adjustments.

The impact of globalization in world markets has impacted industries in different ways depending on the nature of the products or services they offer and the markets they serve. For many companies this has meant seeking higher integration of their value-chain activities across geographical areas in search for efficiencies that come from scale, scope, and learning economies and linking their network of subsidiaries tightly around the world. This process of subsidiary integration requires considerable coordination efforts in order to obtain the desired efficiencies and synergies and these efforts have not always been painless nor have they brought about improved performance (Mitchell et al., 1992; Ushijima, 2002). Therefore, we expect that the intensity by which these globalizing forces are perceived by the firm will determine the degree to which coordination efforts will be undertaken. Figure 5.2 depicts this relationship with the appropriate response located along the diagonal.

Given the dynamic nature of environmental change, particularly in the context of Latin America in the 1990s, we expect to see dramatic changes in both of these dimensions. That is, the pressures firms have experienced from globalization forces have accelerated within the region (and beyond) during this period, calling for a suitable competitive reaction and a concomitant organizational response from these firms. But again, as shown in Figure 5.3, this response needs to be consistent with the underlying changes.

Research Questions

This framework lead us to formulate certain expectations regarding the need for a match between the perception of the intensity of globalization pressures to which

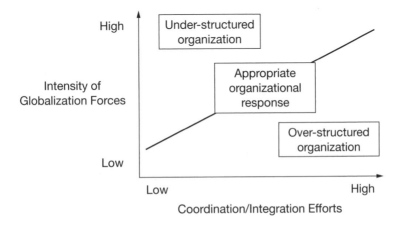

Figure 5.2—Globalization and organizational response.

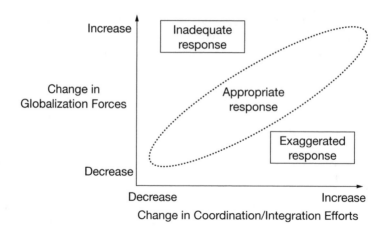

Figure 5.3—Changes in globalization versus changes in inter-subsidiary coordination.

a given firm was subjected during this period and its coordination/integration efforts. The range of organizational responses possible in order to implement higher degrees of coordination and integration is rather broad and should include both 'hard' (structural) and 'soft' (behavioural) approaches. Among the former, the following issues were examined:

- a shift in the locus of decision making and degree of centralization associated with critical product and market choices;
- the degree of formalization of managerial processes and exchanges between subsidiaries and parent company;
- the complexity and extent to which the firm applied regional planning and budgeting systems;
- the frequency and scope of reporting requirements by subsidiary management;
- the intensity of use of home- and third-country (versus local nationals) personnel among the subsidiaries' top executive echelons.

The use of 'softer' coordination mechanisms to achieve similar purposes is also well grounded in the literature. Included in this measure are a number of practices that have been shown to contribute to the sharing of information and the convergence of approaches such as the creation of task forces or permanent cross-country committees, regional brand teams, managerial rotations, the organization of product conferences or planning seminars, and so on. A stronger and more frequent use of such mechanisms should appear as regional integration accelerates.

In parallel with the use of these 'microstructures', we surmise that the development of an appropriate organizational culture through a process of socialization aimed at establishing a uniform set of beliefs, decision-making style, and sense of common values and objectives would be associated with any attempt to bring greater coordination or integration to the regional operations of the company.

Finally, we are fundamentally interested in whether, as predicted by our model, the adjustment of strategy and structures to the prevailing conditions resulted in any performance advantage over competitors. Appropriate responses to such environmental changes should be associated with better performance.

Research Methods

We conducted a mail survey of 449 MNCs in Europe (172) and North America (277) between December 2000 and July 2001. A total of 80 firms were disqualified for various reasons and an additional 86 firms declined to participate, mainly owing to corporate policy. After multiple sampling we obtained 58 usable responses.

Globalization Pressures

A number of measures exist at the national level, among which that developed by A. T. Kearney and the Carnegie Endowment for International Peace is most popular (*Foreign Policy*, 2002). Similarly, there have been multiple attempts to measure the degree of internationalization (DOI) associated with different firms. Early studies used simple proxies for DOI such as the number of foreign subsidiaries or foreign assets as a percentage of total assets. The United Nations Center for Transnational Corporations (UNCTAD, 1995) used a measure consisting of the linear sum of three ratios – sales, assets, and employment – all depicting foreign to total activities. Sullivan (1994) created a reliable DOI scale composed of five variables. Ietto-Gilles (1998) proposed a two-factor approach that combines the qualities of UNCTAD's transnationality index with a measure of the locational spread of MNC activities.

Given our focus, we set out to define an index that reflected the pressures felt by management within a specific industry and regional context. We subscribe to the view expressed by Birkinshaw et al. (1995) that '[f]or an *individual* business, structural forces and competitive actions are both relevant aspects of the environment and form the basis of a comprehensive industry analysis' (p. 638). Thus, our measure of globalization pressures included a set of 'globalization drivers' as well as a sense of competitive reaction.

Second, we needed to deal with an array of industry much larger than that for which objective data is available from existing studies, and we needed to place the evaluation of these pressures in the context of Latin America in the 1990s since previous research had demonstrated the variability of national contexts in industry globalization measures. Therefore, we included a set of 17 measures in our questionnaire that asked the respondents to identify the strength of certain forces within the context of their own industry and region.[13]

Organizational Variables

We also collected information on all hard and soft organizational components listed above for the years 1990 and 2000. To avoid biased responses, we asked if the respondent was also at the firm (or in the same industry) in 1990 and if not how was the information obtained. Answers that appeared unreliable were discarded. In addition, data were collected on the respondent's view of various dimensions of corporate performance, including sales and market share, as well as financial performance relative to the competition for the past three years (1997–2000). They were also asked to judge whether this performance had improved over the decade, the impact of organizational changes on performance changes, and their view of the degree to which any organizational changes prepared the firm to face future conditions in the region.

Control Variables

We also measured a number of other potentially relevant factors, including the experience of the firm in Latin America (more or less than 10 years of experience in the region), the extent of its operations in the region (the number of national subsidiaries in 2000), its continental origins (North American or European), and its main industrial sector. Other control variables included size, the principal form of its corporate structure, the percent of sales that were within subsidiaries of the same company, the type of ownership, and the degree of internationalization of the parent company.

Results and Discussion

In order to examine these research questions, we conducted an extensive mail survey of North American and European MNCs (see box). Here we discuss the key findings from the research and the implications for MNC strategy and structure.

There was strong evidence from the sample that the perceived degree of globalization was significantly larger in 2000 than for 1990. Thus, managers responsible

---

13 The responses to these variables were factor analysed yielding four factors with a combined explanatory power of 69.6 % and Cronbach *alphas* ranging from 0.66 to 0.82. They were: (1) a measure that proxies the degree of differentiation – R&D and advertising intensity, etc. – characteristic of the sector; (2) the barriers to trade and investment across the region for that sector; (3) the degree of market homogeneity; and (4) the prevalence of MNCs in local markets.

for the operations of their companies' activities in the region have experienced a dramatic increase in integration pressures during the decade. As expected, the degree of centralization of decision making for the year 2000 was significantly larger than that for 1990. We also found that regional coordination increased significantly during the decade. Therefore, we can confirm an organizational response that is in accordance with the theoretical expectations.

In order to test various propositions we ran a series of step-wise regressions where each dependent variable was tested against the globalization measures and the control variables.[14] As expected, many of the organizational responses were highly correlated with the degree of globalization pressures, particularly as represented by the differentiation variable. In addition, the experience of the companies in the region appears to have an impact, with older networks exercising a greater degree of control over their subsidiaries than firms whose regional investments are more recent. Similarly, North American firms consistently show a propensity for greater centralization than European firms. Surprisingly, the size of the network does not appear to be significant.

The most interesting results, in our opinion, relate to the performance variables. Figure 5.4 shows the expectations regarding the fit between globalization pressures, organizational responses, and corporate performance. Firms clustered along the diagonal exhibit a measured response to their environmental requirements and, thus, should profit from their managerial wisdom by showing better performance than their rivals. Those above or below the diagonal should suffer from their inability to tailor their responses to environmental conditions and, consequently, should underperform compared to their competitors.

Figures 5.5 to 5.8 present the results of conducting such an analysis of variance tests for companies grouped according to this model. The charts on the left show

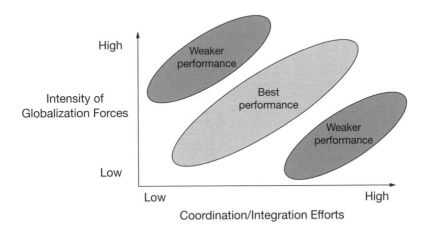

Figure 5.4—Expected linkages between globalization forces, corporate responses and performance.

---

14 For more detail on the statistical tests conducted, see de la Torre et al. (2002).

the mean response for each of the groups of companies, whereas the charts on the right position each of the respondents along two dimensions of globalization and organizational response. We test first (Figure 5.5) a measure of *market* performance that captures both growth in sales and market share for each company relative to their competition. The vertical dimension represents the degree of homogeneity across national markets in terms of consumer behaviour, channels of distribution, and media (among others, a proxy for the underlying pressures for market integration), and on the horizontal axis we measure the degree to which the firms undertook to formalize the relationship between parent company and subsidiaries.

Only two clusters of firms were identifiable in this case, with the firms that 'under-responded' being indistinguishable from those along the diagonal. However, those that overreacted to the need for market standardization across the region did perform significantly worse.

Figure 5.6 uses a different measure of globalization pressures – that is, the degree to which competition in these markets is defined by other multinational companies and the extent to which product standardization is required – but we keep the same measure of market performance as before. In this case, three distinct clusters appear with the 'middle' group (the one along the diagonal, representing the 'appropriately calibrated' response) significantly outperforming those that over or under-reacted. The same results are obtained in Figure 5.7 but this time we measure *financial* performance instead of market performance. Once again, the middle group significantly outperforms the other two.

The last diagrams in Figure 5.8 show a similar analysis but with a measure of the *change* in performance as opposed to a static analysis as in the previous cases. Here, the middle cluster is once more represented by the firms that generated superior improvement in their relative performance over the period when compared with their under- and over-reacting colleagues.

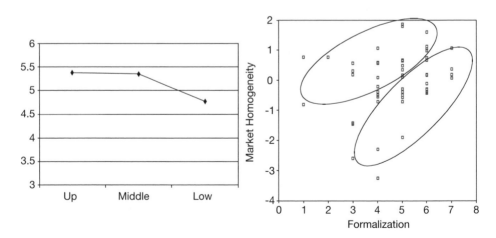

Two distinct clusters (top and middle not significantly different), with $F = 3.547$ and $p > 0.065$.

Figure 5.5—Market performance according to the extent of cross-market homogeneity and the degree of formalization of subsidiary/HQ relationships.

Conclusions

This analysis confirms our initial contention that managers responsible for the Latin American operations of major North American and European multinational companies have experienced a rapid and significant increase in globalization and integration pressures within their industries and region. They have responded by

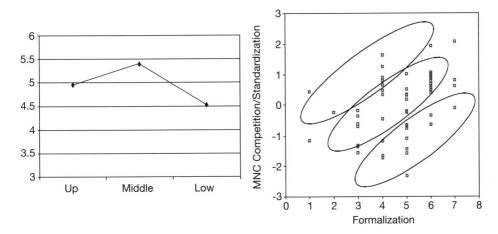

Three significantly distinct clusters, $F = 3.734$ and $p > 0.030$.

Figure 5.6—Market performance according to the intensity of MNC competition/standardization and the degree of formalization of subsidiary/HQ relationships.

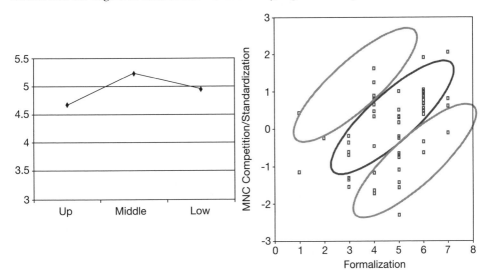

Three significantly distinct clusters, $F = 3.103$ and $p > 0.084$.

Figure 5.7—Financial performance according to the intensity of MNC competition/standardization and the degree of formalization of subsidiary/HQ relationships.

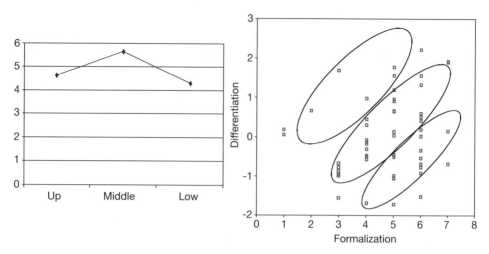

Three significantly distinct clusters, $F = 5.519$ and $p > 0.007$.

Figure 5.8—Change in performance according to the intensity of industry differentiation and the degree of formalization of subsidiary/HQ relationships.

increasing centralization of decision making and by undertaking greater inter-subsidiary coordination of their activities along a myriad of dimensions and across multiple functions and tasks. Furthermore, we conclude that this process of central-ization and formalization of subsidiary relationships was directly and proportionately related to an increase in globalization pressures.

More troublesome, our data suggest that this response is often arbitrary and unmeasured. Multinational corporate managers in the region will just as often over-shoot in their organizational responses (instituting, for example, tight controls and heavy coordination requirements when these are not necessary) as they will under-shoot (maintaining loose inter-subsidiary arrangements in the face of high integration requirements). Our attempts to relate any number of precise and finely tuned orga-nizational mechanisms to the intensity of four different measures of globalization pressures showed mixed or weak results. Whereas centralization of decision making and formalization of parent company–subsidiary relationships were indeed related to management's perception of increases in environmental pressures for greater inte-gration across countries and markets, the other (subtler) managerial mechanisms that we tested showed weak association with any of the forces pushing globalization and integration.

Older networks – those operating in the region for more than 10 years – show a higher propensity to engage in integration efforts. Perhaps this is because they grew in an era of independent and isolated markets and had more catching up to do as conditions changed. One might have assumed, however, that precisely for this reason they faced more obstacles in adapting to the new conditions though the data does not support this view. Newer investors, on the other hand, reacted with looser structures, perhaps because they generally had smaller networks and looked upon their investments as more exploratory in nature.

The fact that North American companies exercised greater control over their networks might be attributed to a simple explanation such as the effects of proximity. European investors may have felt instead that the greater distances (both geographical and cultural, although not necessarily in the case of Iberian companies) argued for greater autonomy. Alternatively, one might reach for a culturally based explanation whereby European MNCs are considered more tolerant of autonomy than their US and Canadian counterparts.

In any event, our most important findings relate to the linkage between corporate performance and the appropriateness of their responses to these environmental pressures. Exaggerated reactions or weak responses on the part of Latin American MNC managers to the requirements for more inter-subsidiary integration appear to lead to lower market and financial performance in most cases. This may come about as stringent centralization snuffs out entrepreneurship and local responsiveness to an extent not justified by competitive conditions. Such over-reaction may impose costs and rigidities on subsidiaries that are not compensated by any gains due to synergies or economies of scale. Whenever we see evidence of under-reaction, the culprit may lie in some degree of organizational inertia or political opposition to the loss of autonomy. Current managers or investors (in the case of joint ventures) may oppose integration as reducing their political power and autonomy, regardless of the economic justification. This is particularly true if the benefits of greater coordination and centralization are not uniformly distributed among a firm's regional operations. Such asymmetric cost/reward structure would engender opposition to change.

In conclusion, our results support the view that globalization is not all or nothing, nor does it apply equally across industries, firms or tasks. A measured and proportional response, one that combines both structural and managerial mechanisms, yields optimal results. Such findings resonate strongly with Stopford and Wells' conclusions, reached nearly three decades ago.

Acknowledgements

The statistical assistance of Paulo Albuquerque and Charlotte Ren, both PhD candidates at the Anderson School at UCLA, is gratefully acknowledged. Nancy Hsieh, Odir Pereira, Jenna Radomile and Mirthala Rangel provided extraordinary assistance in generating questionnaire returns. The financial support of UCLA's Center for International Business Education and Research is also gratefully acknowledged.

6 Risk and the Dynamics of Globalization

Donald R. Lessard[1]

MIT Sloan School of Management

Introduction

This chapter outlines how risk and the various mechanisms firms employ to address risk convey competitive advantages to globally integrated or locally embedded firms and, thus, shape the global landscape of an industry. This is illustrated through a multi-level perspective on a single industry – electrical power including generation, transmission, and distribution.

Following this introduction, the second section briefly reviews the principles of risk and competitive advantage, the third presents a stylized view of the global dynamics of the electrical power industry both in terms of which firms are represented in various countries and which practices are adopted in various countries, and the fourth section focuses on risk as a factor favouring global integration and local embeddedness as a complement to the more traditional scale and learning drivers of globalization and localization.

Risk and Competitive Advantage

While there are many dimensions along which one can classify risk, only one, to list them from 'inside' to 'outside', corresponds to the fundamental responses to these risks. Figure 6.1 presents such a classification for a generic set of activities in the electrical power sector, ranging from 'inside' project risks such as construction or operations risk, or enterprise-level integration risks; mezzo-level competitive and institutional risks; and 'outside' risks including country and world-level macro and market risks.[2]

1 I am grateful to my colleagues at the Brattle Group for providing me with a nuanced view of the evolution of the electrical power industry in several continents in recent years. I also have benefited greatly in developing the implications of the comparative advantage perspective on risk from working first with Nalin Kulatilaka and later with Roger Miller.

2 In examining the risks encountered in 60 large engineering projects, Miller and Lessard (2000) found that roughly one-third fell into each of these categories.

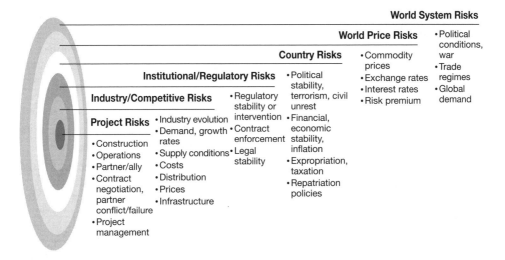

Figure 6.1—Arraying risks from 'inside' to 'outside'.

Regardless of the type of risk, there are only a small number of fundamental possible responses. These include responses that: have the potential actually to change risk drivers and thus alter the stand-alone distribution of cash flows[3] of the affected operation or asset – shaping or mitigating risks; those that have the potential to improve the stand-alone distribution of cash flows of the affected operations conditional on the realization of the risk drivers – real options and real pooling; and those that redistribute risk without affecting the stand-alone distributions of cash flows – financial diversification, hedging and insurance – and thus alter the portfolios of cash flows held by firms or investors.

In an idealized perfect capital market, only the first two categories can add value since individual investors can replicate the latter through financial transactions. Of course, even for publicly traded firms in developed countries these idealized conditions do not hold exactly and it is generally conceded that hedging can add value in the presence of tax asymmetries and agency problems.

For privately held firms as well as firms based in countries with incomplete capital markets, the third category is often important as investors cannot readily reshape their own holdings through financial transactions. It goes without saying that if not selected and managed effectively, all three categories of responses can destroy value.

There is a 'pecking order' of risk management responses to different types of risks. Inside risks of execution or fraud, for example, are best addressed by building an effective organization with properly aligned incentives and other means. Diversification or pooling does not alter the expected loss associated with these

---

3 I focus on the distributions of cash flows to avoid invoking assumptions regarding the completeness of financial markets required in order to make statements regarding the impacts of these actions on the economic value of assets or operations.

errors and insurance will be expensive (relative to the expected losses) because of the moral hazard involved.

Operational risks associated with irreversibly committing resources in the face of uncertainties associated with costs or demand can often be addressed by creating options to allow a greater range of responses in line with future outcomes. These real options, though, are costly, so only some of them will add value. A variant of the real option is real pooling, whereby a firm is able to apply a fixed asset or a fixed capacity to a variety of different demands, reducing the total capacity required to serve them and thus enhancing the distribution of the cash flows for this set of activities. This is different from, and more effective than, financial diversification that simply reduces portfolio variance by mixing different distributions without altering them.

Mezzo-level risks are often ill defined and dependent on affected parties, governments, or regulators. Transforming them through influence, though, is sometimes possible and, if so, will dominate diversification. In contrast, when risks are specific but outside the control of any of the potential parties, shifting or allocating them using contracts or financial markets is the appropriate solution. When risks are broad, systematic, but not controllable, the only approach is to diversify exposure. In portfolios of projects, residual systematic, uncontrollable risks beyond strategic control have to be embraced.

This correspondence of risk and responses is not only conceptual or theoretical, it also holds in practice. In our study of 60 large engineering projects (Miller and Lessard, 2000), we found a strong and statistically significant relationship between types of risk identified and the mechanisms applied.[4]

The relative ability of different firms to effectively employ these mechanisms amounts to a comparative and competitive advantage in risk management. Thus, taking on a particular risk may actually be a source of value. This comparative advantage, in turn, follows from differences in ability to diversify and/or gain access to financial markets, differential information, and differential influence over outcomes.

This concept of comparative advantage in risk management is illustrated in Figure 6.2, based on the case of an independent power-generating plant being built in Argentina by the Chilean firm ENDESA.[5] ENDESA's strategic advantage in Argentina lies largely in its successful prior experience with privatization: it 'knows more about the future of the Argentine power sector than do Argentines'.

Based on its experience as an operator ENDESA has a clear information and influence advantage over operating risk. In fact, this was the strategic rationale for the investment. However, ENDESA may be at a double disadvantage with respect to demand risk. First, Argentine projects may become too large a part of its overall portfolio; second, as a visible 'foreign' firm, it may be singled out for 'contract renegotiation' should terms prove onerous to Argentine consumers. Therefore, ENDESA will shift these risks both to more diversified international players and to Argentine players with greater legitimate voice within Argentina, such as local strategic investors

---

4 The specific categories of risk and the strategies for coping with them are provided in Table 6.1, together with the relevant statistics.

5 This example is based on public information regarding ENDESA's investment in Argentina. See Lessard (1996)

Table 6.1—Type of risk and strategies used in response

Risk (Strategy)	Project (Technical, completion, operational)	Market (Demand and supply)	Social (Stockholders directly affected)	Sovereign (Political, economic changes external to project)
Information/ understanding	178 (Count)	225	35	20
	38.9 (Row %)	49.1	7.6	4.4
	22.6 (Col. %)	26.2	13.2	13.5
	8.6 (Total %)	10.9	1.7	1.0
Design	108	116	13	17
	42.5	45.7	5.1	6.7
	13.7	13.5	4.9	11.5
	5.2	5.6	0.5	0.8
Performance Incentives (inside)	211	233	8	14
	45.3	50.0	1.7	3.0
	26.8	27.1	3.0	9.5
	10.2	11.3	0.4	0.7
Allocation	176	163	16	12
	48.0	44.4	4.4	3.3
	22.3	19.0	6.0	6.1
	8.5	7.9	0.8	0.6
Transformation/ Mitigation (outside)	115	123	194	85
	22.2	23.8	37.5	16.4
	14.6	14.3	72.9	57.4
	5.6	6.0	9.4	4.1

Notes: Counts are of coded mentions of particular strategies in response to particular risk. Multiple responses noted for many risks. Chi-squire statistic 522.83 with 12^0 of freedom, indicating significance at the 0.00000 level.

Entity / Risk Type	Operator/ Strategic Investor	Local Strategic Investor	Local Portfolio Investor	Local Public Authority	Int'l Portfolio Investor	Int'l Policy Lender
Construction						
Delay	+	+?				
Cost	+	+?				
Operations						
Availability	++					
Staffing cost	+	+				
Demand						
Overall				+	+	
Dispatch		+		+		+
Institutional						
Regulation	+	+	+			
Contract Enforce	+	+	+			
Currency						
Inflation					+	
Exchange Rate					+	
Country						
Macropolitical					+	+
Macrofinancial					+	+
World Market						
Oil Prices					+	
Interest Rates					+	

Figure 6.2—Comparative advantage matrix: Power Gen project.

and 'common folk' or, better yet, 'widows and orphans' via pension funds. Ultimately, an independent power-plant project in Argentina is a bet on the viability of the Argentine economic programme.

Examining the electrical power industry is interesting for a variety of reasons. First, it is ubiquitous and firms engaged in the various vertical stages are readily identifiable. Second, it has a discrete beginning, a little more than 120 years ago.[6] Third, the end product/service that it provides is relatively homogenous across countries, which allows price and quality comparisons. Nevertheless, the end product is not traded over long distances and therefore internationalization must take the form of either direct foreign investment or, perhaps, trade in capital goods and services at an upstream level. Finally, it has displayed a fascinating set of ebbs and flows in the degree of globalization, going initially from a locally based industry in lead countries to a quite global industry led by firms from those lead countries to a broadly distributed locally (often state-owned) industry in many countries and back to a mixed picture of private ownership of local continental and global nature. Further, it has very discrete vertical stages, each with its own economics.

Figure 6.3 illustrates the full supply chain for electrical power, ranging at the upstream level from commodity inputs such as hydrocarbons, equipment, and components to the manufacture of large specialized equipment, the provision of engineering services, the provision of software services, the generation of electrical power, the long-distance transmission of electrical power, and finally the distribution of electrical power to the end users.

Illustrative names in the various categories quite clearly make the point regarding globalization. One could argue there are no names associated with hydrocarbons and few names associated with the key components. Nevertheless, the providers of

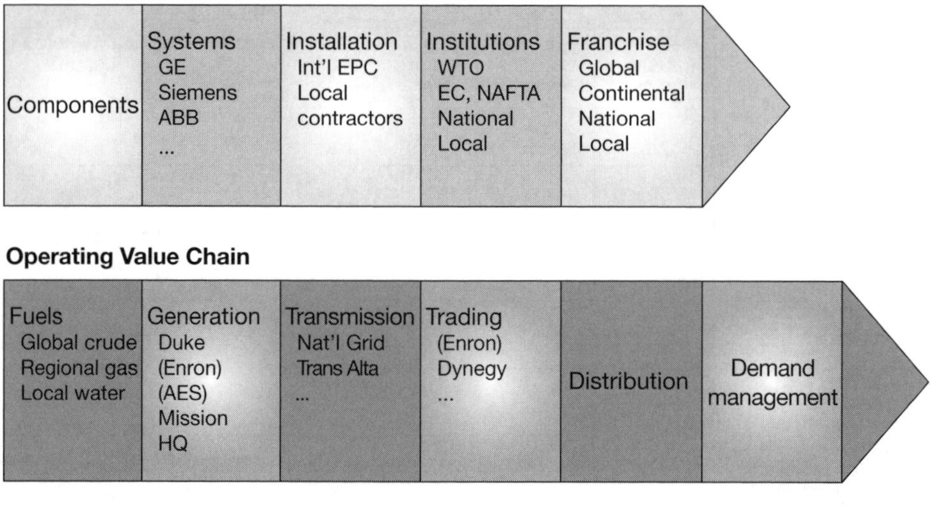

Components	Systems GE Siemens ABB ...	Installation Int'l EPC Local contractors	Institutions WTO EC, NAFTA National Local	Franchise Global Continental National Local

Operating Value Chain

Fuels Global crude Regional gas Local water	Generation Duke (Enron) (AES) Mission HQ	Transmission Nat'l Grid Trans Alta ...	Trading (Enron) Dynegy ...	Distribution	Demand management

Figure 6.3—The electrical power value chain.

---

6 Hughes (1983) provides a comprehensive view of the early years of electrification.

large-scale equipment and construction services are highly concentrated in a small set of global firms.[7] Electrical generation, on the other hand, is broadly distributed among private firms, most of a local nature though with some multinationals. Long-distance transmission tends to be in the hands of national players, either state-owned or privately owned. Distribution is a mixed bag of local operations held by continental or global firms, locally owned private operations, and municipal or state-owned firms, locally owned private operations, and municipal or state-owned operations. This chapter focuses on the three downstream stages: generation; transmission; and distribution.

Looking at the standard factors applied to explain the emergence of multinational firms, the combination of benefits of global integration and local embeddedness, it is clear why the picture is both ambiguous and varied across vertical stages. Economies of scale for generation, transmission, and distribution are exhausted regionally given the large losses associated with the long-distance transmission of power. Therefore, these factors are at best neutral with respect to globalization. On the other hand, the strong system economies within a region, especially for transmission and distribution, call very strongly for local embeddedness. Markets, on the other hand, are quite similar though the channels/commercial practices followed at the downstream distribution stage do vary somewhat. Therefore, these factors are weakly positive for globalization but very strong with respect to local embeddedness.

Regulation is a key variable and clearly militates against global ownership of 'quasi-monopolies' such as distribution but could range from negative to strongly positive for generation and transmission. In fact, the impact of regulation requires a much more dynamic interpretation as there is a learning curve/diffusion aspect that favours globalization and an influence/capture motivation that requires local embeddedness. The existence of a technological gradient – an innovation or set of innovations that has not yet fully diffused – appears to be a powerful argument for globalization whereas the ability to tap local markets and resources calls for embeddedness in only a small number of lead markets.

The Ebb and Flow of Globalization

I am currently working on a set of snapshots taken at major intervals that will show there have been substantial changes, even at a highly qualitative level, in these positions. While it is easy to see that the drivers of global integration and local embeddedness of the three different stages are quite different, it is not so obvious why the degree of globalization at each stage has changed so much over time. The simple answer is regulation though that answer turns government behaviour into a *deus ex machina* and begs the question of why regulation systematically shifts one way or another over time.

---

7 In 2001, only three firms – GE, Alsthom, and Siemens – accounted for more than 80 % of all (large scale) power systems sales (Marsh, 2002).

If one looks more deeply, the ebb and flow of globalization appear to be explained by three factors. The first is the technology gradient, illustrated in Figure 6.4.

When the technology is dynamic and not totally diffused to all markets, it clearly conveys an advantage to lead firms based in lead markets, which tends to push the globalization of the industry. As this technological differential erodes, the push for global integration also erodes.

A second factor is the net-free cash flow position of the asset or system in question. During a period of buildout, electrical power generation, transmission, and distribution are enormously costly and involve large negative cash flows, requiring ready and credible access to capital markets. On the other hand, once a system is built and running, its operating costs are quite low relative to its total recovery and much of the 'fair price' charged is a return on previous capital invested. Therefore one would hypothesize that, depending on the level of free cash flow, the tendency would be to finance one way or the other. One would further expect to see that countries with strong capital markets would emerge as home countries for investment in periods of major buildout and this advantage would erode as net cash flows from operations became more positive.

Therefore, in countries with relatively weak capital markets, one would expect a growth in foreign ownership in periods of buildout, followed by a decline during the 'harvest' period. This brings to mind the fundamental conundrum addressed by Vernon as the 'obsolescing bargain' and elaborated by Moran, Wells, and others over the years.

A third factor is the ideology of regulation. Clearly, there are ebbs and flows in public perceptions of the right way to manage various core activities. While most industries are influenced by the institutional context in which they operate, the role of institutions is especially marked in the case of electrical power.

There are several reasons for this. First, it represents the core infrastructure for any society. Second, it often involves natural monopolies that, in turn, require some form of regulation or other public governance over private activities. Finally, it

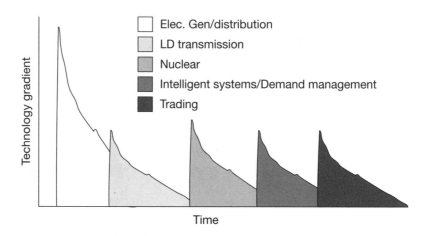

Figure 6.4—Technology gradient over time.

requires very large investments, especially during the rapid buildout phase, that often outstrip the capacity of local private markets for finance.[8]

These institutions, in turn, are dynamic, both reflecting the pendulum between efficiency and abuse as well as the diffusion/demonstration effect of major institutional successes and failures across national borders. Figure 6.5 illustrates the 'regulatory cycle' for electrical power, a cycle that is repeated in similar forms across many other infrastructure industries. The insertions in grey refer to the dominant risks at each stage, which in turn can be linked to the comparative advantage framework.

As a result, we are likely to see three different diffusion patterns over time, sometimes coinciding, sometimes not, that drive the ebb and flow of globalization, technology differentials, capital requirements/net cash flow positions, and ideological patterns. Here we trace each of these through at a highly qualitative and stylized level. A more detailed assessment of each of these stages awaits a future project.

Although I have not yet traced out the ebb and flow of globalization of the electrical power industry over time, the stylized facts are that it had become quite globalized by the early 1900s, reverted to national and often government control between the 1930s and 1950s, and has been slowly reglobalizing beginning in the 1980s, but with a burst in the 1990s with privatization and the demonstration effects of vertical disintegration and deregulation in the UK, New Zealand, China, and the US among others. It is too early to tell if the Enron 'shock' will now send

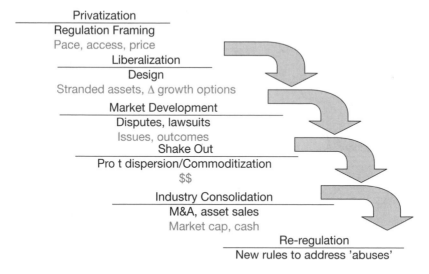

Figure 6.5—The regulatory 'cycle'.

8 It is interesting to note, however, that many of the early systems required the creation of financial systems capable of amassing large capital. Credit Suisse, for example, was created to finance hydro-projects and to this day Electro Watt is a key part of the corporate portfolio despite the fact that few if any synergies remain.

the pendulum in the other direction. These changes have also interacted with the steady erosion of the technological gradient, punctuated and re-established periodically by new innovations.

Risk and Globalization

Risk has been suggested as a major reason for the internationalization or globalization of firms as well as a major obstacle to international investment. While at first glance these may be seen as contradictory views, when the concept of comparative advantage is used to 'unpack' them in terms of the now traditional breakdown of drivers of global integration and drivers for local embeddedness, the story becomes much clearer.

Figure 6.6 illustrates sources of global versus local advantage arising from the types of mechanisms appropriate to the various types of risks.

The management of technical and operational risks requires expertise both in the technology and in organizational design. If the stock of 'undiffused' innovation is large, global integrated firms operating in lead markets (in terms of their technology) will have the advantage. In this case, adding risk to the equation only reinforces the standard arguments for globalization based on 'firm-specific' knowledge-based advantages that can best be exploited through internalization.

As these differentials erode and the technology and management methods become more universally available, this advantage will differ as well. To the extent that the operational risks arise because of local conditions, on the other hand, the advantage is likely to lie with locally based firms unless, of course, globally integrated but locally embedded firms can win on both grounds.

Institutional risks are the most salient in this industry – and not just in emerging markets, as witnessed by the events in California in 2001. Whether these institutions

Risk	Response	Global Advantage	Local Advantage
Technical/Operational	Mitigate	Significant if technology Δ is large	Understand what is appropriate
Institutional	Shape, diversify, mitigate	Breadth, expertise if institutional Δ, friends in high places	Legitimacy, insider knowledge
Macro	Hedge, diversify	Access to financial markets, breadth	None
Market	Hedge, profit from flexibility	Access to financial markets, expertise	Flexibility, ability to offset within portfolio

Figure 6.6—Global vs local advantage in risk bearing.

favour globally integrated firms, locally based firms or locally embedded and globally linked firms is a complex question to which there is no ready answer. If global institutions are at stake, powerful players from major countries will win. If local rules are in play, then local influence will dominate except in colonial or quasi-colonial cases, for example external triad jurisdiction via the IMF, World Bank, or other financial linkages. If ideology and institutional change follow a diffusion pattern internationally, then the ability to carry learning regarding institutional risk from one location to another will reinforce the knowledge-based advantages of the globally integrated firm.

Local ownership, or some other meaningful mechanism for creating local stakeholders, in contrast, is extremely important in all three vertical stages, given the *ex-post* monopoly nature of many of the services provided. Once a concession is granted, once a system for transmission or distribution is built, it tends to be a natural monopoly and it tends to be generating positive cash flows. The argument over who obtains the surpluses and rents becomes the central issue, thus calling for a strong degree of 'local responsiveness' in the traditional sense used by Prahalad and Doz. This is not a question of differentiating the type of kilowatt sold in Canada versus the US. This is the issue of having a local face on the company that wants to raise rates and thereby either 'gouge consumers' or provide its investors with a fair return, depending on one's point of view.

The benefits of flexibility and/or capacity pooling typically extend only to an integrated market that is served by an economically efficient transmission grid. This will be national or continental depending on specific geography and political boundaries. Cross-border ownership does not convey any efficiencies in capital investment relative to local or at least regional ownership. Real options are important in this industry in the form of base load versus peaking capacity, coal versus oil versus gas fired plants, and so on, but most of these options can be constructed and exercised within the continental boundaries.

On the other hand, the potential for risk reduction through diversification may be substantial. However, to the extent that this can be replicated through financial markets, which is likely to be the case for operations in developed countries, such diversification may destroy value. In emerging markets, in contrast, this pure diversification is likely to be valuable since locally based firms cannot match it. But the endogeneity of institutional risks creates a countervailing force. As a result, balance between global integration/diversification and local embeddedness in terms of stakeholders will be desired. Ironically, though, a strengthening of local institutions, and the accompanying increased fluidity of financial flows, could reduce the benefit of global ownership.

The Global OEM: The Transformation of Asian Supplier Companies

Anthony Leung[1] and George S. Yip[2]

[1]Independent Researcher [2]London Business School

A new kind of player, the global original equipment manufacturer (OEM), has joined the ranks of traditional multinational companies. These firms are OEMs in that they supply parts, components, or even complete products to other companies that resell them under their own names. They are global in that they have customers all over the world. These global OEMs represent a new type of multinational company and play an increasingly large role in international trade. Examples include Johnson Electric in micro motors and V-Tech in mobile telephones from Hong Kong; Anam in semiconductors and televisions and Hansol in consumer electronics from Korea; Aztech Systems in personal computers and Creative Technology in multimedia products from Singapore; and Hume in steel-based and air-conditioning products from Malaysia (see Table 7.1).

Traditional multinational companies (MNCs) have sourced from overseas OEMs for nearly three decades. Indeed, by now, the question for most MNCs is not whether to use global sourcing but how to best use it to achieve business objectives. At the same time, some MNCs' overuse of OEMs has compromised critical production capabilities in exchange for cost efficiency. Our theme is that some OEMs have achieved global scope in their own right and now offer their MNC customers not only cost effectiveness but also high quality and reliability. In addition, they increasingly pose a competitive threat to their customers by developing their own brands and selling directly to end-users.

Although little known, many global OEMs have revenues in hundreds of millions of dollars and some are approaching billion-dollar status. Also, while most currently come from Asia, the business model of the global OEM can be applied to many other economies, especially developing ones. What is of interest is that global OEMs have important strategic and operational differences from MNCs, especially those from developed or 'G7' nations. Global OEMs also differ from regular OEMs in the scale and scope of their operations, in their centrality to established MNCs, and in their potential to become full-blown MNCs with their own consumer brands. Especially in Asia, these global OEMs can be more potent regional competitors to G7 MNCs than even other established MNCs.

Table 7.1—Examples of global OEMs

Name	Home Base	Products	Revenues 2001 (US $ Million)
Acer	Taiwan	PCs/Microprocessors	758
Anam Semiconductor	South Korea	Semi-conductors, TVs	172
ASM Pacific	Hong Kong	Electronic tools, Wafers	200
ASUS TEK	Taiwan	Computer Components	2,492
Aztech Systems	Singapore	PCs/Multimedia Products	85
Beyonics	Singapore	Electronic/PC Components	165
Champion Tech	Hong Kong	Telecommunication Parts and Components	193
Creative Tech	Singapore	Multimedia/Semi-conductors	1,222
Da Duck Tech	South Korea	Printed Circuit Boards	269
Daewoo	South Korea	Colour RVs, Consumer Electronics	5,579
Eltek	Singapore	Computer Products	336
Elec & Eltek	Hong Kong	Printed Circuits/Telecom	285
Eng Tech	Malaysia	Electronic Part/Components	44
Hansol	South Korea	Consumer Electronics	264
Invertec	Taiwan	Notebooks/PDAs	2,375
Johnson Electric	Hong Kong	Micro Motors	773
LG Electronic	South Korea	Consumer Electronics	24,616
QPL International	Hong Kong	Integrated Circuits	36
Samsung Electronic	South Korea	Electronics and Appliances	38,269
Shell Electric	Hong Kong	Consumer Electronics and Appliances	283
Taiwan Semiconductor	Taiwan	Semi-conductors	3,363
Uchi Tech	Malaysia	Electronic Components	24
VTech Holdings	Hong Kong	Learning Technologies/Mobile Phone	959
Ya Horning	Malaysia	Electronic Components	19

Global OEMs account for a large percentage of the overall export trade of major Asia-Pacific economies such as Hong Kong, Taiwan, Singapore, Malaysia, Thailand, and South Korea. Their combined revenues are likely to be over $1 trillion. In 2001, total OEM exports from Hong Kong alone reached nearly $200 billion. They are constantly expanding at home and acquiring assets globally, often in G7 countries. Global OEMs have been gradually expanding their worldwide operations during the last 20 years. By now they are well entrenched in the global supply and production networks of traditional MNCs. Yet, because they hold few, if any, consumer brands, global OEMs have received little attention in business or academic media and publications.

Johnson Electric, a Hong Kong-based producer of micro motors, provides one of the best examples of this new type of global OEM. It sells nearly $800 million a year to MNC customers such as Plymouth and United Technologies, both large US companies. Johnson's global headquarters and management are in Hong Kong and it has manufacturing facilities in China and Thailand and advanced engineering process facilities in Germany and Hong Kong. Johnson has wholly owned subsidiaries in the US and Japan, sales offices in the UK, Hong Kong, Singapore, China, and Thailand, and sales partners in Germany, France, Italy, Taiwan, Korea, Spain, Argentina, and Brazil.

Another Hong Kong global OEM, VTech, has become one of the world's leading consumer electronic corporations. It designs, manufactures, markets, and sells electronic learning and telephone communications products. It has an extensive international distribution network and had worldwide sales of nearly $1 billion in 2001.

This chapter highlights the essential characteristics of global OEMs and identifies how they differ from traditional G7-based MNCs. We focus on Hong Kong-based global OEMs to illustrate this new type of global firm although we also provide examples of global OEMs from Taiwan, Singapore, Malaysia, and South Korea. By better understanding their strategies, modes of operation and international expansion, we aim to shed light on how they can be both potent competitors to and helpful partners for G7-based MNCs.

Asian Bases of Global OEMS

Although other countries and regions, especially Mexico and Poland, also have important OEM firms, Asia has by far the largest number. Within Asia, the key home bases for OEMs are Hong Kong, Malaysia, Singapore, Taiwan, and South Korea, with Thailand and the Philippines playing lesser roles. In the future China and India should also produce many global OEMs.

The key Asian home bases have the following in common: skilled and motivated labour forces; low wages (or access to contiguous low-wage labour pools as in the case of Hong Kong's use of mainland China); strong trade and transportation infrastructures; favourable government policies; initially small domestic markets that spur an outward search for customers; an entrepreneurial class that is also able to acquire the managerial skills needed to work with large, complex MNC customers; and a moderate level of technological expertise.

Interestingly, these Asian bases for OEMs lack one advantage that has helped other countries to become OEM bases – proximity to a large developed market, as in the case of Mexico (the US) and Poland (Germany). South Korea provides a partial exception. Its OEM businesses have benefited from both nearness to Japan and a moderate-sized domestic market. In consequence, many Korean global OEMs are parts of larger companies, typically *chaebols* such as Samsung and LG that have both substantial branded business and unbranded OEM business.

Research Methodology

Data for identifying the special characteristics and globalization patterns of global OEMs were gathered in three steps:

Step 1 – Literature search and question formulation. We began by reviewing company reports, industry directories, trade web sites, advertising, and articles in trade magazines. From this we developed a list of specific questions focused on company configuration, market focus, products and orientation, research and development, production, distribution, marketing, and international and foreign market entry modes.

Step 2 – Discussions. Using the above questions, we held discussions with personal acquaintances and friends who are active in the Hong Kong manufacturing sector. We spoke with owners, substantial shareholders, or senior managers of OEM firms. These discussions helped to confirm and refine what we found from the literature review. We also used these discussions to refine questions to use in more formal interviews with five OEM firms.

Step 3 – Interviews with five OEMs. We conducted interviews with owners and senior mangers of five Hong Kong-based OEMs in order to provide additional insights into the critical differences between traditional MNCs and global OEMs. The interviews took place at either the office or factory of the owners or senior managers. On average, each interview lasted about 45 minutes to one hour. The discussions were preceded with a brief tour of each firm's facility. These owners/senior managers were friends of the authors. All of them have been involved in the OEM field for over 25 years.

What's Different about Global OEMs?

In describing how global OEMs differ from traditional MNCs we will focus on the distinctive characteristics of the *typical* global OEM. Hence we will not discuss all the different variations possible.

Instead of taking on pre-eminent global leaders, global OEMs focus on supplying them with parts and components that are typically more mature in terms of the product life cycle. They have the capacity to produce high-quality products at low price, to provide just-in-time delivery, and to achieve global scale economies. They have strong and efficient domestic and offshore production bases. They have demonstrated that their modes of operation can bypass the drawback of a small domestic consumption base and can avoid the costly process of developing the brands and products that are needed to be competitive in newer industries.

Consequently, global OEMs offer an alternative model of development for firms from emerging economies that lack the experience and resources to compete with dominant firms from larger, more developed economies. This model differs from that of most Japanese companies, which grew first in their large domestic market and were thus able to develop strong brand names and final products. Even those Japanese companies (such as NEC, Toshiba, and Hitachi) that started as OEM component suppliers to US MNCs were able to leverage the size of the domestic Japanese market to develop branded consumer products. Korean companies, with their moderate-sized domestic market, provide a mix of Japanese style and global OEM style in their internationalization strategies. Global OEMs from the smaller Asian economies, such as Hong Kong and Singapore, provide the purest cases.

We now look in detail at how global OEMs differ from traditional MNCs in terms of: company configuration, market focus, business and product orientation, research and development, production, distribution, marketing, and internationalization and foreign market entry modes (summarized in Table 7.2).

Company Configuration

Global OEMs differ in company configuration from traditional MNCs in terms of their place of incorporation, location of operating centres, company names, and ownership.

Place of Incorporation

While most traditional MNCs incorporate in their home countries, most global OEMs incorporate in international tax havens such as Bermuda or the Cayman Islands in order to realize tax advantages and international trade privileges. But they seldom establish a presence or set up actual operations in such countries. In the case of Hong Kong global OEMs, political security provides another motivation for incorporating offshore. The fact that the Hong Kong government does not distinguish between foreign or local registration means that many indigenous firms are free to register and perform major functions in Hong Kong while incorporated in another country for tax advantages. These firms also have the added advantage of being protected by a foreign government.

Principal Operation Centres (Head Offices)

Despite being incorporated in foreign countries, global OEMs still base their head offices in their native countries for conducting major day-to-day operations. Most Hong Kong global OEMs hold foreign incorporation in Bermuda or the Cayman Islands. But they base their head offices or principal centre of operations in Hong Kong.

Company Names

Global OEMs tend to use Western names as their firm name or trade name rather than indigenous ones in order to enhance respect and credibility in both Asia-Pacific and

Table 7.2—Comparison of traditional G7-based MNCs and Asian global OEMs

Features	Traditional MNCs	Asian Global OEMs
Company Configuration	Incorporated in home country Mostly publicly listed G7-based head office Use indigenous company name Regional offices to run operations	Incorporated in overseas tax havens Mostly private moving to partial public listing Asia-based head office Use foreign (Western) company name Regional offices to reach MNC customers
Market Focus	Domestic markets first as base for later global expansion	Foreign markets first Minimal domestic market
Business and Product Orientation	Mainly branded final goods Some parts and components Full business system	Mostly intermediate parts and goods Some final products Mainly OEM, some ODM Narrow part of business system
R&D	Extensive R&D to develop proprietary technology and products	No R&D, but some moving to ODM
Production	Some domestic production, increasingly sourcing offshore from own subsidiaries or OEMs	Extensive domestic production Strong offshore production base in China or Asia-Pacific, some in North America & Europe Just-in-time delivery Economies of scale
Distribution	Strong global networks	Strong networks that plug into those of MNC customers Mostly regional rather than global Dependent on local infrastructure
Marketing	Media promotion of brands Exploit appeal of Western popular images and life-styles Emphasize technology and quality	Direct selling to small number of MNC customers Appeal on low price, high quality, reliability, and adaptability
International and Foreign Market Entry Modes	Single mode initially Export globally License out technology Joint ventures to gain market access or production Investment to help trade Foreign subsidiaries to run businesses Foreign acquisitions to expand	Multiple modes early Export to developed economies License in technology Joint ventures to provide production Investment to add production capacity Foreign subsidiaries to work with customers Foreign acquisitions to gain technology and brands

other countries. In addition, if global OEMs with Western names establish plants or acquire assets in Western countries, the general public there might have less apprehension that their local firms or assets are being acquired or controlled by Asian firms.

Some examples in the electronics industry include Johnson Electric, Elec & Eltek, VTech, Varitronic, Shell Electric, Grande Holdings, Tembray, Tomei Holdings, and Truly International. In the fashion sector, Giordano was a name created by a Hong

Kong company, while DKNY, started by a US company, now has half of its sales volume in the Asia-Pacific region and sources significant amounts of its products, fabrics, textiles, and garments from there. Although Giordano and DKNY both market under these names through their own international channels, a large part of their business comes from supplying products for rebranding by G7 multinationals.

Global OEMs in Singapore, Taiwan, and South Korea also use Western names, not surprising in the case of Singapore, which is basically a bilingual country with both Chinese and English as official languages. In the electronics industry, some of the most successful OEMs all use Western names: Acer Computer from Taiwan; Creative Technology and IPC from Singapore; and LG (formerly Lucky Goldstar) from South Korea.

Ownership Structure

Most traditional MNCs are public companies. Global OEMs feature a mixture of public and private ownership. In recent years, many have gone public in order to raise money for expansion. Often, such OEMs acquire overseas assets shortly after they list on a stock exchange. For example, one year after listing on the Hong Kong Stock Exchange Techtronic Industries acquired 51 % of Gimelli Productions AG of Switzerland, one of the largest manufacturers of dental health care products in the world. This enabled Techtronic to explore the development and production of dental health care products in Hong Kong. One year later, it also acquired 75 % of Solarwide Industries Limited, a US producer of solar and electronic products.

There are also some very successful family owned firms that are not listed on any stock exchange. Some of the most successful of these private firms hold large market shares within the Asia-Pacific region and have supply partnership arrangements with leading multinationals such as Eastman Kodak, Tommy Hilfiger, and Levi Strauss. Hawking Industries, a private Hong Kong optics firm, is one of the best examples. It holds a large market share (the details guarded as a family secret) in the optics field (cameras and various forms of lenses) in Asia-Pacific, has production plants in China and many Asia-Pacific countries, and offices in London, Chicago, and New York. Its customers include Kodak, Nikon, and Konica. Hong Kong's Burringtex is one of the world's largest garment producers, manufacturing for numerous US brand names including JC Penney, Sears, Saks Fifth Avenue, Liz Claiborne, Nautica, The Gap, Izod, Ralph Lauren, and LL Bean.

Market Focus

Typically, G7-based MNCs have first established a stronghold in their domestic markets before they target and sell overseas. Large home-market customer bases also helped them to build brands that could be extended overseas. The appeal of Western life-styles and fashions (and now also Japanese fashions) further strengthened the appeal of Western and Japanese brands. Global OEMs from emerging Asian economies have lacked both large domestic bases and internationally appealing life-styles (with

Hong Kong perhaps an exception for mainland China). With indigenous cultural heritages unfamiliar to G7 consumers, firms from emerging Asian nations find it much more difficult to directly market their products to the rest of the world.

So, in the case of Hong Kong, OEMs sell mainly to overseas markets and to MNC customers. These markets include Europe, North America, Australia, China, Taiwan, Japan, Korea, and some parts of South America and Africa. One of the major benefits of having multiple market targets is that these firms are far less affected by events in any single country or region. In fact, Hong Kong OEMs fared relatively well during the Asian financial crisis of the late 1990s.

Business and Product Orientation

Global OEMs have business and product orientations quite different from those of traditional MNCs. To a large extent, global OEMs complement traditional MNCs in the global market by providing intermediate products or unbranded final products. In addition, while many MNCs focus on the first few stages (R&D and product design) and the last few stages (marketing, selling, and service) of the value chain, global OEMs focus on the middle stages (production).

Global OEMs provide products of high quality but low price that usually meet high technical specifications, such as ISO standards. Another important feature of successful global OEMs is that their products have a high degree of reliability, one reason being to avoid eventual consumer warranty problems for their MNC customers, which increasingly use extended warranties as a marketing tool, particularly in consumer electronics. Global OEMs also have to be able to make quick changes in product features with minimal notification time. Adaptability has become one of the most highly regarded features of successful global OEMs, as product direction and preferred features change rapidly in today's fast-moving consumer electronic, computer, and other markets.

With these product capabilities, some global OEMs have become world leaders in production. For example, Hong Kong's Johnson Electric has since the 1990s been the world's top producer of electronic motors for toys and ranked 828 by market capitalization in *Business Week's* Global Top 1000 companies for 2002.

Korea's Gold Peak Industries has become the second-largest supplier to the world's leading battery maker, Duracell (a US firm) and, in fact, acquired Duracell's rechargeable lithium ion battery division and US factory in 1998. Gold Peak will continue to market both its own brand and the Duracell brand and also supply OEM customers. The Duracell acquisition will allow Gold Peak to expand in the US and to also benefit from Duracell's research and development in advanced battery technologies.

Tomei (of Hong Kong) has since 1991 been the world's largest producer of polyvaricon capacitors (the tuners on pre-digital radios) and the third-largest maker of personal cassette players and also holds 5 % of the world market for earphones. These firms would probably not have achieved such a high level of global success had they not started as pure OEMs.

Research and Development

OEMs, by their nature, have little need to undertake product research and development. They manufacture products according to specifications and instructions received from their MNC customers. Most often the products are mature and hence pose much lower technical, product design, and market demand risks. So global OEMs can avoid the costs incurred by traditional MNCs in R&D, frequent product introductions, and adapting products for different national markets. (At the same time, global OEMs may need to invest in process R&D to continually reduce their production costs and enhance efficiency.)

The cost advantage from this low R&D strategy is, of course, offset by the lower margins that can be obtained from the global OEMs' undifferentiated products. Some OEMs are extending their activities to become 'Original Design Manufacturers or Contractors' (ODMs or ODCs). ODMs are similar to OEMs in most ways except that they also design the products that they make. But, as with OEMs, the ODMs' products are sold under the MNC customers' brand names. Still, the ODM route increases profit margins and capabilities. Hence, particularly in Hong Kong, some policy makers and management writers suggest that OEMs should do more design work for MNCs if they want to remain competitive in the future.

Production

Global OEMs focus on low-cost efficient production, just-in-time delivery, and aggressively seek low-cost production sites.

Low-cost Production

Global OEMs need to achieve scale economies in order to stay viable and competitive. Their main operating objective is to produce the largest volume in the least possible time at the lowest costs. To some extent, given that they mainly produce standardized parts and components, they tend to realize scale economies more easily then firms that produce a wide range of non-standardized and differentiated products for different parts of the globe. Also, by providing globally standardized products to a few global customers, these OEMs can enjoy long production runs of a limited number of products.

Global OEMs also reduce their production costs by focusing on fast-growing sectors such as computers, telecommunications, and consumer audio, where different MNC customers purchase common parts and components. Many global OEMs supply common parts and products for global brand names such as Hitachi, Sanyo/Fisher, JC Penney, Wal-Mart, and AT&T.

Lastly, global OEMs can achieve very high production utilization. For example, some Hong Kong OEMs operate their facilities three shifts per day non-stop for many months of the year.

Just-in-time Delivery

A critical part of what traditional MNCs buy from global OEMs is just-in-time delivery (JIT). As parts of MNCs' global business systems or value chains, global OEMs must meet exact, pre-determined production schedules or else stall the entire production chain. Also, in today's fast-moving consumer fashions, consumer electronic, and computer markets, where product cycles are short, there is profound pressure to get products out to the retail sector as soon as possible. To a large extent, this JIT capability also depends on the transportation infrastructure of the country where the OEM's major production facilities are located.

Location of Production

Most often, global OEMs have major production bases in their native countries. Increasingly, however, more global OEMs have been expanding their production capacity to even lower-cost production areas – in both nearby areas or in other regional emerging economies. So even more than traditional MNCs, global OEMs are in a constant hunt for locations that offer tax advantages, special privileges, efficient and low-cost labour, and reasonably good transportation infrastructure for international trade.

Traditional MNCs, on the other hand, tend to retain the production of most current products or of the most advanced parts and components in their home country. They outsource to OEMs usually only the less-advanced components and parts in order to protect trade secrets and technical advantages.

Production Expansion Patterns

Global OEMs expand their production in a number of stages. In the case of Hong Kong global OEMs, they first operate with manufacturing facilities in Hong Kong only. Once they have established themselves in Hong Kong and built a strong working relationship with MNC customers, they advance into their second stage of expansion. They expand into China's mainland or the rest of Asia. In particular, they tend to locate in mainland China in order to increase production capacity and avoid the high production costs in Hong Kong.

Most tend to locate their additional facilities in one of the rapidly developing economic zones, such as the Pearl Delta Region in Southern China. That zone's infrastructure is relatively developed and has a large pool of low-cost labour. Access to a large work force is a particular advantage for more capital-intensive concerns in that it allows them readily to adjust the size of the work force to seasonal demands to ensure optimal employment of capital.

At the third stage, they list their firms on the Hong Kong stock exchange to raise a larger amount of liquid assets for developing or acquiring newer or additional production facilities. In addition to China, some OEMs establish plants or acquire production assets in the US and Europe. Others establish overseas offices to strengthen their presence in various markets.

Distribution

As part of the global production chains of MNCs, global OEMs must themselves have efficient and reliable distribution networks. This holds particularly in fast-moving industries such as fashion, consumer electronics, telecommunications, and computers. But a company's efficient distribution network depends on the smooth functioning of national infrastructure systems. However, not all emerging economies have an efficient and modern infrastructure system that can support a global network. So it is not surprising that global OEMs have emerged first in those economies with good trade and transportation infrastructure.

Hong Kong-based Shell Electric Manufacturing, for example, maintains marketing and distribution centres in Hong Kong, China, North America, and Europe to support its annual sales of over $200 million in DVD players, VCD players, audio amplifiers and speakers, home theatre video equipment, ceiling and table fans, vacuum cleaners, air grill ovens, telephone products, and decorative lighting products. Presently, Shell has the world's largest electric fan production capacity, at over five million units a year.

With the adoption of Internet technology, many global OEMs now manage their global distribution systems even more effectively. Today, practically all major global OEMs have their own web sites and email contact accounts for customers. The Internet should also further increase the reach of global OEMs and reduce their dependence on individual MNC customers.

Marketing

As producers mainly of parts and components, most global OEMs do not advertise their products in popular consumer-oriented media and hence are unknown to the general public. They concentrate their marketing efforts on direct selling to their immediate customers, mostly traditional MNCs in G7 countries. In contrast, MNCs generally heavily promote their own brand or trade names. MNCs' products can be purchased in major commercial outlets and are promoted in major public media. Although leading global OEMs now advertise in major trade journals or directories and have set up web pages to attract customers, their main sources of sales still come via referrals from colleagues, family connections, and business contacts.

Global OEMs and their host economies are now waking up to the disadvantages of having few brand names of their own. Larger and more forward-looking OEMs, such as Acer and Johnson, are now seeking to build up their own brand names. One barrier is that most such companies are owned by individual entrepreneurs or families who are uncomfortable with the idea of investing in an intangible such as a brand. Furthermore, surrounded by many producers of counterfeit goods, local entrepreneurs have shied away from creating their own brands for fear of becoming hostages to fortune.

Internationalization and Foreign Market Entry Modes

Traditionally, MNCs have selected distinct modes of foreign market entry, particularly direct exporting, licensing, joint venturing, and wholly/partially owned foreign direct investment (FDI). Each mode provides different degrees of control, flexibility, and risk. Historically, MNCs tended to progress through an export phase before switching to market-seeking FDI and then to cost-oriented FDI. In the final stage, manufacturing, and even demand in some cases, leaves the country of the original innovation.

Increasing globalization has speeded up the internationalization process and younger firms, in particular, tend to follow different sequences of foreign entry or jump straight into more demanding entry modes. Global OEMs differ from established MNCs in that foreign sales come before domestic sales, which may never even occur. In addition, global OEMs often use all of the major market entry modes simultaneously.

Direct Export

Global OEMs mainly export to other states in the same region or to foreign countries where major established MNCs are based. Conversely, many G7-based MNCs have set up offices in OEM bases such as Hong Kong, Taiwan, Singapore, or Malaysia for direct sourcing in these countries or in the region. These offices simply seek out suitable OEMs and order parts and components from them. The OEMs take responsibility for the production of the specific orders and for shipment to the agreed foreign destinations.

Licensing

While traditional MNCs use licensing as a way of exploiting their technological or other know-how, global OEMs use licensing to obtain such know-how because they undertake very little product research and development of their own. In recent years, OEMs have bought licences to mass-produce personal computers and parts, semi-conductors, and multimedia and telecommunication products. For example, VTech gained wireless phone technology from foreign firms including AT&T and Telus (Canada).

Joint Ventures

Traditional MNCs commonly use international joint ventures as a way to obtain access to foreign markets or as a way of obtaining lower-cost production. Global OEMs cannot help in the market access objective but they do provide the lower-cost production. Hong Kong's Hawking Industries, for example, has set up a joint venture with Eastman Kodak to target the China market and to tap into the US market, with Hawking producing the optics for Kodak to make the final camera and camera accessories. Johnson Electronic has a joint venture with a Chinese state-owned enterprise to produce carbon bushes for automotive and other fractional horsepower motors in Shenzhen.

Foreign Direct Investment

Most traditional MNCs initiate FDI in countries that are target markets in order to avoid trade barriers, reduce production and transportation costs, cut delivery times, and the like. Often, a large proportion of initial FDI by MNCs relates to foreign warehousing and distribution facilitates, with production facilities coming later. FDI by global OEMs follows an opposite pattern. For them, FDI comes early as a way to achieve low-cost production rather than to seek markets. For example, many Hong Kong OEMs attempt to increase their production capacity and reduce costs by undertaking FDI in mainland China. Potential sales to mainland customers count as a secondary benefit only.

Foreign Subsidiaries

Traditional MNCs set up foreign subsidiaries for a wide variety of reasons but primarily to run their business better in a foreign location. Global OEMs have similar objectives for their foreign subsidiaries but these units tend to have more focused aims – to work closely with a small number of large customers. In time they will also be able to use these subsidiaries as bases for expansion under their own names.

Foreign Acquisitions

Traditional MNCs from developed nations typically make foreign acquisitions as ways to increase local market access and share – essentially downstream activities. In contrast, global OEMs are now becoming strong enough to make their own acquisitions, though as ways to obtain upstream assets such as technology and brands. VTech purchased some of Lucent Technologies' production assets in the US in order to obtain 10 years' exclusive right to use the AT&T brand name on wire line telephone products and accessories in the US and Canada. This acquisition enabled VTech to establish a stronger presence in these markets.

Champion Tech, a Hong Kong producer of telecommunications and personal computer parts and components, has acquired a number of European subsidiaries and set up offices in the UK and mainland Europe in order to consolidate and expand its market coverage there. In the UK, its subsidiaries include Multitude Electronic Place in Basingstoke and it has set up sales offices in Dublin, Berlin, Dusseldorf, Hamburg, and Hanover as well as in Austria. Other Asian global OEMs have undertaken similar patterns of overseas acquisitions. For example, Korea's LG Electronic acquired Zenith, a major producer of US personal computers, and Samsung acquired AST Research, another US computer firm, to strengthen its global market presence.

Conclusions and Implications

In summary, there are many ways in which global OEMs differ from traditional multinational companies. In addition, these global OEMs act in ways that go well beyond traditional OEMs and hence constitute a new type of multinational company. They are dynamic enterprises, constantly expanding both in global markets and adding activities beyond production. Global OEMs have not only developed but also thrived with such capabilities. They have established a reputation for being especially skilled in coordinating a myriad of downstream production activities and in managing production of world-class quality and reliability.

In recent years, they have made significant acquisitions of firms in G7 countries as bases to further expand their activities in those countries. They are starting to develop their own brands and to move beyond OEM status.

Global OEMs offer an alternative model of development and competitive strategy for governments and firms in many emerging economies. Instead of competing directly with pre-eminent global competitors, governments in emerging economies should try to foster the conditions and infrastructure that support OEM firms. Having a strong emphasis on building an export-led economy with OEM firms will help developing countries to overcome a small domestic consumption base and the costly process of developing brands and building research and development at home.

Firms from such economies should emphasize building the critical characteristics of successful OEMs. Gaining a foothold as an OEM for global customers will enable them to become more experienced in efficient production and in handling international trade before advancing overseas and establishing a sustainable position in global markets. They could also specialize in producing certain parts and components in fast-growing industries. This way they may face less competition from OEMs that are based in other emerging economies.

Acknowledgement

The authors thank Anna M. Dempster, Cambridge University, for her helpful comments.

8 Designing Multinational Organizations: Is It All Over Now?

Lawrence G. Franko

College of Management, University of Massachusetts Boston and Thomas Weisel Asset Management, LLC

The problem of 'fit' between organizational structure and a corporate strategy that combined high degrees of both product and geographical diversification was a central issue in the seminal work of John Stopford and Louis Wells, *Managing the Multinational Enterprise*, in 1972.

The strategic and structural evolution of firms was hypothesized to follow the trajectories mapped in Figure 8.1. Successful multinational firms whose strategy concentrated on a narrow range of products moved from a stage of quasi-autonomous foreign subsidiaries, through the use of international divisions, to 'global' functional or regional structures. Firms diversifying primarily by product, but also geographically, moved from autonomous subsidiary and international division stages through to worldwide product divisions.

But what were firms that had high degrees of both product and geographical dispersion to do? The search for new responses to these new problems was the subject of Chapter 6 of Stopford and Wells' book. And the options explored were 'mixed', 'grid', or 'matrix' structures. These seemed the most likely ways to solve the structural problems posed by a strategy of extensive and simultaneous product and geographical diversification.

My own work on continental European companies within the Harvard Multinational Enterprise project built on the Stopford–Wells framework. It needed a few modifications to allow for the considerably greater and longer use of the 'mother–daughter' (in US parlance 'autonomous subsidiary') stage of headquarters to national subsidiary relations. But an evolution towards global, regional, and worldwide product structures and the beginning of moves towards matrix and mixed structures was again apparent.

What was noteworthy was the fact that such strategic problems, and structural solutions to them, were at that time considered the normal, almost inevitable, consequence of the growth and development of large, successful corporations. Chandler's famous work *Strategy and Structure*, which was the foundation on which we built our examination of multinational enterprise strategy and structure, was read primarily as a

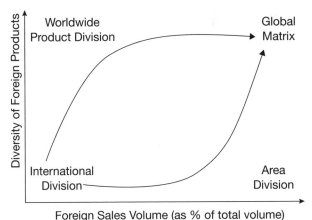

Figure 8.1—The Stopford and Wells model (reprinted with permission from Stopford and Wells, 1972).

story of growth leading to the accumulation of resources and capabilities by firms. This – with the inevitability implied by a stages model – led to increasing organizational complexity and to the adoption of multidivisional structures in response.

Chandler, to be sure, recognized some exceptions to this 'inevitable' process in his chapters on industries not accepting, or only partially accepting, the new structure. For example, he wrote: 'Because the copper companies are mining and processing enterprises producing a relatively few types of products for a well-defined market, they have been under less pressure to concern themselves with organizational matters. Their only administrative challenges have been in the improvement of the administrative control of the departmental headquarters and the central office.'

Such firms and industries appeared, however, to be clustered in what even in the 1960s were considered hopelessly 'old economy' activities like mining and metals.

Chandler also included a critical caveat that today looks prophetic: 'Further researchers in the growth and administration of American industry and business must consider the importance of the market. That the expansion and government of industrial enterprises in a market economy should be closely related to the changing nature of the market seems obvious enough. Yet many writers dealing with principles of business administration, often discuss leadership, communication, and structure with only passing reference to the market.'

Still, with his finding in *Strategy and Structure* that diversification strategies and multidivisional structures were clustered in electronics and chemicals – the 1960s' 'knowledge-intensive industries of the future' – readers took away the clear message that the successful large firms of the 20th century were, and would be, the ones that dealt best with the internal structural and administrative issues inherent in managing complexity.

The tale told by the Harvard Multinational Enterprise project of the early 1970s was thus to Chandler rather as the *Odyssey* to the *Iliad* or, perhaps more accurately, as Virgil to Homer. The story, the stages, and the sense of classical inevitability of it all were enriched and extended but the transition to the new Rome of a market-driven era was only hinted at, if noted at all.

Indeed, as recently as 1989 it could still be taken as axiomatic that it was both desirable and feasible for firms that were diversified both by product and by geography to develop 'multidimensional strategic capabilities'. Based on an examination of GE, ITT, Philips, Matsushita, Unilever, NEC, Ericsson, Kao and Procter & Gamble, Bartlett and Ghoshal argued that the circle of many product activities in many countries could be still be squared – but not by matrix structures with dual or multiple reporting lines (the matrix was by then recognized to have been a largely failed experiment). Rather, what was needed was to build broader organizational capabilities that transcended formal structure, for example through developing extra-hierarchical communications channels, interpersonal relationships, and reward and punishment systems.

The Future Wasn't What It Used to Be . . .

Not a lot has been heard lately about internal corporate, 'visible hand' solutions to the problems of product, market, and geographical diversity. Equally, there haven't been many recent success stories about some of the companies pursuing such strategies back in the 1970s such as ITT, W R Grace, Sperry Rand, and Celanese. And while Monsanto and Texas Instruments have been in the news from time to time, it is their restructurings and product line simplifications, not organizational innovations, that have provided the stories.

What happened? It seems that the predominant solution to the problems raised by corporate strategies of simultaneous product and geographical diversification was not the grid, or the matrix, or even transnational solutions but rather the diminution in importance of the visible hand of corporate management compared to the 'invisible hand' of financial and product markets. To borrow from another discipline's metaphor, corporate 'inner-directedness' came to be, if not wholly replaced by, then at least strongly constrained by the 'outer-directedness' of financial and product markets.

One of the first signs of change occurred during the 1980s when diversification strategies, especially those of the conglomerate variety, fell into disfavour. Not only did many of the highly diversified firms come visibly to underperform more focused rivals but finance theorists and their followers in the mutual fund and institutional investment world also launched an assault on such strategies. It was often pointed out that, at least in countries with developed stock markets, shareholders could build portfolios diversified by industry, company, and asset class on their own without paying corporate managers to do it for them. Agency theorists chimed in, accusing managers of often diversifying for reasons of self-interested empire building.

Back when Stopford, Wells, and I were writing about multinational organizational design, we were writing in an era rather innocent of such notions and of others such as 'the market for corporate control' and 'shareholder value'. We lived largely in a world where management and ownership were separated and where managers did not yet conceive of themselves as being agents of shareholder principals. Corporate managements could dream of and implement multiproduct, multinational empires unlimited by pesky external constraints like shareholders and raiders. Junk-bond financing of upstart new entrants and hostile takeover bids had yet to be invented. The institutionalization of equity ownership and the consequent empowerment of mutual and pension fund managers to pressure corporate managers for improved financial performance and segment transparency had only just begun.

To be sure, managerial hubris and management separation from dispersed and disorganized owners were not the only pillars supporting visible hand solutions to multinational corporate resource allocation and structural problems. The notion of a quasi-omnipotent managerial 'technostructure' was more than merely a caricature conjured up by the political left. Many managers rather liked being told that they had great power. The alleged dominance of the visible hand thus had a none too subtle appeal to management. It also received considerable intellectual underpinning from the business school and consulting intelligentsia. Moreover, there was much in the external environment that supported the model.

Supporting the Primacy of the Visible Hand

The intellectual case for stressing the importance of internal structuring of the enterprise as opposed to its interactions with specific markets had at least two main doctrinal streams.

First there was the school of 'management by the numbers independent of industry' aka 'a good manager can manage any business'. This is often identified with Harold Geneen of ITT but was preached in many a business school classroom before his tenure at the head of that company.

Later, in the 1970s and 1980s, the gospel of within-the-firm, non-market resource allocation came to be preached in another form. This was also a matrix. But, though iconic, it was not organizational but designed by the Boston Consulting Group as a conceptual framework for non-market, internal resource allocation among diverse product activities. Businesses were classified as high market-share, low-growth 'cash cows', low-growth, low-share 'dogs', high-growth, high-share 'stars', and high-growth, low-share 'question marks'. The 'free cash flow' from mature activities, or cash cows, was to be allocated to stars or question marks inside a corporate framework.

The assumption was that managers knew best how to allocate resources among businesses. Today, shareholders – especially of the institutional variety – view free cash flow, cash flow net of capital expenditures to sustain core businesses, as something to be returned to them, ere it be squandered on corporate empire building via value-destroying investments in overcapacity or overpriced acquisitions.

Internal Corporate Strains

But even during the 1970s, extreme complexity began to put strain on the self-contained, quasi-extra-market world of some of the most product-diversified and geographically spread multinationals. It did not take a rocket scientist to suspect that there was something vastly more time consuming and costly in coordinating a firm with 1,200 (often unrelated) products produced in more than 100 countries than there was in a company with a handful of products made in optimal, world-scale factories in half a dozen locations.

Even for firms not attempting to implement orthodox organizational matrices, the complexity of proliferating product and geographical divisions and 'strategic business units' (SBUs) was often producing questionable results. The BCG matrix had not only spawned a host of strategy-consulting imitators. It had also begun to be used by some to structure organizations, to determine personnel and staffing decisions, and to mould culture in organizations according to the differentiated 'key success factors' of high-growth attractive versus low-growth unattractive, and high market-share versus low market-share businesses. Dynamic entrepreneurs were to go in this box, grey-suited bean counters into another, ruthless opportunists in yet another division and so on.

But again, what was tempting in theory was often problematic in practice. For every seemingly happy Swiss Confederation of business and corporate cultural diversity, there were as many or more Afghanistans riven by conflicts among the divisional warlords and their tribes. When conflicts over resource allocation were (quasi) resolved, they too often resulted not in economic, but political and 'fair-share', divisions of resources.

Perhaps the most piquant summation of the dilemmas of strategic and structural complexity I ever encountered was in the mid-1970s during a programme for IBM executives in Paris on which I was teaching about multinational corporate organization. My talk involved going down a list of structural archetypes and discussing firms that used them and why. I was just coming to Philips and the matrix when a member of the group began to laugh in a manner not entirely consistent with the decorous, white shirt and tie culture of the IBM of the time. (Maybe it was the effect of the wine IBM allowed at lunch in France, but not elsewhere . . .) When asked what was so funny about such a very serious Dutch company, the gentleman said: 'Sorry to laugh. Actually, Philips is my favorite company. I sell computers to them. Their administrative systems are so complex that where most companies need one, they need three.' Indeed, a quick and dirty check suggested that the information technology and administrative overhead budgets as a percentage of sales of Philips *were* significantly above that of its competitors.

It was a luxury the external environment was not about to permit for much longer.

The Decline of Negotiable Environments

1. Trade Barriers Come Down

If much of the business ideology of the 1960s and 1970s supported the primacy of the visible hand of management, so did many elements in the external environment.

Back in the 1960s the world's product markets were also geographically divided into semi-sealed units called 'nations', grouped only occasionally into trading blocs – several of which were designed more to keep former colonies as private hunting preserves than to encourage free, cross-border trade. Although tariff barriers were coming down, many non-tariff barriers remained. The European single market had not arrived nor had the single currency to facilitate comparison-shopping across borders. The very term 'multinational enterprise', coined sometime in the 1950s, reflected the primacy of multi*national* operations.

Whether international operations were structured along 'mother–daughter' lines, or international divisions with autonomous national subsidiary structures, or subject to regional coordination, or had grid or matrix-like 'dotted' or dual cross-border reporting lines, they were based on the primacy of nation states as markets and negotiating partners. The geographical, and especially the nation state, dimension of the Stopford–Wells model had to be given pride of place in international business operations.

With fits and starts, the story of the international business environment from 1970 to 2000 has, however, been a fairly continuous one of the opening of international trade, the creation of regional and world markets, and the arrival of more and more globally oriented competitors. The walls of the 'negotiable environment', a term first used to describe the business climate of governmentally sanctioned trade barriers, currency controls, and tolerated cartels and collusions of the inter-war and early post-second world war years first gradually gave way, then – at least relative to what it had been – crumbled.

Successive trade rounds led to open markets and a boom in world trade and the GATT became the WTO. The ever-expanding European Community moved from reducing tariff barriers to the single market and free trade and on to monetary union and the euro. Infatuations with 'national champion' companies and that oxymoron 'state enterprise' are little more than a memory in the developed world and not much more than an embarrassing, expensive relic in most of the rest, including the once-communist lands. The statist ideologies and dependency theories of Raul Prebisch and others who commended closed, national markets to the 'third world' were proven bankrupt by the world trade oriented successes first of the Asian 'gang of four' and then by 'capitalist communism' in China. And the most closed-market, statist ideology of them all collapsed along with the Berlin Wall and the disintegration of the USSR.

2. The Japanese Competitive Thrust

The decline in trade barriers and the rise of outward-looking, non-statist growth and development models might not on their own have provided sufficient force for shifting firms' attention to efficiency seeking, and then from internal structuring to the external configuration of the firm. However, the challenge of the centrally directed, global thrust of the Japanese surely did.

The late Ray Vernon, the guiding spirit of the Multinational Enterprise Project at the Harvard Business School when Stopford, Wells, myself and others were embarking on their careers, used to argue that, left to their own devices in the new world of globalizing markets, US and European firms would, after initial thrusts and challenges into each others' territories, exchange hostages and by and large settle down to a life still pretty much defined by geographically compartmental-ized markets. After all, many were starting from that point. They were used to a world of nation states in which many of the firms already had long-established national 'daughter companies' or 'autonomous subsidiaries'. Organizationally, product and functional matrix overlays may have been added but the factories and sales teams were still geographically segmented. There were costs sunk in mini replicas of home country multiproduct factories to protect and much physical, human and psychic capital invested in dealing with a world of nation states to defend from obsolescence.

Multinational enterprise was in fact not a new phenomenon. Bayer, DuPont, GE, Siemens, Asea Brown Boveri, Philips, RCA, Ford, and Fiat had long got along in an early 20th century world of trade and currency barriers and of tacit or explicit market division and cross-licensing accords: a world which was the antithesis of globalization. Moreover, US and European firms actually believed that they were in business to have high and growing profits. Or if reported 'profit' was a dirty political term, embarrassing, or just tax-inefficient for the often family-dominated companies of continental Europe, the aim was to augment 'owner's wealth', that is, re-invested cash flow.

The Japanese, for reasons embedded in their culture of corporate-group, *keiretsu* rivalry, put volume and sales growth first, with profit a secondary matter or one considered to be a long-term by-product of volume increases that promised, via the experience curve, ever-decreasing costs and eventual profits as cumulative quantities shipped increased. Aided by periods when the Japanese yen was seriously undervalued versus the dollar and other Western currencies, the Japanese cut prices, took market share, and, in a manner inscrutable to many shell-shocked European and US managers, didn't stop until they had dominated or conquered markets entirely.

Moreover, Japanese firms achieved their global successes largely with efficiency-oriented, centrally coordinated, worldwide product-division structures that contained world-scale manufacturing activities, not multitudes of nation-by-nation, daughter-company replicas of mother-country operations.

Many of the Japanese challengers were quite diversified by product line and by geographical spread of markets. But, although they were increasingly multinational in manufacturing, locations of production were far less dispersed than in most US and European firms. And when foreign production was embarked upon, it was much more likely to be of optimal economic scale, located in low-cost locations, and designed to be used as a source of product for world, not national or regional, markets. Product-diversified Japanese firms also faced fewer structural and administrative challenges than did their Western counterparts, not only because of the homogeneity of Japanese culture and staffing, but also because, unlike the often Lego-like construction-through-acquisition of product portfolios in the West, Japanese product diversification had occurred organically.

When product-market complexity threatened to overwhelm structure in Japanese firms, they were inclined, well before the deconglomeration and divestment waves in the West, to spin off (and yet retain linkages as part of 'groups') particular activities as they developed distinctive management, personnel, and market-interface needs. Rather than bogging down in internal restructuring, Japanese 'groups' often developed by a process analogous to amoebic cellular division. Furakawa Electric begat Fuji Electric, which begat Fujitsu, which begat Fanuc and Panafacom. This development also led to a series of autonomous business entities, not to an over-arching corporate control structure and bureaucracy.

The Japanese challenge was most manifest in the 1980s (see Table 1), but it in fact started much earlier. Matsushita was already gaining ground on Philips in the late 1960s. Japanese bearing companies started picking off the daughter companies of Sweden's SKF in the early 1970s. In the hands of companies like Canon, Sony, Toyota, Honda, and Fuji Photo, it remains more than formidable to this day. One should not confuse the decline of the Japanese 'growth model' and the recession in Japan with the fate of these world-class competitors. They have more than learned the art of 'managing around a black hole' of domestic demand, to reprise a term coined by Stopford in another context. The Japanese juggernaut – the manufacturing part of Japanese enterprise that is globally oriented and not tied to the moribund, over-regulated, rigid domestic economy – rolls on.

Table 8.1—Major winners and losers in global corporate competition, 1980s

Industry	Winners	Losers
Aerospace	British Aerospace Allied-Signal	Dassault
Autos	* Toyota	British Leyland
Chemicals	AKZO	DSM
Computers	* Fujitsu * Canon Apple	CDC Sperry ICL
Electronics	* Hitachi ABB * Sony * NEC	ITT Westinghouse RCA Western Electric
Steel	* Kobe Pohang (POSCO)	US Steel Bethlehem
Non-Elec. Mach	* Mitsubishi Heavy * Komatsu	FMC Combust. Eng.
Non-Ferr. Metals	* Sumitomo Metal Mining	Inco
Petroleum	PetroVen (PDVSA)	Gulf
Pharma	Abbot	Warner-Lambert
Textiles & Apparel	* Teijin	Burlington JP Stevens Springs
Tyres	* Bridgestone	Dunlop Firestone Uniroyal

Source: World Market Share Corporate Data Base, as reported in Franko, 1991.
Companies gaining and losing major shares in total sales of world markets in global industries.
(Japanese firms marked *)

Faced with the Japanese challenge, a challenge piled on top of increased demands from the financial markets for profitability, 'lean and mean' became more than a slogan for Western firms. The inefficiencies of complex product-cum-geographical diversification strategies, and of the complex matrix, grid and mixed structures that accompanied them, were no longer viable.

3. Financial Market Pressures

Although corporate managements were coming under pressure to globalize and move from reorganizing to restructuring by the opening of world markets and by Japanese global competition, the final push came in the late 1990s via change in financial and capital markets. The first tidings became manifest in the 1980s in the US with the junk bond financed development of the market for corporate control and the rise of the hostile takeover. The raiders and takeover artists and leveraged buy-out (LBO) firms were quite unsentimental about keeping underperforming activities inside firms just because they had always been there, or waiting for internal corporate reorganizations to produce – perhaps, maybe someday – results. Especially in LBOd firms, the 'sword of debt' forced quick disposals and sales of under-performing assets and of the people who managed and worked in them.

Unsurprisingly, entrenched managers in many large firms were bitterly opposed to the continuation of this vigorous threat to their empires, their discretionary powers, and their pocketbooks – sheer company size having long since come to correlate better with top-management compensation and social prestige than profitability or returns to shareholders. They used all available means to succeed in turning the law into an instrument to protect corporate incumbents. Yet the Maginot Lines they threw up barely halted capital market pressures for efficiency and share-holder value. In spite of the roadblocks of poison pills, shark-repellents, and raider-deterrent laws, the takeovers, carve-ups, and external restructurings continued through the 1990s.

Ironically, much of the cause for the continuing pressure on management to become ever more efficiency oriented was due to the interests of people rarely identified with those of management as a class: teachers, public employees, and unionized workers. For it was they who were the beneficiaries of new fiduciaries with acronyms like CALPERS (California Public Employees Retirement System) and CALSTERS (California State Teachers Retirement System) which were about to apply concentrated pressure on corporate managers, first in the US then around the world, to focus on shareholder interests above all.

The last quarter of the 20th century saw the rise of 'fiduciary capitalism' in the US and a return to concentrated share ownership after a half-century interval. However, as Lynn Stout has written (2001): 'This time, share ownership is consolidated not in the hands of wealthy individuals like Henry Ford or Andrew Carnegie, but in the hands of wealthy institutions. In particular, public and private pension funds now hold a size-able portion of the outstanding equity of the largest US firms. These fiduciary institutions have both the incentive and the ability to throw their weight around in the corporate boardroom that widely dispersed individual investors don't and can't.'

Having come to possess fiduciary ownership of almost 60 % of the 1,000 largest US corporations by 1997, these institutional investors have increasingly used 'voice' as well as 'exit' in dealing with underperforming companies. They have transformed the principal–agent relationship between shareholders and corporate managements. The pressure of the fiduciary capitalism in the US then began to spread.

Financial markets, and especially equity markets, were not globally integrated 30, even 15, years ago. Even many developed countries then had currency and other controls that severely inhibited cross-border stock investments and other financial flows. Not until the late 1980s did US pension and mutual funds began to do more than dip a toe into the waters of international equity investing. But by the mid-1990s US institutional investors had a large enough share ownership in non-US firms to begin to follow on with the same sort of pressure and influence on managements they had come to exercise on domestic firms. And they were not alone. Funded pension plans, the rise of mutual funds in Europe and elsewhere as a part of pension reform aimed at shoring up soon-to-be-insolvent government retirement programmes have brought, and are increasingly bringing, an institutional shareholder culture to even the non-Anglo-Saxon world.

Corporate managements contemplating product-cum-geographical diversification strategies and structures are now operating between the scissor blades of globalization. On one side are increasingly competitive international goods markets; on the other there are the ever more interlinked, ever more institutionalized, financial markets.

The implication is clear: discretionary managerial options for allocating resources by the visible hand of organizational design have been greatly narrowed. Cross-border competition increasingly limits the amount of time and money that managements can burn trying out complex structures, and buttressing them with information systems, culture-building exercises, management training, and organizational development meetings. Institutional investors, when not harassing managers in presentations and conferences with warnings not to use free cash flow for value-destroying acquisitions, impose 'conglomerate discounts' on firms that attempt to resist the assertion that investors can build their own diversified portfolios and do not need managements to do it for them.

Markets rule. Many-product, many-nation strategies, and the matrix, grid, or even many-product divisions and SBUs – all organizational structures once thought to support those strategies – are a people and time-intensive luxury no longer permitted by the markets. I think it was James Carville who said that he would like to be reincarnated as the bond market rather than as president or pope because that was where the real political power was in the US, a conclusion he drew from the pressures successfully put on the Clinton administration to shelve its more grandiose government visible hand spending plans during its first years in office.

In the business world, the real power of the securities markets, and of product and labour markets, has similarly constrained the visible hand of management and the results are manifest.

ITT's conglomerate configuration and its matrix structure are long gone. Its name, which originally signified a telecommunications business, the remains of which were eventually acquired by France's Alcatel, now is found on a medium-size industrial components manufacturer. W R Grace survives as a $1.5bn-turnover, vastly slimmed-down, focused speciality chemicals firm, not even of *Fortune* 500 size. (It is number 827 on the *Fortune* 1000 for the year 2000.) Its once famous Latin American shipping activity was disposed of long ago, and it divested many 'non-core' packaging, water treatment, organic chemicals, oil and gas production and services businesses during the 1990s.

Corning finally solved its problem of great product-geography complexity by selling and spinning off its consumer products and health care services activities. Volvo's matrix was abandoned and non-vehicle activities were divested some time ago, and its best-known business, autos, has become part of Ford's luxury automotive group.

Swedish-Swiss ABB, once known as Asea Brown Boveri, and once an exponent of the product-nation matrix, has spun off much of its heavy equipment manufacturing activity and simplified its organizational structure. ABB's matrix, rather than being a final evolutionary stage, was like many an international division before, not a destination but a transition, one perhaps useful in making the sometimes psychologically wrenching adjustment of taking decision-making power and status away from national subsidiary barons and moving it to global product managers.

After a battering by Japanese and other competitors, Philips, too, speaks no more of matrices but of worldwide product divisions and (external) restructuring via a continuing refocusing on a smaller number of scale-efficient activities in fewer countries with fewer people. It has even thought previously unthinkable thoughts in public, including contemplating the ending of its consumer electronics activities in the US should they continue to be unsuccessful.

Enron: Light on Opacity

The latest demise of an overly complex firm, Enron, will surely accelerate the pressures. Even before the Enron debacle and its knock-on effects on Tyco, institutional shareholders were becoming increasingly intolerant of the opacity and complexity of multi-activity firms. Tyco's decision to end its life as an acquisitive conglomerate and break itself into four separate companies was its means of attempting to avoid the dreaded 'conglomerate discount' imposed by the financial markets – read institutional investors – on firms whose operations are deemed non-transparent.

Not only are the markets intolerant of product-cum-geographical complexity, they are allergic to mere product complexity. The inability to manage multi-product plus multi-country diversification was at the root of the demise of ITT, the decline of W R Grace, and the travails of Philips and Texas Instruments. Even the decline and fall of Enron had a significant international component in the form of its disastrous Indian power venture and unsuccessful Brazilian and UK utility projects. But Tyco (and Hanson and Tomkins before) was punished mainly for simple product diversification. Thus, the strategic and structural options available to firms competing in the global economy have narrowed yet further. Not only are grid, mixed, and matrix structures, and the strategies that call for them, off the table but so, it seems, are strategies and structures that require more than a handful of product divisions. Firms who trespass these boundaries are only too likely to be viewed by the financial markets as ripe for dismantling.

Until the late 1990s, it might have been arguable that the constraining of managerial strategic and structural options to a narrow portion of the Stopford–Wells model applied mostly to the world of Anglo-Saxon capitalism, or what some in the French political left refer to as *le capitalisme sauvage.* Yet, like the Gulf Stream, the corporate restructuring and divestments and shareholder-focused capitalism that had come earlier to the US and the UK eventually came to the Continent. Alcatel simplified what had once been, literally, the Compagnie Générale d'Electricité and then broke itself apart and, with part of an also split-up and de-matrixed ABB, formed Alstom as a separate heavy-engineering firm. Lagardère de-conglomerated. Hoechst spun off and divested its traditional chemicals companies and became Aventis, a focused pharmaceutical firm. Nokia and Ericsson thrived (more than did less-focused Motorola) only after paring down to their wireless technology essentials – at least before that whole market hit a speed bump. Unilever divested chemicals. And so on.

True, firms like Bayer and Norsk Hydro defend the old multi-product, multi-geography faith but the financial community is circling these holdouts and asking 'when will the conglomerate discount get to be too painful for their shareholders?'

The GE Exception

'But what about GE? (Some readers may have been wanting to ask this for some time now.) It produces and sells many unrelated products, doesn't it? GE stock doesn't sell at a conglomerate discount. And you yourself have praised it for its push to internationalize in your latest review of global corporate competition. It can be done.'

There are at least four obvious retorts: (1) Jack Welch. (2) A clear criterion for deciding what businesses to be in – the Welch rule of 'be number one or two, fix to be number one or two, or sell'. (3) The fact that there are exceptions to every rule. That bumblebees fly does not mean that they should be taken as a general template for aeronautical design. (4) Difficult strategies and structures can, perhaps, work for a while – even a long while – especially when a huge investment has indeed been made in the Bartlett–Ghoshal 'transnational solution' by transcending formal structure through the rigorous building of a common culture, including the Crotonville management development boot camp.

Still, even GE has not escaped criticism for creative accounting and 'earnings management' and recessions have a way of revealing inefficiencies that good times mask. Will the house that Jack built (or, more accurately, rescued from once going the way of previous conglomerates) last?

There are also at least two less obvious retorts. One I learned from speaking with GE executives. To wit: 'the giant cuts itself up into midgets when it goes to market'. Not everything, it seems, is matrixed or transnationalled.

Another relates to GE's chosen fields. Perhaps GE is not quite the unalloyed, triumphal success story implied by its stock price. Many of the businesses it abandoned were in global, or rapidly globalizing, industries, for example consumer electronics, semiconductors, computers and peripherals, and wireless communications. Several that it still manages – US appliances, the NBC and CNBC broadcasting networks, military jet engines, medical electronics, lighting, some of the finance activities – are somewhat, or even very, sheltered from the cold winds of global corporate competition and undervalued currencies. Time-intensive, expensive, multi-domestic or transitional/transnational structures and processes housed within – and transnationalled – across worldwide product groups are surely more feasible when the global competitive winds blow less ferociously. It is probably heresy to say so, but could not part of GE's secret of success have been a judicious retreat to safer ground?

Are There Structural Dilemmas Remaining?

Has shareholder capitalism solved all dilemmas of multinational corporate organization? My tone so far might seem to suggest that my answer would be a resounding 'yes' and even that I might join Richard Foster and argue that firms should 'become markets', i.e. that strategic management's main business ought to be the buying and selling of businesses.

However, I do not concur. Not only does the business history of the 'buying businesses', or the M&A part of this injunction, suggest that even related business acquisitions are fraught with peril but Foster's ode to Enron and its 'asset-less' or 'asset-lite' strategy puts me in mind of some of the loopier edges of efficient market theory. I am reminded of the saw, to paraphrase slightly, about how, if one sees a real asset lying in the street don't bother to do the management work of picking it up because in an efficient world, if the asset really existed 'the market' would have already picked it up.

It also seems doubtful that investors ('the market') would much appreciate the change. How can one decide what to invest in if the object of the investment, thanks to a constantly changing kaleidoscope of activities, is itself a (highly) moving target? This is one of many reasons why the institutional investment firm with which I work wouldn't touch Enron.

No, the ancient advice to shoemakers to stick to their lasts and to do their work well seems much more pertinent. An article by John Kay I was reading in the *Financial Times* with my morning coffee today (a postmortem on yet another corporate calamity, Marconi) brought home the point with almost Texan bluntness and simplicity. The job of a company manager is not to be a 'meta-mutual-fund' buyer and seller of elements of a shifting portfolio, it is to 'run a business that adds value by means of the services it provides to customers'. Businesses 'add value if their superior delivery [to customers] enables them to command a premium price or if they design their operations in such a way that they meet these needs at lower cost'.

Designing superior products or services and the delivery thereof and/or designing lower-cost ways of meeting customer needs in a global market would still seem to provide a goodly number of practical challenges for organizational and structural design.

The financial markets have come to like focus. They have been largely weaned off their former infatuation with the regular increases in earnings per share that acquisitive conglomerates could produce for a time. There is also evidence and theory to suggest that markets like product-market focus spread across many geographical markets, what might be called focused multinationality or transnationality. Markets appear to accord higher valuations to product-focused but geographically spread firms than they do to product-diversified companies of either a domestic or multi-national scope, at least in the US. Part of this is due to a clear perception that the risk-reduction benefits to corporate income streams of operations spread across geographical markets with uncorrelated or imperfectly correlated economic cycles are more tangible and predictable than are those of product diversification. Multinational firms within specific industries typically have lower variability in their income streams than do non-multinational competitors dependent on the vicissitudes of the economic cycle in one market (for example, Ford with great multinationality versus Chrysler with virtually none); they are rewarded with lower 'betas', a lower cost of capital and higher market valuations.

What is focused and what is not, however, still remains quite a bit in the eye of the beholder. Much room for the art of management remains. Many highly successful firms are not focused exclusively on a *single* product. De-mergers and corporate break-ups often do seem to unlock shareholder value, though not invariably so. Economies of scope as well as those of scale do exist. Companies like IBM, American Express, and Disney, which have a diversified pallet of related activities, may be able to leverage their brands across them in order to obtain economies in cross-selling and distributing multiple products and services.

Moreover, the problem for multinational managers of how to weigh global effi-ciency versus national responsiveness may be lessening as industries globalize. But it surely will not go away as long as distinctive nations, political-economic systems, cultures, and tastes continue to exist. Indeed, some industries, such as processed foods and defence, may long remain tilted towards the local or multi-domestic end of the scale.

The problems of organizational renewal and the management of innovation in a globalizing world remain. One of the great opportunities available to MNEs, but not to domestic firms, is that they face and can respond to stimuli in diverse countries, markets, and cultures. Ideas generated in some countries and regions may prove transferable to many elsewhere. Yet many of the 'old' structures were designed around the assumption, explicit or implicit, that their main function was transferring home-country innovations out to lower-income, lesser-developed foreign lands. Now, however, many of the then lesser-developed are developed or if not developed quite yet, very capable indeed. Successful multinational firms in the future may prosper not mainly by transmitting products and ideas from the centre to the periphery but by transmitting them from centre to centre.

The problem of productively transnationalizing research and development, and of squaring the circle of the need for broad R&D for corporate renewal and a focused product line, may prove especially acute. Or need all R&D be carried out within the firm? Could it not, as has occurred in the relationship between traditional pharma-ceutical companies and biotechnology start-ups, be more successful if outsourced or put at some distance from the corporate organization in a joint-venture or 'virtual' partner or subsidiary?

Thus, choosing an optimal (related) diversification strategy, and an international structure to support it, seems still to be very much an art, not a science. But some strategies and structures have become more equal than others, at least in a globalizing world.

A Personal End-note: Breaking Up Is Hard to Do

I must confess to the reader that I am not a totally dispassionate, objective observer of these phenomena. During my own teaching career I have had some curious experiences directly relevant to structural and corporate change. There were some rather fractious moments in Geneva at CEI (now IMD) with managers from Philips, our then single largest client firm, triggered by my raising questions as to whether they really could efficiently manage 1,200 products in 150 countries. (One of the Philips folks got up during a class and gave me a longish lecture on the error of my thoughts.) I've had a few similar moments with folks from Bayer.

There were also some strange discussions with top managers at Volvo about how matrix/grid organizations really functioned. From these I privately began wondering whether what might really be going on was that top management was too busy with other pursuits to bother choosing between product diversification and geographical expansion. Maybe they had adopted a matrix structure so that the people who actually worked in the organization would battle it out for themselves. This impression was further reinforced when I came back to the US in the 1980s and spent some time lecturing and consulting in my new backyard (Concord, Massachusetts) with, among others, another now-departed 'matrixed' firm, DEC.

And then there was December 1981 or thereabouts in Moscow when I was invited – along with other mostly European and Japanese luminaries, some of whom, like me because of my Ukranian name, were apparently (in my case quite erroneously) thought to be sympathetic to the Soviet cause – to help them save their economic system. To my utter amazement, it turned out that my book on European multinationals had been much more thoroughly read in Soviet circles than it had been in the West. Why, I asked? 'Because you have examined many non-market solutions to the resource-allocation problems of large multi-product, multi-ethnic organizations – like ours,' was the answer.

They seemed sincerely puzzled by my insistence that resource allocation was usually a more efficient process in a market-driven, rather than a bureaucratically or politically driven, context.

9 The Customer-focused Multinational: Revisiting the Stopford and Wells Model in an Era of Global Customers

Julian Birkinshaw and Siri Terjesen
London Business School

There is a well-established line of thinking on multinational enterprises' (MNE) strategy and structure beginning with John Stopford's doctoral thesis work in 1972. But since the early 1990s this line of research has almost dried up. There continue to be occasional studies of strategy and structure in the MNE but for the most part research has moved on to other issues such as the changing roles of foreign subsidiaries, knowledge flows inside MNEs, and studies of the evolution of these types of corporations.

Here we argue that we need to revisit issues of MNE strategy and structure in MNEs but that rather than focusing on classic factors such as number and diversity of countries, we need to start looking more broadly at other dimensions around which MNEs are now structuring their activities.

The main structural dimensions of the 1970s and 1980s were countries, business units, and functions. Today we can identify a number of other dimensions that appear to be equally valid. One is the *global account structure* for customers who expect to be supplied in a coordinated and consistent way across multiple countries and business lines. A second is the *industry sector structure*, commonly seen in professional services firms, for servicing a set of customers in a focused and knowledgeable way. And a third is the *solutions-based structure* in which the customer-facing unit pulls together the offerings of various business units and third parties to provide greater value-added for customers.

We will discuss each of these types of structure in detail, looking at the reasons why each has emerged, how it works, and its costs and benefits. We will also address the broader question of why the emphasis in MNE structures has shifted over the last decade towards these customer-focused designs. The primary reason, we argue, is that the opportunities for growth and increased profitability are shifting downstream, towards the provision of value-added services and solutions for customers. Many large MNEs have undertaken this shift in emphasis, including GE, ABB, Ford, and Unilever. And while some have failed, others have made the transition very effectively and have been rewarded with superior margins.

This broad shift in emphasis has two important consequences, both of which will be discussed in some detail.

The first is the risk of creating an organization structure that becomes so complex it is unworkable. Often these new dimensions of structure – global accounts, industry sectors, and solutions – are placed on top of an existing organization structure, resulting in a four- or five-dimension matrix. This creates complexity, blurring of roles, and administrative overload. As a result, many MNEs are experimenting with ways of simplifying their structures. They are looking at how they can reduce their portfolio of businesses, outsourcing major activities, and making use of market-like mechanisms for structuring internal relationships.

The second consequence is the potential decline in the importance of geography as a design variable. Many MNEs almost completely disregard the traditional country unit of operation (particularly in the developed world) as other structural dimensions become more important. Our belief is that there are major risks in going down this route and we will examine some of the approaches MNEs are using to counteract this tendency.

First, let's examine how approaches to MNE organization have evolved over the years. The classic path of development, as elaborated by Stopford and Wells in 1972, was for a firm to adopt an 'international division' structure while domestic business was still dominant and then to move to either an 'area division' or 'global product division' structure as its business became truly international (with percentage of foreign sales and foreign product diversity as the key factors).

The area division structure, as represented by Philips, Shell, and Nestlé in the 1970s, gave enormous power to countries and regions but made coordination of product development and manufacturing across countries very difficult. The global product division structure, as adopted by Matsushita, GE, and many other MNEs, had the opposite characteristics – very clear accountability for production assets on a worldwide basis but little sensitivity to the differences in customer demand from country to country. Stopford and Wells also speculated that the global matrix would emerge as the structure of choice as firms reached high levels of both foreign product diversity and foreign sales. (See Figure 9.1.)

The strategy–structure school of thought popularized by Stopford and Wells gave way in the 1980s to a rather more behavioural or process-oriented body of literature. Chris Bartlett's doctoral thesis in 1979 showed that a sample of pharmaceutical and food-products firms had stayed with a formal 'international division' structure long past the point at which they would have been predicted to adopt an area or global product division. His interpretation was that these firms had managed the transition to global scope by changing their management systems and culture rather than their formal reporting structure. Concepts such as the 'transnational' corporation developed by Bartlett and Sumantra Ghoshal in 1989 and the 'heterarchy' were developed as rather normative guides to *how* MNEs should manage their worldwide activities.

These concepts in turn helped to push a number of new lines of research, such as the evolution in subsidiary roles, the coordination of international R&D, and the transfer of knowledge within the MNE.

Figure 9.1—The Stopford and Wells model (reprinted with permission from Stopford and Wells, 1972).

Even so, many MNEs ended up developing formal matrix structures. There was a wave of popularity for the matrix in the early 1980s but most firms retreated from the pure form – in which country and business unit held equal power – in favour of a model in which one side or other dominated. The matrix gained renewed popularity in the 1990s thanks largely to the then success of ABB and its CEO Percy Barnevik's appetite for publicity. But ABB ultimately found the balanced matrix to be unworkable and in 1997 shifted towards a global business unit structure.

Today's MNE literature has moved a long way away from its original emphasis on strategy and structure. There is increasing interest in various aspects of MNE structure and particularly in the customer-facing part of the organization. There has been detailed research done on global account management and there are a few studies looking explicitly at the emergence of customer and solution-based structures.

Second, there is some discussion of the problems of too much complexity inside MNEs, for example the challenges of working with multi-dimensional matrix structures and the approaches that can be used to reduce complexity. Other studies have looked at the use of market-like mechanisms within the firm as a way of simplifying bureaucracy and at the need to break up and simplify MNEs that have become too large and complex.

Interestingly, part of the problem here appears to stem from the enormous popularity of Bartlett and Ghoshal's transnational model. Many firms that embraced their ideas ended up adopting structural approaches to delivering the demands for integration, responsiveness, and learning at the same time, even though this was not Bartlett and Ghoshal's intention. As a result, they created administrative structures that were complex, bureaucratic, and inward looking.

Taken as a whole, we see a need to bring organization design issues back into consideration as a central part of understanding how MNEs work. There is some evidence of MNEs experimenting with new ways of structuring their activities and it is therefore important for the academic community to document and make sense of these innovations.

There is also a sense that organization structure has been neglected for most of the past decade as researchers have focused their attention on other issues. While organization structure is never the whole story, it is – and always has been – an important part of the story. Our purpose in the remainder of this chapter is to try to shed some light on the variety of customer-facing structures we see in existence today.

New Demands, New Responses

MNEs face no end of challenges and threats in today's business environment – from new and disruptive technologies to political changes in emerging markets, and the rise of non-governmental organizations (NGO) such as Greenpeace. In the context of this discussion, however, some changes are more relevant than others. So rather than consider a whole variety of macroeconomic and political factors, we prefer to focus on a number of rather specific changes. These are as follows.

- *The emergence of global customers looking for integrated offerings.* Of course, customers have been global in scope for decades but increasingly they are now demanding integrated offerings from their suppliers – the right, for example, to buy the same product at the same price and service level in every country around the world. And even in industries where local regulations prohibit such integrated offerings (for example, pharmaceuticals), the emergence of global distributors has the same effect.
- *The emergence of new focused competitors who compete globally in one product area rather than attempt to provide a broad product line (for example, Palm versus Philips).* These new competitors typically reveal just how slow moving and bureaucratic incumbent MNEs have become. To take such competitors on, some MNEs use heavyweight development teams to cut across the traditional lines of structure; others focus on their ability to bundle together a variety of different products and services.
- *Changes in industry boundaries, with many cases of convergence and deregulation.* These changes are creating both the opportunity and the need for MNEs to pull together new services and solutions for customers who do not think in terms of traditional industry boundaries.
- *Increasing competition in traditional core business (for example, from low-cost countries), leading to shrinking margins and anaemic growth rates.* In searching for new sources of growth and margins, many MNEs have started to look downstream – towards value-added services and solutions they can sell alongside their traditional products.

What is the best way of meeting these new demands within an existing organization structure? The usual approach is to put in place informal or temporary coalitions rather than create entirely new arrangements. To manage a global customer, for example, a first stage would be to appoint a global account manager whose role was to act as the internal coordinator of all the different businesses that sold to the customer. And if that were not sufficient, a cross-business team would be created with representatives from each business area. Such structures are typically kept informal but still overlay all existing structures.

But while this sort of ad hoc solution is valid, it can quickly run out of control. It is not uncommon for a mid-level executive in a large MNE to have his 'line' job and then three or four additional responsibilities, each of which involves some form of coordination along one of these other dimensions.

Unfortunately, this approach quickly reaches the limits to internal coordination. Human beings can only process so much information and will simplify, prioritize, and shut out extraneous data when the burden becomes too great. Working in a two-dimensional matrix is not easy but most managers can just about cope with the different and often conflicting priorities of two bosses. But once the individual starts to work with three, four, or five dimensions the information overload becomes too great. Priorities get confused, and focus is lost. This has all sorts of side effects. Most obviously, people turn inward and expend their energies on internal activities rather than on things that directly add value to the customer. Equally, there is typically a loss of entrepreneurial spirit and of momentum.

Is it possible to avoid these problems? Not entirely. But our analysis suggests that there are certainly approaches the MNE can take to avoid the 'logjam' in coordination that is often experienced. Let's begin with a few broad observations before moving on to the specifics.

First, *while simpler organization structures are desirable, it is not possible to get rid of complexity altogether* because the demands on MNEs will continue to be multi-faceted and ever changing. As the principle of requisite variety states, an organization needs to be as complex as the environment in which it operates. So it is necessary to take a careful look at the various parts of the organization and decide which parts *need* multi-dimensional complex structures and which parts can get away with simpler arrangements.

Second, *the increasing importance of attributes such as flexibility, focus, and speed point towards the need for more customer-focused organization structures*. ABB, for example, created a business to sell full service and maintenance contracts for oil refineries. It essentially sits between the ABB product businesses and the customer, buying in products and expertise from those businesses and adding value through its own industry-specific knowledge.

Third, *we would argue that a large part of the complexity faced by MNEs can best be addressed in the customer-focused parts of the organization*. Global account managers and their like are the 'boundary-spanners' whose role is to soak up and interpret the complexity of the business environment and provide some stability to those in the core of the organization. This also makes intuitive sense because the global account manager attempts to bring together the multiple demands of the customer, prioritize them, and then liaise with other parts of the organization to deliver on the customer's orders.

Fourth, and following from the last point, *there is considerable scope in most MNEs to simplify the supply side*. For example, Ericsson increasingly uses contract manufacturers to make its digital switches and ship them around the world. Working closely with external manufacturers creates its own challenges but the point is that the supply operation does not need to be wrapped up in the global matrix. Other MNEs have created distinct 'front end' and 'back end' business units that deal with each other on a quasi-market basis.

Types of Customer-focused Structures

To try to make sense of today's various customer-focused structures, we propose the following framework. It focuses on two aspects of the relationship with the customer.

The first is the extent to which the MNE provides an integrated presence in front of the customer – perhaps through the designation of a global account manager or by creating a dedicated unit around a particular customer. The creation of such structures can be driven either by the customer demanding a single point of contact or by the proactive efforts of the MNE.

The second is the level of value-added in the customer interface. The lowest level of value-added is represented by a one-off product sale. Higher levels of value-added are such things as a long-term contract, the provision of a service contract alongside the product, or the provision of a bundled 'solution'. These higher levels of value-added often require new types of customer-focused structures. And as before, the creation of such structures can be driven from both the customer and vendor side of the relationship.

These two variables form the basis of our framework. (See Figure 9.2.) The bottom-left corner represents what we can call the traditional model. Here, the MNE sells to its customers on a country-by-country basis rather than on an integrated basis. And it focuses on its product sales, rather than on services or solutions. The appropriate organization model can be any of the traditional structures – the global product division, the area division, or the global matrix.

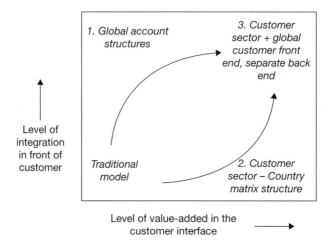

Figure 9.2—Framework for customer-focused structures in the MNE.

However, as we have already argued, we see a number of broad changes that are pushing MNEs away from this traditional model towards new customer-focused structures. Let us consider in turn the appropriate structures for each of the other quadrants in the framework.

1. High Level of Integration in Front of the Customer

The standard response to customers seeking a coordinated presence from their suppliers is to create some sort of global account management structure on top of the existing country-based sales organization. In its simplest form this is little more than a single individual charged with coordinating the MNE's offerings in multiple countries. But in many MNEs global account structures are now highly sophisticated, with whole teams supporting key customers, information systems dedicated to measuring customer profitability, and complex incentive systems to credit both global account managers and country sales people with sales.

In terms of the framework presented above, global account structures do not apply exclusively to the top-left quadrant. Rather, they occupy a spectrum from the top left through to the top right, with the simpler ones concerned only about coordination of sales on a worldwide basis and the more complex ones also concerned about the higher value-added opportunities at the interface with the customer. Three broad variants can be identified.

Global coordination. Here the global account manager has to coordinate the disparate country-based operations of the MNE towards a particular customer. Ericsson's first attempt at creating global account managers in the early 1990s was a coordination model. One individual, for example, became the global account manager for Cable & Wireless, which involved first of all getting to grips with all Ericsson's current projects for Cable & Wireless, and then finding ways of coordinating and adding value to them.

In a similar way, Electrolux created a global account coordinator in response to Shell's demand for a global purchasing deal for all its commercial refrigeration equipment. This form of global account management is relatively cheap to implement and avoids complexity but it is often very difficult to make work. Both the Ericsson and Electrolux examples were only partial successes because the global account managers did not have sufficient time or authority to really make their coordination role work effectively. So, for example, while they could agree a deal in principle with their global customer, they were often powerless to implement it in every country around the world.

Global matrix. This approach gives greater power to global account managers to enable them to do their job more effectively. It essentially works as a matrix within the sales organization, with countries on one axis and global accounts on the other. For example, Hewlett-Packard's global account manager for Volkswagen would be responsible for all sales made to VW around the world and would have people working directly for him or her in each major VW market.

This approach ensures a high-quality and coordinated service to Volkswagen in all its plants around the world but the price is a higher level of structural complexity in HP's sales organization. It also involves considerable investment in new IT systems and incentive programmes that double-count sales on both dimensions of the matrix. Many MNEs have adopted this structure. Ericsson evolved from the coordinating role to the matrix structure in the late 1990s. HP used this model throughout the 1990s until its recent changes (see below). It is also used in 3M, ICI, and BT.

Dedicated customer units. The third variant of the global account structure is to create dedicated units around key customers. This approach essentially pulls key accounts out of the traditional sales organization and gives them dedicated teams that report exclusively to a global account manager. Examples of this can be found most clearly in the world of contract manufacturing. For example, companies like Solectron, Flextronics, and Celestica have entire groups dedicated to their major customers like IBM, Ericsson, or Motorola. The automotive supply industry also works in this way with teams dedicated to the big auto companies like Ford and Volkswagen. And on a smaller scale some IT services companies are also structured this way. For example, Pink Elephant, a medium-sized Dutch IT company, has dedicated teams for most of its major customers like Shell, ING, and ABN-Amro.

This structure is designed to offer both a coordinated and a higher value-added set of services to the customer and takes us towards the top-right quadrant of the framework (see below). Its primary benefit, of course, is the level of customization and dedication that can be given to a particular customer. However, it is potentially a very expensive model that can only be justified for very large customers. It can dilute the attention shown to other customers that do not justify a dedicated unit. It also creates a high degree of dependency on a few core customers. MNEs that have adopted this structure observe it is very difficult to think beyond the short-term demands of those customers. It is also difficult to take business away from them (even if it is not very profitable business).

2. High Level of Value-added in Customer Interface

The most effective way of delivering a higher level of value-added in the customer interface is through a sector or market-focused structure on top of the existing country-based sales organization. In other words, individuals working in the customer-facing part of the organization will have both a country base as well as a sector base. The country is typically their home base (in terms of salary, career development, and a place to work) but the sector is where the work gets done and where the sector-specific knowledge is built up.

While this is a relatively new model for industrial companies, professional services firms have been organized this way for decades. The reason for this should be self-apparent – professional service firms are by definition concerned with creating value-added relationships with their customers through the advice they offer or the expertise they provide. So in order to understand the structure that suits this contingency best, it makes sense to review the model that professional services firms have developed.

One example is Accenture (formerly Andersen Consulting). It was traditionally structured in three dimensions – countries, customer sectors, and competencies (skill bases such as strategy, technology, process, organization and human performance). Employees were hired into a particular country and competency and then gradually pushed into one or two customer sectors depending on where demand lay. However, the company has now evolved its structure away from a competency orientation in favour of a client sector-oriented model. Since 1999, the company has realigned itself around clients' specific needs across four industries (communications and high technology, financial services, products, and resources) and eight service lines (strategy and business architecture, human performance, customer relationship management, finance and performance management, supply chain management, technology research and innovation, solutions engineering, and solutions operations).

McKinsey operates a similar model. It is structured into countries and solution practices. The practices span both specific industry and functional areas of expertise. A consultant will be based in a geographical office and be involved in one or more practices that reflect his or her client base, for example telecommunications or marketing. A consultant's project and affiliation with the firm will be predominantly regional. In the firm's larger practices (for example Chicago or London), a consultant is aligned primarily to his or her customer sector such as telecoms. In comparatively small practices (for example, Sao Paolo), geography is a consultant's primary allegiance.

These two examples illustrate the importance of the customer sector. The underlying logic is simply that sector-specific knowledge is central to the role of advising and adding value to the customer, so as a result it is necessary to work with a rather complex matrix structure that incorporates geography, competency, and sector.

Product-based companies have begun to adopt elements of the professional services model as a way of creating greater value-added with their customers. For example, in the computer industry it is now commonplace for the sales force to be structured around products, countries, and also customer sectors (sometimes called industry 'verticals'). Again, the logic is that computer usage in the telecoms industry will be rather different to usage in the oil and gas industry, so to stay competitive a computer company has to have deep industry expertise.

Most product-based companies still see their product units (or occasionally their countries) as their primary reporting line. In a few cases, however, this is also beginning to change. Reuters, for example, was traditionally organized around its primary products (editorial content, information systems, and so on) but recently went through a major restructuring and it is now organized around four customer segments – investment banking and brokerage, treasury, asset management, and media and corporates. The first three segments serve financial markets; the last enables Reuters to mobilize resources in a 'broader corporate context'.

According to CEO Tom Glocer: 'In reorganizing the company from its earlier geographic and product structure to run along customer segments we sought, literally, to put the customer at the heart of the business. But to meet our long-term revenue aspirations, we know we must convert this customer focus into the highest-quality products and truly great service. We will deliver on these goals by aligning our company from front to back with our customers, understanding their sophisticated workflow in areas such as straight through processing, capturing these requirements, and then delivering better products faster' (Annual report, 2000).

While one should never take quotes from annual reports at face value, this statement underlines the central idea of a sector-based organization structure, namely that it represents a way for the sales organization to focus on the customer base first and products second. In Reuters' case, this shift in structure is aided by the fact that there is a close alignment between its products and sectors – information services to large banks and brokerages and editorial content to media companies.

While sector-focused structures obviously make it easier to add value in the customer interface, they also lead to some additional challenges. First, they represent an additional line of reporting that typically sits on top of the existing country-based sales structure.

This often manifests itself in extremely complex team structures. For example, if IBM is preparing a bid to sell a project to Shell, it needs people from the relevant countries, from the right product groups, from the oil and gas sector, as well as people who can relate to strategic partners such as SAP or Oracle.

The second major problem is that sector-focused structures tend to herald a split between the front-end (demand side) and back-end (supply side) parts of the MNE. In professional services firms this is not really an issue because there is no supply-side organization. But in product-based companies the front end begins to find itself separated from the back end that is actually developing and manufacturing the products. This creates a variety of issues – transfer prices between the front and back ends, sourcing of third-party products, and the location of the marketing function. We will discuss this problem in detail in the next section, where it becomes really acute.

3. High Integration in Front of Customer and High Value-added in Customer Interface

While there are still many examples of MNEs that focus on either cross-national integration *or* higher value-added in the customer interface, the two dimensions increasingly go together and this is where true customer-focused structures come into their own. Such companies as IBM, HP, ABB, Citibank, and EDS have all moved through one or other of the previous structures towards a model that delivers on both dimensions simultaneously.

The central feature of this model is a clear split between the front-end and back-end parts of the MNE. So HP, for example, has two customer-focused businesses (front-end) that are structured around a combination of customers, sectors, and countries (see below for details) and two product-focused businesses (back-end) that develop and manufacture products. The structure of the customer-oriented front end varies from case to case but is typically divided first into customer sectors, with specific global customers within that, and then with countries as a secondary line of reporting.

The front-end/back-end structure has a number of interesting features and while it represents the leading edge in terms of adding value in the customer interface, it also has a substantial number of problems. But before getting into these general points it is worth describing a few examples of how it works in practice.

IBM

The world's largest computer company developed a form of front-end/back-end structure during the early 1990s. This structure emerged in part through the enormous success of IBM's global services business, which grew rapidly during Lou Gerstner's tenure as CEO and now accounts for around 43 % of the company's $80 billion revenues.

Central to the philosophy of IBM's customer-facing operations was the idea that the company would sell whatever combination of products and services the customer requested, whether that meant sourcing the products from inside IBM or selling competitors' machines. So product development units could sell directly to customers but also function as internal suppliers to the firm's solution units (Global Industries) that serve industry segments. There was also the Global Services organization that developed products into solutions. IBM established strong centralized functions to manage this front-end/back-end relationship, including a finance centre to manage the solutions business, internal transfer pricing, and regional leadership groups that focus on resource allocation.

Hewlett-Packard

HP is the second-largest computer company in the world. Until 2000 it was organized in a highly decentralized fashion with as many as 83 product units ('divisions'), each responsible for developing and manufacturing its own products. The customer interface was managed through a global sales organization, split by country first and with a global account management structure overlaid on top.

This structure was effective for much of HP's 60-year history and helped to create strong managers and an impressive record in product development. On the other hand, customers faced numerous sales and marketing staff and the company was so focused on small projects that it missed the boat on large initiatives such as the development of a firm-wide Internet strategy. There was also a great deal of internal bureaucracy.

When Carly Fiorina became HP's CEO in 2000 she quickly moved towards a new customer-focused structure, in large part to address the concern that HP was missing out on big growth opportunities in the industry. The result was a structure with two back-end units, developing computers and printers, and two front-end units focused on corporate sales and consumer sales. (Originally, there were two other units: a front-end digital appliance product development group and a back-end consulting services unit.)

The goal of this structure was to give customers (corporates in particular) a single point of contact and to enable HP to provide integrated solutions across all of its product and service areas. The new organization was also intended to help executives running the back-end units to focus their resources on a smaller number of core initiatives.

This new structure has had mixed reviews. Many HP executives enthuse about the success and say that modifications are helping to simplify the structure and make it more effective. Others are less positive, describing how the new organization created disorder and failed to get buy-in across the company. Some employees were also discouraged by their decreased lack of control and financial responsibility. According to one employee: 'The front-back thing has been a complete, unmitigated failure' (quoted in *Business Week*, 4 Jan 2002). It is also not entirely clear that the customer has been able to reap benefits. According to one customer: 'It's beyond my ability to communicate our frustration . . . it's painful to watch them screw up million-dollar deals' (as quoted in *Business Week*, 5 July 2001).

These two examples are provided to illustrate in broad terms how front-end/back-end structures work and the sorts of benefits the MNEs in question believe they offer. In IBM's case, the structure appears to work well. But HP represents work-in-progress and it is too soon to say whether or not they have got it right.

What are the challenges in making front-end/back-end structures work? There are two broad problem areas, both of which require careful management.

First, the link between the front-end and the back-end is far from simple. Back-end businesses complain that they no longer have a direct connection to their market place and that they are being asked to accept lower margins on their products, which are often sold as part of a bundled offering. Front-end businesses, in turn, complain that they do not get the level of customization and attention they need from the back-end businesses and that they spend a great deal of time haggling over transfer prices.

To make this work, the usual model is to move to market-based transfer pricing and indeed allow front-end businesses to source from third parties if necessary. But a strong centre is also needed to mediate disputes, such as when a front-end business wants to source a competitor's product rather than the one produced by the back-end business.

The second problem is that as the front-end business gets closer to its customers and starts providing complete 'solutions' to their problems, it will typically move away from relying on its traditional product offerings. One of the key features of a solutions-based business is that it has to be prepared to 'include strange bedfellows' as part of its offering. This can mean working with new partners in very different industries as well as sourcing competitors' products. A related problem is that the skills the MNE needs to manage its traditional back-end businesses will typically be very different from the skills it needs to manage its new front-end businesses.

In sum, then, the front-end/back-end structure offers many benefits but also opens up new management problems. It also raises the rather awkward question of where the MNE's boundaries should lie. IBM global services, for example, could be spun off as a separate entity with little damage to its competitiveness.

Conclusions

The purpose of this final section is to revisit a number of the issues that have emerged during the course of the discussion and to try to develop some broad conclusions.

The first task is to relate these structures to the original Stopford and Wells model. At one level these new dimensions of structure can be seen as adding to the original three dimensions of product, country, and function (because these dimensions are still important). However, given the difficulties of working in multi-dimensional matrix organizations, the reality is that they end up competing with the traditional dimensions. This competition is resolved in many cases by ignoring geography. And in the front-end/back-end model it is resolved through separation – product issues are managed in the back end and customer and country issues in the front end.

The provisional conclusion, then, is that the classic structures identified by Stopford and Wells (product division, area division, product–area matrix) are no longer leading edge. They still exist, of course, but the issue for large MNEs has shifted downstream towards the customer interface. And this requires a variety of new structural solutions.

Before taking this discussion about new structural solutions too far, it is worth underlining the point made earlier regarding Bartlett's doctoral thesis work and the subsequent literature on the process perspective. As before, structure is an important starting point in developing an organization to deliver on the MNE's chosen strategy but of equal or greater importance is the development of the appropriate management systems and supporting culture. Indeed, one could argue that all the structures discussed here actually fit quite nicely into the original definition of the 'transnational solution' – the need to deliver global integration, national (read customer) responsiveness, and worldwide learning. The structural dimensions may have changed but the principles remain the same.

A couple of loose ends should also be addressed.

First, what is the fate of the 'back end' or supply side of the organization in this shift towards customer-centred structures? To a certain degree it can be simplified and outsourced and there are gains to be had in taking this approach if only through the reduction of complexity. But of course there are also enormous negative implications for the competitiveness of the MNE if this model is taken too far.

For example, HP relies on a constant stream of innovative technologies for its competitive advantage so unless the front-end and back-end parts of the company can continue to work effectively together they are in trouble. So while it probably makes sense for MNEs to get out of commodity manufacturing and to simplify large parts of their supply chain in that way, they have wisely recognized as central to their long-term competitiveness the importance of strong design and development capabilities and the need to integrate them with their customer-focused operations.

Second, it is worth commenting on the apparent decline in the importance of geography in structuring MNEs. As already observed, the country dimension is often relegated to fourth or fifth place in terms of organizational priorities, below the customer, the segment, the product area, and the function. This may indeed be appropriate in many cases but it is worth remembering that while deals can be done at a global level, implementation is conducted on a local-for-local basis. Most service operations, for example, rely entirely on local capabilities and relationships.

So while the high-level structure of the MNE may have little space for country-level management, it has to find its way back into the organization chart at an operational level. And of course country management is still of great importance in the developing world, where such things as government relations are central to success.

10 Geography as a Design Variable

D. Eleanor Westney

MIT Sloan School of Management

Stopford and Wells' pioneering 1972 study *Managing the Multinational Enterprise* begins by identifying the organizational design challenges in multinational enterprises (MNEs) and the ongoing experimentation induced by those challenges:

'Few organizations in the past have equalled today's multinational enterprises in sheer size and complexity ... Nevertheless, businessmen have found ways of organizing the multinational enterprise that enable them to control and coordinate the activities of the various units. For some multinational enterprises, however, continued growth is reducing the effectiveness of past solutions to the problems of control and coordination. New forms of organizational structure are being developed. Whether they will enable the manager to overcome the problems of the largest and most complex multinational firms is not yet certain.'

It is a statement that could have been written today, with surprisingly little change. Indeed, in Jeffrey Garten's recent study, *The Mind of the CEO*, the chapter on 'Being Global' finds that the challenges and uncertainties of design for large and complex MNEs loom as large for today's CEOs as they did three decades ago:

'How to organize a company for global operations? Even the most internationally experienced business leaders continue to experiment, for no one has the right formula.'

Arguably the design challenges are even more salient today, given the considerably increased complexity and geographical scope of the MNEs that dominate the economic landscape of the early 21st century. The most geographically extended MNE covered in *Managing the Multinational Enterprise* had manufacturing operations in 29 countries; today it is not unusual for MNEs to have production operations in two or three times as many locations.

Geographical scope remains the defining feature of the MNE. However, the role geography does and should play in the design of the MNE is an increasingly complex problem. Both the concept of organization design and the role of geography in design have changed considerably over the last three decades. Design today encompasses formal linking mechanisms and formal management systems (including incentive structures) as well as the first-order design parameter of the 'boxes' of the organization chart on which the first generation of research on MNE design focused.

In many multinational enterprises, the country subsidiary, whose role as the basic building block of MNE design could be taken for granted in the early 1970s, has given way to smaller, more focused sub-national units that are often more closely connected to their counterparts in other countries than to other sub-units in the same country.

This chapter explores the changing views of geography in the organization design of MNEs over the last three decades, uses organizational changes in one MNE (ABB) as a window on the evolving role of geography as a design variable, and concludes by identifying some areas for future research and analysis in the management of MNEs.

Organization Design of MNEs

The first wave of research on the organization design of MNEs, of which Stopford's work was the most influential both at the time and in succeeding decades, built on Alfred Chandler's strategy and structure paradigm. Chandler focused on the relationship between business diversification strategy and formal structure; Stopford and other researchers added the relationship between international diversification and structure.

The Chandlerian paradigm defined structure in terms of the first-order design parameter: that is, the domain of the level of management reporting directly to the CEO, defined in terms of function, business, or geography. Chandler's early work assumed that for corporations adopting a multi-divisional structure, in which the first-order design parameter was the business, the second-order design parameter would be function.

In the international business (IB) field, researchers assumed that for the MNE, if geography were not the first-order design parameter it would be the second. In other words, in a worldwide functional or business organization the units reporting to the function or business head would be based on geography, either region or country. But in fact, very few empirical studies in this tradition extended their analysis below the first level of the organization chart.

Chandler developed his basic proposition – that diversification strategy drove changes in formal structure – inductively, from a set of detailed case studies, but it was soon given theoretical underpinning by the development of contingency theory and by the variant of contingency theory called information-processing theory.

Both approaches postulated that organization design should meet the demands imposed by the external environment, which was characterized in terms of variables such as uncertainty and diversity. Information-processing theory, as its name indicates, focused on the information environment of the firm and analysed design as a system for processing information. In the 1980s, a small but influential stream of research on MNE design adapted the information-processing approach to the study of MNE structures, still with a primary focus on the first-order design parameter of the firm.

The second half of the 1980s marked a turning point in the study of the MNE, marked by changes both in the empirical phenomenon and in the concepts and theories that dominated its analysis. For the world's largest MNEs, which had been the major focus of the analysis of MNE organization design, the focus of managerial interest shifted from the internationalization process to the challenges of effectively managing dispersed operations – from how to expand abroad to how to integrate activities across borders.

In the IB field, the central themes driving research expanded from the analysis of the competitive advantages that enabled a firm to extend its reach internationally to the competitive advantages a firm could derive from being international.

As the focus of MNE strategy shifted, so did the focus of MNE organizational analysis, from a typology based on formal structure to a set of ideal types based on the dispersion and distribution of capabilities and the direction and density of cross-border networks. The labels for these ideal types – variants of multi-domestic, global, transnational – denoted both the strategy and the organizational model associated with the strategy.

This highly influential approach to MNE organization eschewed the analysis of formal organizational structure in favour of processes (ranging from the very general, such as learning and local responsiveness, to the specific, such as management development) and networks, especially networks linking activities across locations.

This approach to MNE organization was in step with – even, arguably, in advance of – work in the field of organization studies on the 'new organization' emerging in the US – the flat, flexible, and networked organizational form that by the late 1980s was widely seen as superseding the bureaucratic, hierarchical corporate structures that had dominated the American industrial landscape for decades.

The main drivers of the emergence of the 'new organization' were usually portrayed as rapidly evolving information technologies (beginning with the distributed computing of the PC era) but both changes in the work force and competition from flatter and more networked Japanese firms were also invoked to explain the change.

Both the new approach to MNE organization and the work on the new US organizational forms tended to eschew the analysis of the 'boxes' of the organization chart – and for many of the same reasons. For both organizational researchers and those who worked in the rapidly evolving organizations of the information economy, the formal structures seemed to capture less and less of the reality of contemporary organizations. These were characterized by work processes that routinely crossed formal sub-unit boundaries, by temporary structures such as project teams and task forces, and by informal networks that were increasingly important in taking effective action. Even more than the work on MNE organization, the writing about the new organizations ignored formal design in favor of ideal types and metaphors – shamrock, pizza, spaghetti – to describe the new forms.

Scepticism about the relevance of formal structure was reinforced by the rise of two theoretical paradigms: institutional theory in organizational sociology; and the dynamic capabilities approach in the strategy field.

Institutional theory challenged contingency theory explanations of formal organizational structure by arguing that the variety of organizational forms was far more limited than the variety of environments defined in resource or contingency theory terms, and that the environmental influences that shaped the formal organizational structure were social.

Organizations adopted formal structures in imitation of other organizations seen as more successful (mimetic isomorphism) to fit the beliefs and expectations of key internal stakeholder groups (normative isomorphism) or because certain structures were imposed by and required for interaction with more powerful organizations in the environment (coercive isomorphism).

Organizations could be seen as strategic in their choice of organization structure but their strategies were those of legitimization and social signalling, not business strategies as conventionally described in the strategy or IB field, and their choice was severely constrained by the small number of institutionally accepted and familiar structures.

The dynamic capabilities approach posed a very different challenge by pointing out that firms in similar environments and with similar formal structures achieved very different levels of competitive success. Therefore the search for the sources of competitive advantage would need to burrow more deeply into the organization than the first- (or even second-) order design parameters on which so much earlier research had focused.

But the recognition that a key element of an organizational capability was the capacity to cross internal boundaries speedily and effectively meant that organization design, in the broader meaning of the term, again became a potential focus of interest. Organization design not only sets up boundaries that then must be bridged in order to take effective or innovative actions, but also establishes many of the key bridging mechanisms, such as project teams, task forces, liaison or coordinator positions, IT systems and their access rules, and planning systems.

The absence of these increasingly important formal linking structures from the formal organization chart was one of the main reasons that the 'organogram' received so little respect in the late 1980s and early 1990s. But these linking mechanisms are as much a part of the formal design as the units they connect. By the late 1990s, the analysis of organization design gave as much attention to formal linking mechanisms as it did to the 'grouping' of activities that generated the formal organization chart.

There are also signs of a revival of interest in formal design in the study of MNEs, grounded not only in a broader concept of organization design but also in several dramatic recent reorganization efforts in MNEs that had long been held up as exemplars of a particular design.

Procter & Gamble, for example, changed from its geographical organization to a global business structure in 1999, a move which received initially favourable coverage from the business press but which quickly roused major resistance from within the company and cost the CEO who directed the effort his job after only 18 months in office. In 2001 ABB abandoned its much-praised geography–business matrix for a new design less oriented to geography but no less complex (discussed in detail below).

In these and in other, less widely publicised cases of change, the redesign quite deliberately lowered the salience of geography as a design variable. In the last decade, it has sometimes seemed that geography was becoming a third- or even fourth-level design variable as companies moved to break down what they saw as 'country silos' in order to improve cross-border integration.

One aspect of the changing role of geography in MNE design has been its changing meaning. Since the earliest studies of the MNE, geography as a design variable has meant 'country' at a basic level and some aggregation of country-based units into regions at a higher level. The phrase 'country subsidiary' continues to dominate the IB literature, even when it is accompanied by an acknowledgement that the unit in question may be located in a particular country but is not a 'country sub' in the classic meaning of the term: that is, an organizational unit that manages the value-adding activities of the MNE in that country.

Japanese MNEs seem to have been the first to replace the classic country subsidiary with a set of smaller, more focused units that reported to their counterparts in the home organization rather than to an umbrella country unit. In the case of the Japanese MNEs, the basic units were functionally specialized, with manufacturing subsidiaries organizationally separate from marketing subsidiaries. In diversified electronics firms, units were even further specialized by product line, with separate manufacturing subsidiaries for TVs and tape recorders, for example.

This was initially regarded as an aberration and as one indicator among many that the Japanese MNEs were 'immature' or at an early stage of their international development. However, the approach proved to be a harbinger of similar moves by Western MNEs to reach below the country level for the basic building blocks of the organizational architecture.

A major design issue has therefore come to be whether to have these units report to a country organizational unit or to have non-geographical cross-border lines of coordination and control (for example, by function or product).

One set of factors complicating the design is the changing meaning of geography – or of location, to use the currently prevailing phrase used in the strategy field. Location has ceased to be synonymous with country; furthermore, location increasingly has different meanings for different functions. Julian Birkinshaw points out in Chapter 9 that the country is too small to define the market for a growing number of firms, whose customers are defined by boundary-transcending sectors or global firms. On the other hand, other researchers have asserted that for innovation activities in both R&D and production, the country is too large a unit and that location is defined by the sub-national 'cluster' or 'hot spot'.

These discussions, however, are built on the 'input–throughput–output' model of organization that dominates the strategy field, in which an organization is a system designed to take inputs from the environment, add value to them, and earn a return on its activities by disposing of its product or service, in competition with others, in output markets.

In this model, the environment is a resource environment – a source of inputs, a market for outputs, and an arena of competition for those inputs and markets. The relevant level of the location environment in this model may well either transcend the country or operate at a much more focused sub-national level.

Organization theorists remind us, however, that organizations are not simply value-adding systems designed to achieve strategic goals. They are also cultural and political systems. Country remains a powerful identity-shaping factor and an environment that forms mental models and basic assumptions; it is also readily invoked to mobilize interests and build coalitions (see, for example, Birkinshaw's work on subsidiary initiatives in MNEs). It is the very power of country as a cultural and political environment that makes it such a problematic variable for MNEs as they work to develop architectures that facilitate cross-border integration.

Some of the complexities and changes in the role of geography in the design of MNEs are well illustrated by the organization design of ABB, a company that – notwithstanding its recent troubles – has been the focus of organizational research and discussion since its creation in 1988.

The Organization Design of ABB

ABB's organization design probably received more attention in the 1990s than was given to all other MNEs combined, both from the business press and from academics. It was seen as an exemplar not only in the IB field, as a geography–business matrix that worked, but much more broadly in the field of organization studies as the epitome of the 'new organization' – flat, flexible, densely networked both internally and externally, and global. That it was a 'new organization' in a decidedly old industry only increased its fascination. It seemed to demonstrate that the organizational revolution of the late 20th century was transforming even industries born a century earlier. As one popular business book put it, 'Asea Brown Boveri is seen by more and more global business leaders as the model of the way that organizations will have to operate to thrive in the 21st century – that is, streamlined in structure, rapid in transferring information, having employees who are highly empowered, committed to continuous learning, running world-class HRD programs, and team-working and networking globally. ABB appears not only first in the alphabetical listing of companies, but also as one of the first among global learning organizations' (Marquand and Reynolds, 1996, p. 149).

The widespread fascination with ABB began with the process that created the company in 1988 with the merger of two companies in the electrical engineering business: Asea of Sweden (founded in 1890) and Brown Boveri of Switzerland (founded in 1891). The process seemed to follow with reassuring precision the 'structure follows strategy' model of organization design. Percy Barnevik, the CEO of the new ABB, presented his analysis of the industry environment facing the new company and the strategic direction in which the company should move: a focus on the electric power industry; improved efficiencies through cross-border coordination combined with responsiveness to local customers; and international acquisitions to expand the geographical reach of the company. He also set out the basic features of the organization design: a business–geography matrix.

The use of the matrix structure was controversial since few companies had been able to make a business–geography matrix work effectively. The innovative feature of ABB's design was less the matrix itself than the form it took. The basic building block of the organization was the local operating company (which quickly came to be called a BU – business unit – within ABB, although it did not fit the standard business usage of the term to describe a multi-product, multi-functional, multi-market business unit).

These companies were units that were focused on a single business and market within a country. Each reported both to a 'business area' (BA) manager and a country manager. In many cases the local operating company was literally a company: it was separately incorporated as a wholly owned subsidiary. The local operating company usually contained two to five profit centres and an average of 200 employees. In spite of hyperbolic business press articles claiming that 'everyone in ABB works for two managers', in fact the local operating company manager was the only position in the company to report formally along two dimensions (see Figure 10.1).

Both the BA manager and the country manager in turn reported to a member of the Executive Committee (EC). In the case of the BA, the reporting line was to a 'business segment', managed by an EC member. The fact that only one layer of management stood between the manager of the local operating company and top management made ABB an extremely flat organization.

Its perceived flatness was reinforced by Barnevik's highly publicized decision to reduce headquarters' staff to 10 % of the level of the aggregated HQ staff of the two companies. Operational decision making was pushed down to the local operating company. One of the features of ABB's design that appealed to many of its admirers was the empowerment of this basic unit, the local operating company. Christopher Bartlett and Sumantra Ghoshal describe the role of one such manager whose original employer, Westinghouse, sold the division for which he worked to ABB: 'From being an effective operational implementer working hard to be an effective part of a massive corporate machine, he was now cast in the role of an entrepreneurial initiator with full responsibility and accountability for the development of his own frontline company . . . In short, he began seeing his job not simply as implementing the latest corporate program but as building a viable, enduring business.'

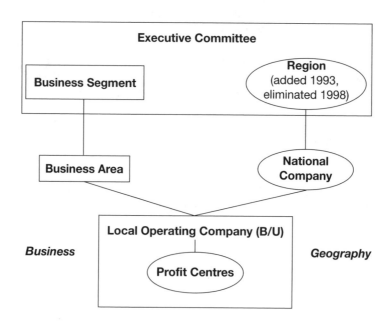

Figure 10.1—ABB's organization structure 1988.

ABB's organization design not only empowered local operating company managers; it made relative costs transparent at a much lower level of the organization than had previously been possible and allowed ABB to increase its efficiency both in the former Asea and Brown Boveri operations and in the companies ABB acquired in its drive to expand into North America and Eastern Europe after the merger.

Transparency and efforts to improve efficiency were aided by a much-touted linking mechanism: ABACUS, a company-wide information system that collected monthly performance data from all the profit centres, put it into a standard currency, and provided standard monthly reports for managers at the BA, country, and Executive Committee levels. It also included a 'drill-down' capability that allowed top management to dig deeper into the performance numbers by business area and by country.

But ABACUS was only one of many structured linking mechanisms in the organization design. Indeed, David Nadler and Michael Tushman used ABB as the exemplar in the chapter on linking mechanisms in their 1997 book *Competing by Design*. The formal linking mechanisms were especially numerous across local operating companies, especially within the BA and included BA boards (advising the BA managers), BA functional councils, BA task forces, and local operating company steering committees.

The business area brought together local operating companies within it across countries; the country management linked operating companies within the country across business areas. However, there were far fewer formal linking mechanisms at the country level than at the BA level. Initially this was probably because building a network within the new BA structure was much the more urgent task, whereas the country had long provided a strong base for internal integration across businesses. But over time, the imbalance in the linking mechanisms began to affect the balance of the matrix, tilting it away from geography towards the business side.

ABB's design had many advantages beyond combining cross-border integration and efficiency on the business side of the matrix with responsiveness to local markets on the country side, which made it such a widely used exemplar in IB classes. International expansion by acquisition was a cornerstone of ABB's strategy in its first eight years and the structure of small focused building blocks in the form of the local operating companies enabled ABB to integrate acquisitions rapidly.

Breaking acquired companies into product-specific local operating companies (or into profit centres that could fit under local operating companies where these were already established) transformed the acquired company's structure and with it the old political system, making even large companies such as Combustion Engineering and Westinghouse's power business readily digestible. This was particularly valuable for a small-country-based company like ABB making acquisitions in large countries like the US, where an integrated country subsidiary would be resistant to external control and cross-border integration.

The design also provided valuable flexibility as the business portfolio of ABB changed over the 1990s. Business areas could be re-defined and business segments re-configured with ease because the local operating companies, which grew in number as ABB expanded through acquisitions, could be re-assigned to different business areas, which themselves could be re-grouped into different business segments, without tearing up the organization – indeed, without significant impact on its operations.

The number of BAs, for example, went from 40 in 1988 to 65 in 1991 and was reduced to 50 in 1993. The business segments were re-configured roughly every three to four years. The relative ease with which BAs and segments could be re-configured also aided the process of exit from businesses, such as the shedding of Transportation into a joint venture with Siemens and the spin-off of Power Generation.

The evolution of ABB's businesses over the 1990s created some strains for the organization design, however. Geography was increasingly problematic. While the BAs were grouped into segments in the 1988 design, the country organizations reported to individual Executive Committee members on a somewhat ad hoc basis. As ABB's geographical reach expanded, Barnevik decided in 1993 to add a regional level to the design, paralleling the segment level on the business side, clustering countries into three geographical regions.

In 1998, however, the reorganization initiated by Goran Lindahl when he took over as CEO eliminated the regional level, on the grounds that staffing had grown and was creating unnecessary costs. The business press tended to portray this change in dramatic terms; the *Financial Times*, for example, led its story on ABB's 1998 reorganization with the sentence: 'ABB, the much admired engineering conglomerate, has scrapped the matrix management structure put in place by Percy Barnevik, the man who turned the company into a world-class competitor . . . .' In fact, of course, the matrix continued to exist: formally, ABB reverted to the 1988 original design.

But to the extent that the balance of the matrix had shifted over the decade from the geographical to the business side, the pundits were not totally wide of the mark. The much stronger linking mechanisms on the business side (noted above) were certainly a factor in this. But so was the changing business environment.

In the electrical power businesses of generation, transmission, and distribution, the privatization of utilities, growing competition from increasingly capable specialized local and regional competitors in the components businesses, and intensifying global competition in power systems all meant that the pressures for efficiency and cross-border integration were rising while the value of local responsiveness was eroding.

The fast-growing industrial equipment businesses were from the beginning more strongly subject to pressures for cross-border integration, and their growing weight in ABB's businesses reinforced the environmental 'tilt' away from local responsiveness and the diminishing value of a geography–business matrix.

Moreover, many of the most promising areas for revenue and profit growth were in systems that integrated products produced by different BAs. However, linkages across the BAs were not built into a design whose primary linking mechanisms had been focused on cross-border integration within each BA. Cross-BA integration was left to the country organization. But not only were the linking mechanisms at this level under-developed, it was increasingly clear that in a growing number of ABB's businesses the country was not the appropriate level for cross-BA integration. A growing number of key customers were global or regional, not national.

Finally, the autonomy and entrepreneurship of the local operating companies, so important for achieving cost reductions and growth in individual products in the early years of the new structure, were potentially problematic as the business strategy increasingly emphasized 'solutions' and multi-product systems. The measurement of the local operating companies on financial performance meant that internal transfer pricing was a matter of considerable and often fierce (and time-consuming) negotiation.

These problems might have been manageable with changes in linking mechanisms and alignment processes (particularly performance measurement and incentive systems at the local operating company level). But in 2001, a new CEO, Jorgen Centerman, decided to undertake a radical re-design of the company, abolishing the business–geography matrix in favour of a design that had become increasingly common in companies in the IT industry in the late 1990s: a 'front-end/back-end' organization.

The front-end/back-end organization design was developed by companies that produced a wide range of products based on different product and process technologies but combined into complex systems for which the customer wanted one point of interaction for sales and service. A business unit organization in this kind of industry means the customer interacts with multiple units and bears the primary responsibility for integration. A functional organization, on the other hand, can provide 'one face' to the customer but has difficulty speedily integrating technology development and production.

In the front-end/back-end design, the 'back end' is composed of business units, each of which incorporates technology development, manufacturing, and production logistics (this last increasingly important as companies increasingly outsource components and subsystems) but not marketing and customer interface, which go to the 'front end'. The back-end structure provides the close integration between technology development and production that is needed in fast-changing technological environments. Another advantage of the back-end structure is that organizational units can be defined by technology and also by 'location' in terms of hot spot or advantaged cluster rather than by country (following the 'metanational' organizing principle).

The front end is organized by market, either by customer segment or by geography, and includes not only the obvious activities of marketing, sales, and distribution but also technical support and customer service.

This organization design depends heavily on effective linkage mechanisms between the front and back ends. Ideally, the front end drives the back end, in terms of feeding user needs into technology development and ensuring that production is paced to sales. Many of the IT companies that moved to a front-end/back-end design did so from a functional organization. This transformation is hard enough for a functionally organized engineering-based company, in which back-end functions, especially technology development, have traditionally held most of the power and dominated the culture. But moving from an engineering-based business unit organization to this design can be extremely difficult, because it involves rending the business units into two functional parts.

ABB's move to this organization, like its choice of the matrix over a decade earlier, was driven, at least ostensibly, by its strategy (although an institutional theorist would be tempted to see a strong element of mimetic isomorphism with the then-soaring IT companies, induced perhaps in part by Centerman's own background in ABB's automation business).

Centerman described the strategic goal as being 'to boost growth by helping customers become more successful in a business environment of accelerating globalization, deregulation, consolidation, and e-commerce'. ABB had come to recognize that a high proportion of its sales came from less than a quarter of its customers and that improving its relationships with those customers required much better gathering, consolidation, and use of customer information.

In his announcement of the new organization design in January 2001, Centerman invoked the Internet as a vehicle for doing a better job of selling to and supporting customers, positioning the new 'customer-centric design' as focusing the organization on using IT more effectively to link its customers, its suppliers, and the key groups within the company.

ABB was to become a customer-driven exemplar of 'mass customization' and the knowledge-based company. The extent to which Centerman was invoking the then-current jargon of the Internet age was not lost on a somewhat sceptical business press (see for example the generally favourable but slightly dubious article in *The Economist* 2001).

The new design (see Figure 10.2) changed ABB's structure from the business–geography matrix to a structure of two back-end units (power technologies and automation technologies) and four main customer units, with the customer segment defined not by geography but by industry (utilities, oil and gas, process industries,

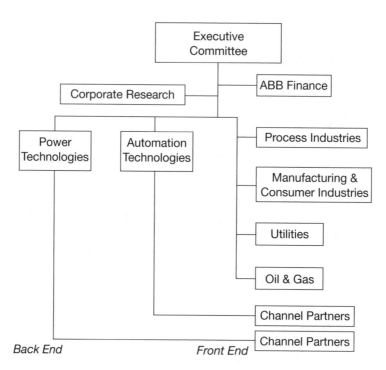

Figure 10.2—ABB's organization structure 2001.

and manufacturing and consumer industries). In addition, each of the two back-end units had a front-end unit to distribute products through intermediaries (known as 'channel partners'). One of the main goals of the back-end structure was to integrate technology development across the businesses in each of the two main sectors of ABB's technology. Of course the main goal of the front-end structure was to increase ABB's capabilities for creating value for customers, especially customers that transcended country borders.

Recognizing how great the reorganization challenge was likely to be, ABB also set up a 'corporate transformation' unit to guide the reorganization. It was clear to most managers in the company that this would not be an easy change. It was not possible to follow the relatively painless pattern of the reorganizations of the 1990s, which left the local operating companies intact. The new organization saw the operating companies as part of the problem that the new design was trying to fix. Some of the local operating companies have been moved into either the back or the front end; others are being divided into sub-units and integrated with other similar sub-units.

At first glance, it appears that geography has become a less salient design variable in the new ABB. However, one further development is that ABB has begun to consolidate its independent operating companies at the country level, setting up integrated national subsidiaries in a number of countries. How these will fit into the new front-end/back-end structure is not completely clear but geography remains one of the challenges and may emerge as a second- or third-order design parameter.

ABB's organizational transformation has been complicated by serious financial problems, scandals over the extremely generous retirement packages given to Barnevik and Lindahl, the two former CEOs, and the apparently forced resignation of Centerman himself in September 2002.

ABB has seen its image change from that of an exemplar of the 21st century organization to that of 'the troubled Swiss–Swedish engineering company'. Its future revival depends heavily on how well it manages the organizational transformation process and how effectively it can build the linking mechanisms that make the difference between the success and failure of a front-end/back-end organization.

Implications for Future Research

This chapter advocates the restoration of the analysis of organization design to the mainstream of the study of MNEs. Compared to the era in which the first generation of analysis of the design of MNEs was developed, both the empirical phenomena influencing MNE design and the analytical tools and frameworks of organization design itself seem more complex and the task of developing a research agenda more daunting.

Established MNEs like ABB face the difficult challenges of making their organizations more responsive to shifting environmental pressures and changing strategic goals. Newly emerging MNEs – today's 'born global' firms – might seem to have more freedom in how they design their international operations but that freedom may be more apparent than real; the range of structural design choices open to them remains quite limited.

In both types of firms, managers face the challenges of identifying and building effective designs that accommodate their evolving global strategies with even less guidance from research than was provided by IB scholars three decades ago.

What research agenda might we build in the IB field to provide a more solid grounding for the design of MNEs and for understanding more clearly the role of design in MNE strategy, activity, and performance?

In one respect at least, researchers in IB have an advantage over their colleagues in the organization design field, in that the design variable of central interest is obvious: it is geography. But to grasp the role of geography as a design variable, it is necessary to move beyond the focus on the first-order design parameter that characterized the early research on MNE design.

One approach is to reverse the 'top-down' analysis of much organization design research and start 'bottom-up' – from the basic building blocks of the organization chart (the analogue of the local operating company in ABB). Sometimes these are the profit and cost centres; sometimes, as in ABB, they are the units that have managerial decision-making responsibility for a set of profit centres.

It is also necessary to go beyond the formal 'boxes' of the organization chart to incorporate linking mechanisms and alignment systems, the design elements that underpin the formal structure and that largely determine the success of the organization relative to others with similar formal structures (for a summary of these mechanisms, see Figure 10.3). For example, analysing formal linking mechanisms and looking at the density and direction of those linkages are essential for understanding not only the organization design but also the networks that have been so much a focus of analysis in IB in the 1990s. Formal linking mechanisms are not the only determinant of network structure but they are critically important in shaping and in changing it and their analysis is a necessary if not sufficient condition for understanding the network dynamics of the MNE.

In research on MNEs, geography remains at the heart of our inquiries. As an alternative to beginning the search for the basic building blocks of the organization with the overall organization chart, the IB researcher can begin with a specific country or set of countries and look at what formal sub-units exist within that geography, how they are grouped, and when – indeed if – geography (country or region) becomes a formal structural parameter.

In the IB field we have tacitly abandoned the assumption that the country subsidiary is the basic building block of the MNE – but we have not been quick to identify what alternatives have been developed, what the strengths and weaknesses of those alternatives might be, and what their relationship is to different aspects of geography.

Most studies of MNEs in the last decade or so that have tacitly assumed that the key geographical unit is the business unit within the country (that is, that geography is the second-order design parameter). But as we have seen in ABB, companies are increasingly trying to adopt designs (such as front-end/back-end) that try to accommodate the different valence that geography has for different parts of the value chain – which may well further complicate the configuration of units within a country.

Useful as business-focused studies have been, it is of growing importance to augment these with studies that look at the entire range of units located within a country and examine not only the formal grouping structure and cross-border linking mechanisms but also the linking mechanisms that connect different units within a country.

Companies are increasingly recognizing that the result of over a decade of carving functional and geographical structures into worldwide business units has been the replacement of functional and geographical silos with business unit silos. This raises the possibility that geography will once again become an important factor in developing the cross-business synergies that are so important a source of corporate value creation. The design tools for doing this may well be geographically based (within country or within region) linking mechanisms rather than a reversion to formal geographical grouping structures.

MNE research in the last decade and a half has been focused, understandably, on cross-border integration; we need to recapture in the coming decade the analysis of within-geography integration.

In developing the next generation of MNE design research, we must not lose one of the key features of the first generation: the linkage between strategy and structure. Our concepts of strategy have moved beyond the focus on diversification that anchored the earlier work but the strategy–structure linkage remains crucial to the analysis of organization design. Indeed, diversification is still an important element of strategy although currently the focus is often on migration from lower to higher value-added activities within the same businesses.

But as we saw in the case of ABB, we must also assess the capacity of the organization design to accommodate strategies of cross-border acquisition and of business divestiture as well as the changing balance among the three strategic parameters of efficiency, local responsiveness, and learning that have dominated our analyses of MNE strategy.

Finally, we need to augment the input–throughput–output model of the organization that has dominated the analysis of organization design with the recognition that the organization is also a political and a socio-cultural system. As we saw with ABB, the extent of an organizational redesign can be influenced as strongly by a CEO's desire to change the political and the cultural nature of the company as it is by the need to respond to changing environmental constraints.

Organization design is not only important in its own right; it is a major factor shaping power and influence, identity, and mind-set within the company. One of the problems of studies of organization design is that they are perceived, sometimes with all too much justification, as boring – as involving lists and typologies, charts and pedestrian descriptions of the 'X department was merged into Y, and A into B' variety.

The implication of design for action in organizations is all too often left out of the analyses. One of the reasons the ABB case was so widely used in IB was that we had much richer information not only on ABB's design but also on what it was like to try to take action in ABB, thanks in large part to the detailed descriptions provided by Chris Bartlett's HBS cases and by Bartlett and Ghoshal in *The Individualized Corporation* (1997). Enriching our studies of organization design by examining the implications of design for those who live and work in the organization, at several levels, is one of the most difficult but potentially rewarding paths for the next generation of analysis of the organization design of MNEs.

1. Key Grouping Criteria:

- Activity:
    - Function
    - Process (e.g. business process)
- Product
- Market/customer:
    - Geography
    - Customer segment
- Hybrid:
    - Matrix
    - Front end/back end

2. Key Linking Mechanisms

- Formal reporting structures (e.g. 'dotted line' reporting)
- Liaison roles (information conduit – e.g. 'community of practice leader')
- Integrator roles (ensuring information sharing – e.g. 'core technology champion')
- Permanent cross-unit groups (e.g. Technology Councils)
- Temporary cross-unit groups (e.g. project teams)
- Information technology systems (e.g. shared data bases, shared CAD tools)
- Planning processes (e.g. scenario building)

3. Key Alignment Systems
(Alignment – Ensuring that people and organizational units have the resources and the motivation to carry out the activities needed if the company is to achieve its strategic goals)
- Performance metrics
- Rewards and incentives
- Resource allocation
- Human Resource Development (recruitment, training, tracking, planning)

Based on Nadler and Tushman, 1997.

Figure 10.3—Elements of strategic design.

11 Regional Organizations: Beware of the Pitfalls

Paul Verdin[1], Venkat Subramanian[1], Alice de Koning[2], Eline Van Poeck[3]*

[1]Solvay Business School, [2]Georgia State University and [3]K. U. Leuven

While in the 1990s globalization pushed many companies to try to establish global organizations (such as global business units, R&D departments, global account management, to name only a few) in search of maximum efficiency, it has now become abundantly clear that a truly 'global' organization is a reality for only a happy few – and some of these have not been very happy lately.

Indeed, even when companies managed to keep their global stance over time, their pro-global message has not always been very convincing as they increasingly lost touch with local markets or the cost of complexity overruled any theoretical scale economies. All this has given rise to the recently evident counter-measures of international companies as they begin to pay renewed attention to their local strategies.

Here we would first like to discuss how the regional approach could be a way of dealing with the continuous challenge of balancing global–local tensions. After reviewing some recent examples of companies re-addressing the balancing problem, we will explore the advantages of the regional approach as an organizational form that may help to combine the advantages of globalization (efficiency) and localization (responsiveness).

Our main point, however, is to go beyond this blueprint argument by pointing out that regionalization should not be seen as the panacea for all globalization pressures and limitations. The extent to which a regional strategy may be a feasible response for a particular company will always depend on the dynamics in its 'international playing field' on the one hand, and the current state of its own organizational development on the other.

There is more to regionalization than just being a useful blueprint. Regionalizing is an approach by which a company may dynamically adjust to changing external conditions of convergence or divergence in markets as well as to overcome internal constraints to changing the organization and building a 'critical mass' of capabilities contributing to the company's worldwide competitive advantage.

---

* This chapter has benefited from comments by Patrick Verghote, KU Leuven.

A Renewed Search for Localization

The benefits of localization, even in supposedly 'global' businesses, have long been identified. As early as the 1980s, in some industries, such as white goods, national players were more profitable than those favouring global strategies because of fragmentation of demand and diminishing scale economies.[1] In other industries, the potential of scale economies has always been questionable and the widespread consolidation across industries has been raising even more questions for profitability, such as in the temporary labour services industry.[2]

In recent years, these early warning signals have turned into a major crescendo that has been precipitated by the severe performance problems of several former global stalwarts. Companies in a variety of industries are changing track by pushing through a more local strategy as a response to the difficulties produced by their earlier integrative global strategy.

One of the most publicized and dramatic shifts came from Coca-Cola and its 'think local, act local' strategic priority.[3] A push for innovation and initiative at all levels and markets became the new priority in order to restore the connection with local realities. The manager of Coke in Belgium formulated the challenge as follows: evolving 'from Global Master to a Global Network of Local Champions'. His CEO put it this way: 'In our recent past, we succeeded because we understood and appealed to global commonalities. In our future, we'll succeed because we will also understand and appeal to local differences. The 21st century demands nothing less.'[4]

At P&G, the former CEO, Dirk Jager, came under serious pressure for trying 'too much too fast' with his globalization drive, as poor performance results were increasingly difficult to ignore. His successor, A.G. Lafley, labelled a 'revolutionary with a relaxed approach', was hired to 'restore balance' and re-establish regional and even local decision making and accountability.[5] The new credo became to do best locally what should be done locally, and similarly for regional or global activity.

McDonald's, one of the best-known global companies, now wishes to be known as a 'network of local entrepreneurs'. 'We are a decentralized entrepreneurial network of locally owned stores that is very flexible and adapts very well to local conditions,' said Jack Greenberg, CEO, presumably not only driven by public relations concerns raised by anti-globalization activists.[6]

HSBC, once using the motto of a 'global bank' in advertising campaigns, now likes to present itself as 'the world's local bank', emphasizing the diversity and complexity of today's world, not dissimilar to the strategic positioning of the Belgian-based Interbrew company, which has propelled itself into a top world player with the motto 'the world's local brewer'.[7]

---

1 Baden-Fuller and Stopford (1991).

2 See *Temporary Work Services Industry* Note, Van Heck and Verdin (1996).

3 Douglas Daft, CEO, Coca-Cola, in preparation of strategy and organizational change plan, spring 2000.

4 *Financial Times*, 01-02-00.

5 *Financial Times*, 15-08-02.

6 *Foreign Policy*, May–June 2000.

7 This development even prompted legal action by Interbrew accusing HSBC of plagiarism.

In another 'global industry', pharmaceuticals, GSK (GlaxoSmithKline),[8] the largest global player, spun off research units as it became clear that global innovation and R&D are not necessarily better off by simply multiplying the number of researchers.

Even in the case of ABB, long known for its pioneering attempts to marry the global and local (and as well-known proponents of the 'think global–act local' motto), one could wonder whether its global matrix organizations dedicated to the simultaneous pursuit of global and local dimensions (across all businesses) did not produce an enormous duplication of effort.[9] The company may have created global product centres and local country organizations that at best duplicated efforts, and at worst created the complexity that distracted management from creating customer value.

In light of these developments marking a renewed trend to rediscover or re-establish the value of local business and to avoid unnecessary costs of global complexity, the regional organization re-emerges as a viable alternative.

1. Regionalization as an Optimal Solution

What organizational model allows a company to balance efficiency and responsiveness? It all depends, so the answer goes, on what is the right level of global integration and local responsiveness in the various activities and functions of the organization.[10] As the examples above imply, in the past many may have responded to the attractions of the global economy without due consideration for the limits of scale, scope or geographical coverage or for the still required responsiveness to local markets.

Earlier work on regional organizations tried to expand the rather one-dimensional and dichotomous global–local discussion by introducing the intermediary choice of regionalization.[11] Regionalization might be an optimal solution to achieve a balance between integration and responsiveness, if the minimum scale of efficiency can already be achieved at the regional level. The costs of integrating globally may not be justified by further efficiencies.

Even in some apparently 'global industries', such as automobiles, the convergence of customers' needs is far from global, and yet no longer specific to a single nation either.[12] The economics of this particular industry may favour a federation of regional organizations, each one able to derive greater economies of scale and scope than national organizations, while still remaining responsive to the market. 'Global' organizations then at best may mean 'multi-regional' organizations.[13]

The need for a dynamic approach. This argument in favour of regionalization is intrinsically rich, though it may risk stereotyping the problem. It may create the potentially dangerous impression that an international company can function effectively as

---

8 *Financial Times*, 25-01-02.
9 *Fortune*, 18-11-02.
10 Prahalad and Doz (1987).
11 E.g. Morrison et al. (1991).
12 Schlie and Yip (2000).
13 De Koning et al. (1999).

long as it chooses and implements the 'right' blueprint. The regional approach is obviously not a panacea for all the globalization pressures and limitations a company may be facing.

We are living and working in an increasingly dynamic and changing environment. Real and perceived benefits of internationalization or globalization keep changing at different levels of the organization and in different parts of the business. While the idea of a network of regional hubs connecting local subsidiaries may be a more flexible option, achieving this 'right-sizing' in response to changing environmental conditions remains a continuous challenge.

The challenge consists of approaching the local–global dilemma in a more dynamic context, where the goal is not to identify the perfect fixed point on the local–global range, but rather to provide a framework for analysing and continuously reflecting on the repercussions of the local–global tension in a changing international playing field.

We call the 'international playing field' the maximum degree of globalization benefits one can realistically and profitably achieve, given the economics of the business (amount of cross-border cost advantages or network benefits) and company's chosen strategy on the one hand, and the many limits on globalization on the other hand, as influenced by differences in cultures, regulations, and languages among national countries.

This international playing field, however, is anything but a static concept. At any time, either the globalization pressures could be falling, or the localization pressures could start waning, as illustrated in Figure 11.1 (see next section). Whatever specific factors drive the changes in the international playing field, it would be dangerous to expect the global–local balance within companies to remain unchanged.

For example, Europe used to be an amalgam of national markets, each operating according to its own (lack of?) logic, and requiring a tailored approach, limiting substantially the potential of realizing significant cross-border opportunities. The European integration attempts, pushed among others by the 'Europe 1992 programme' and the Euro introduction, however, have changed the name of the game significantly. As a result, for most companies the international playing field was extended, but expectations were often overextended, further pushed by the recent globalization hype. There have been examples of some independent operators internationalizing 'too little, too slowly', like independent DAF in the truck industry, but there have been many more examples of companies attempting to go 'too far too fast'. Many of these examples are also just now beginning to unravel, like the questionable pan-European (and worldwide) consolidation in paradoxically local business such as the temporary labour industry or the retail financial services sector.

Only an ongoing analysis and monitoring of the changing situation can prevent a company from over-globalizing (too much, too soon) or under-globalizing (too little internationalization, too late). Such an ongoing process can help it avoid the need to make dramatic adjustments to the strategy after the damage has been done. The situation of Coca-Cola cited above is only one example.

In answering the question *what organizational model allows a company to reach maximum cost benefits or network benefits?* we are left with the uncomfortable and stereotypical answer *it depends*. The appropriate organizational model is a moving target, because so much depends on the changing economics of the business and technology, unpredictable patterns of market convergence or renewed divergence shifting barriers to integration that change slower than anticipated, and divergence of realities versus perceptions in the market, and the organizational capabilities of the company to integrate across borders.

The task of achieving a competitive edge on the international playing field is a difficult, continuous and context-specific challenge for every company to face. What may be good for one company today may become a one-way ticket to failure tomorrow. For instance, what may have been successful national strategies in the 1980s in the white goods industry need not necessarily be the case in 2002. What may be a good step for one company at a specific time may be exactly the wrong one for another company, even at the same moment and in the same industry. What may have been an appropriate – and belated – approach by Unilever when it announced a dramatic reduction in its portfolio of different brands (from 1,600 to 400) a couple of years ago probably would have been the wrong move for arch-rival P&G, which had started to successfully streamline its portfolio and build up pan-European or even global brands already more than twenty years ago. Each company's strategic and organizational context leads it to different approaches towards greater or lesser integration.

2. Regionalization as Part of a Process

Overcoming internal barriers. Regionalization may be the best way to go for a company *if* its international playing field as determined by the economics of the business and the external market and other barriers emerges to be at the regional level. However, we could also view regionalization as part of a wider and continuing process, highlighting the importance of organizational barriers and internal political considerations in a dynamic context.

Even for companies that find that the intended benefits of internationalization stretch to the global level, a case can be made for first attempting a regional organization. Giving up on some potential scale economies (or other benefits) at the global level may be justifiable even though that may seem like a deliberate 'under-shooting' strategy.

The rationale for such an approach can be found in the organizational constraints. Creating regional hubs can be part of a deliberate strategy to overcome internal resistance, taking a 'step-by-step' or 'go slow' (organizational) strategy on the path to globalization. In other words, regionalization can become a stepping-stone on the road towards a full globalization strategy.

We believe this argument is particularly relevant:

- when the company culture favours a more gradual, step-by-step approach to change (and there is no urgency to dramatically change that culture);
- when there is no significant externally driven crisis in terms of the business environment, customer expectations or pressures from financial markets;
- when top management can be expected to stay in leadership sufficiently long to bring the whole process to a successful completion;
- when there is interest, motivation and capacity to capture and capitalize on the organizational learning in the process, to be leveraged later across the company's global organization;

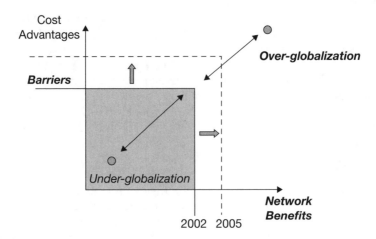

Figure 11.1—The international playing field. The relevant international playing field is constantly changing as a result of changing globalization opportunities (cost advantages and network benefits) and changing globalization barriers (market divergence, regulation, technology, political and other 'external' barriers). Therefore, risks of over- or under-globalization strategies are always imminent and need to be balanced against time required to make necessary organizational adjustments.

- when significant uncertainty exists with regard to the exact nature or sustainable benefit of a global organization.

Making the jump from local to global in these cases may be too ambitious or too risky, even if the company ultimately has good reason to aim for a global strategy. Regionalization may be a good testing and learning ground for the management of the integration processes and may enable the development of organizational learning and capabilities required to make an efficient cross-border organization work. Such was the case of P&G during its twenty years of development of its European organization.[14]

In addition, an initial regionalization strategy allows for better monitoring of the intended results: if one cannot show *and capture* the intended benefits clearly at the regional level, how then could one expect to achieve them at an even more abstract, remote – and usually harder to manage – level like 'global'. Regionalization then, although clearly a deliberate 'sub-optimizing' strategy (instead of an ideal blueprint), can act as a very important lever and checkpoint on the grand globalization journey.

One could argue that this is exactly the journey that P&G was on, except that having reached regional scale and efficiencies, the jump towards 'global' as heralded by Jager seemed 'too much too soon' on the back of what had been a very gradual regional integration process.[15]

---

14 Bartlett et al. (1999).

15 As Claude Marcel, Vice President R&D of P&G, put it, 'It (the regional integration strategy) was an act of faith, by now (the globalization drive), it has become a religion.' See *Procter and Gamble Europe: Ariel Ultra's Eurobrand Strategy*, INSEAD-HBS Case Study.

The process of regionalizing while on the way to creating global integration could be and has been observed as a somewhat involuntary phenomenon in several companies.[16] Our argument is that regionalization could be turned into an explicit and intermediate objective in the context of a deliberate internal globalization strategy process. This strategy obviously is not without its perils.

The Risks of this Approach

The risks of a deliberate 'undershooting' approach to globalization should not be neglected. In general terms, the risks can be linked to some of the well-known inconveniences of any 'slow and steady' strategy in the management of organizational change processes,[17] including:

- loss of dynamism and critical mass; risk of getting stuck in the process;
- top management turnover and lack of sustained leadership;
- shifts in priorities, lack of long term vision or commitment;
- unwillingness or inability to push beyond the unavoidable intermediary tensions in the course of the process;
- time running out due to market or business developments or more dramatic events occurring on the external front (political, economic, etc.);
- build-up of internal resistances (usually at the local level) rather than dealing with them;
- inability to take decisive decisions when faced with difficult alternatives or trade-offs.

In addition, if the move towards regional does not imply a more than proportional dismantling at the local or national level, the risk of failure and stalling is not imaginary. Many companies have recently discovered that their change processes have created an additional layer of overhead and costs, and another source of complicating or even stifling bureaucracy and political power, without achieving sufficient integration benefits.

Some companies instinctively created headquarters at the regional level to facilitate the formulation and implementation of regional strategies, without paying sufficient attention to how national subsidiaries will cede, share and create resources to the RHQ.[18] Often, such RHQs turned out to be no more than coordination centres without real authority (read bottom line responsibility) to overcome internal barriers and create shared consensus for greater integration at the regional level. As a result, several multinationals, especially some early adopters of regional platforms such as P&G and 3M,[19] have already taken significant steps to scale back some of their newly built organizations in Europe.

---

16 As documented e.g. by Malnight (1995, 1996).

17 As further illustrated in the discussion on 'slow and steady' versus 'shock therapy' approach towards regional integration in De Koning et al. (1997).

18 See Schutte (1998) for an overview of RHQ formation and their role in the global organisation.

19 Bartlett et al. (1999); Van Heck and Verdin (1996).

This phenomenon can obviously take many different shapes and colours. A few years ago, in a large pharmaceutical company, the drive towards an effective pan-European organization was stifled, not because of the usual opposition from some of the traditional country 'barons' – in fact most of the country managers were highly in favour, and they were not even country nationals anymore – but because it was viewed by many of them as 'an attempt by the Brits to centralize everything back in London!' (the location of the newly declared European HQ).

Another more subtle, yet not far-fetched or imaginary example came from a large European financial services group, where the Spanish country manager, who in good times was no strong supporter of the new pan-European initiatives directed from the Swiss headquarters, all of a sudden became a supporter of the intermediate step towards regionalization: he sold headquarters the idea of 'the Iberian peninsula' just about when his own business in Spain came under pressure and the results in Portugal started brightening up, much to the aggravation of his Portuguese colleague.

As one country manager put it, voicing his frustration over similar political developments at the regional level: 'I have always been a promoter of pan-European synergies. (. . .) Of course there should be sound economic and strategic reasoning behind decisions either to centralise/share resources – along business/segment lines or functional areas – or reinforce local units. (. . .) Unfortunately some decisions are still being taken based on the "reason of power" instead of the "power of reason".'[20]

Such processes, when not carefully anticipated and managed, risk leading to more – not less – frustration and inefficiencies. The change process then moves away from what was or should have been the original driving force and ultimate objective: to provide more efficient and better value to the customer.

An alternative approach to achieving regional efficiency therefore may consist in doing exactly the opposite: overshoot to a global organizational structure to break resistance in order to at least achieve a 'compromise' or a 'fall back' position at the lower regional level. One can argue that such is exactly what happened with some ambitious and highly publicized 'global' projects, like for instance in the car industry with 'the global car platform' by Fiat and the pioneering 'world car project' from Ford Mondeo. In summary, we believe that from a process management perspective, there could be very good reasons to 'over' or 'undershoot' in terms of globalization strategy and organization (thereby providing another potential interpretation of the situation as depicted in Figure 11.1) and the regionalization approach can be part of such a process.

3. Regionalization as a Way to Generate Critical Mass

Another important strategic advantage for a successful international company may be the extent to which it manages to leverage – better still initiate and develop – competencies, know-how and innovation across the organization, wherever they emerge.[21] The real challenge is to create a feasible process of sensing the dispersed

---

20 E-mail correspondence to one of the authors, justifying his resignation over the issue.
21 E.g. Bartlett and Ghoshal (1989); Verdin and Van Heck (2001).

knowledge throughout the company, mobilizing it through the network in order to innovate creatively and exploiting the innovations efficiently.[22]

A valuable source of competitive advantage for a multinational is the potential to leverage multiple perspectives and knowledge across borders, and access location-specific knowledge as it arises. But the major trend over the recent decades has been the steady marginalization of subsidiaries, particularly those far-flung ones that churn out the products supplied by the parent into the local market. A pursuit of global efficiencies has made the already challenging role of subsidiaries to have an influence on the global strategy even more daunting.

It has been argued that subsidiary growth and hence its importance is driven by its distinctive capabilities, which are location specific (maybe because the subsidiary operates in an industry cluster) but its leverage is non-location specific, and valuable to the company's global competitive advantage.[23] A subsidiary that is able to gain a worldwide mandate for a specific product or a capability by being explicitly acknowledged by the rest of the global organization (and the headquarters in particular) also has the potential to provide the diversity and balance to strategy.[24]

Building a network around strong regional organizations instead of country subsidiaries may provide a pragmatic solution to this problem by building critical mass within the organization as the weight and significance of integrated regions may be better equipped to combine the diverse perspectives, knowledge and competencies of the local subsidiaries.[25] Regional cross-border organizations are situated in much larger markets and can produce more easily the critical mass of skills and knowledge necessary to create sustainable competitive advantages.

This argument seems particularly valid for regional development within multinationals that are based outside that particular region, like American or Japanese multinationals in Europe. Combining the strengths and competencies at the regional level may allow diverse units to 'speak with one voice' and to be heard in distant headquarters (in much the same way that the development of regional European policies and the introduction of the Euro has been argued to be an important strategy for Europe to play a bigger role on the world stage).

Regional hubs that integrate the operations and perspectives of many subsidiaries should be more than new structures and layers in a hierarchy. They can function as dynamic learning platforms, which allow knowledge to be created and shared across borders. The creation of a pan-European R&D organization at P&G, for instance, was not only inspired by the significant cost savings to be expected, but equally by the prospect of quicker development and time-to-market of new products within the region as well as across regions on a global level.

---

22 As pointed out by Doz et al. (2001).

23 Birkinshaw (1996).

24 Frost et al. (2002).

25 De Koning et al. (1999).

Limitations of the Regional Approach

In the concept of a 'metanational', the regional organization could play the role of a 'magnet', sucking up the diverse perspectives and ideas throughout the different subsidiaries and leveraging them through the network. The regional organization can then be seen as the channel through which knowledge can be captured and managed. However, there are important caveats with this argument.

First of all, one should not expect critical mass to be created automatically, if no specific structures have been established for this purpose. One should not expect the regional organization to function as a magnet if nobody in this structure has been given the explicit task of melding the knowledge that has been gathered from diverse sources.[26] Subsidiaries, even at the regional level, may need support in terms of money, recognition and internal champions to be able to create some structure and processes to identify opportunities for building knowledge and also filter out options that may be no more than attempts to hoard resources from other parts of the company.[27]

In the regional organization, as indeed in any organizational device intended to play this magnet role, unlocking the potential or dispersed knowledge in the network may be the exception rather than the rule if there is nothing inside the structure to encourage the process of creating critical mass. 'While it is no one's role or responsibility to make this kind of thing happen, it can only happen by happy coincidence.'[28] Thinking in terms of 'blueprint' or 'organization structure' at the regional level therefore can prove more than harmful; it is the management processes that accompany the structure which really will make the difference.

Secondly, the question arises if the regional organization really can play this magnet role in the sense of locating and attracting the various parts or 'pockets' of knowledge and innovation potential, *wherever they are located*. The move to regional headquarters or hubs could be a means to over-rule the excessive dominance of the traditionally more powerful parts of the organization – usually the home country and other large countries in the organization. But the potential also exists for regionalization to just shift the problem: who will have the largest influence and access to the regional level?

Going back to the experience of our Spanish country manager cited above, suddenly favouring a move towards a pan-European organization, the manager's case could have been made stronger and more credible if the intent was to pool the capabilities and complementary skills and assets in the region to create innovations that increase the firm's worldwide competitive advantage.

Care must be taken therefore to prevent turning the regional organization into a tool to re-confirm the 'power of size' (dominance of the largest countries) or the 'tyranny of the average'. The result would thereby ignore the potential richness of

---

26 As Doz et al. (2001) argue.

27 See Birkinshaw et al. (1998) and Birkinshaw and Hood (2001) about the importance of structured processes to subsidiary development.

28 Doz et al. (2001, p. 98).

the greatest diversity present in every corner of the company. For it is diversity and conflict that will remain the breeding ground for new ideas rather than integration or uniformity; as the French saying goes: *'Du choc des idées éclate la lumière'* ('Out of the clash of ideas emerges the light').

This means a formidable challenge in which a regional organization could be a useful device or learning platform. Regional organizations should not be created solely as a response to regulatory, political and economic changes, such as the development of trading blocs, but as a pragmatic response to the changing dynamics in the company's external environment and with proper attention to its potential role to be part of a wider organizational development process, required for taking advantage of newly emerging opportunities.

12 The Metanational: The Next Step in the Evolution of the Multinational Enterprise

Yves Doz, José Santos, Peter Williamson
INSEAD

Introduction

Researchers have long been interested in the question of why, from a theoretical perspective, the multinational enterprise (MNE) exists as an organizational form. Early work on this issue proposed that the MNE was an answer to market failure in the effective exploitation of intangible assets overseas. These ideas were further developed by Kogut and Zander (1993) who postulated that the multinational was an efficient mechanism to transfer complex knowledge across borders. But implicit in this work is a fundamental, but seldomly stated, assumption: that a company *first* gains competitive advantage through strategic innovation at home and *then* exploits its advantage internationally. Or, as Bartlett and Ghoshal put it (1989, p. 115): 'A firm invests abroad to derive further profit from innovations developed for the domestic market.' We have termed this behaviour *'projection'* because it focuses on transferring and exploiting advantages built at home into overseas environments.

While projection has obviously been a profitable strategy in the past, this chapter argues that it is facing diminishing returns as the costs of distance fall and markets have become more efficient mechanisms for transfer of resources, information and knowledge. We contend that in the future the competitive advantage of the multinational enterprise will come, not so much from its efficiency in transferring resources, information and knowledge, but from its unique potential for radical innovation by melding and leveraging distinctive knowledge drawn from diverse geographical contexts around the world. We show that this source of innovation advantage and the existence of a new organizational form that is uniquely capable of building and exploiting this type of advantage are the logical 'next step' in the evolution of the multinational enterprize. The potential for this kind of innovation advantage has always existed (one past instance is Airbus), but it was seldom exploited in practice because the cost of bringing together dispersed pieces of knowledge was simply too high. Once the costs fell sufficiently, multinational companies would begin to exploit this source of advantage that was uniquely open to them.

Our research set out to discover whether this new organizational form, which we termed the 'metanational company', was in fact emerging, and what kind of new structures and management processes might be necessary to make it work effectively.[1] We concluded that today some companies are pioneering the metanational organization, but to do so requires both important changes in mind-sets and the augmentation of the structures and processes used to manage a traditional MNE with fundamentally new ones (Doz et al., 2001).

Were We Mistaking History for Theory?

One does not have to look far to understand why conventional wisdom on the internationalization of firms is based on the assumption that a company first gains competitive advantage at home via some unique combination of supply and demand conditions that usually make its home both the lead market and the fount of knowledge for its business (Porter, 1990). A classic case in point is IKEA, taking its innovative design and application of the 'cash & carry' concept to furniture from Sweden to other countries as income levels increased and baby boomers' home creation waves crested. Once their operations spread around the globe and encompass multiple product lines, fledgling MNEs manage the resulting complex interactions and interfaces between products, functions, and geographies through matrix organizations (Stopford and Wells, 1972). Within these multidimensional organizations they carefully manage the balance between the advantages of global integration and those of local responsiveness to reflect external economic, competitive and political demands (Prahalad and Doz, 1987).

But, in building theories of internationalization from the experience of these firms, are we drawing universal theory from a singular moment in history? While history is not necessarily atheoretical, as researchers we must be careful with how and where we generalize from historical observations. These internationalization patterns may have been true of the German chemical industry in the nineteenth century, of American automobiles and farm equipment at the beginning of the twentieth century, or more recently of Japanese consumer electronics. Today, we are no longer dealing with corporate internationalization in a not-yet international world, but with internationalization in an already global world. This is not just a world of instant communication and fast and inexpensive transportation, but also a world where, contrary to the examples just cited, knowledge relevant to a particular industry is distributed worldwide. No single location exercises undisputed knowledge leadership anymore. New firms may not even start in one place either: contrary to the proverbial image of the garage entrepreneur, many of today's entrepreneurs, their cosmopolitan mind-set inherited from their experience in multinational companies, think from day one about how to build a global business. The world is changing on

---

1 We use the prefix *meta* – from the Greek term for 'beyond' – to emphasize a key point: metanational companies do not draw their competitive advantage from their home country, nor even from a set of national subsidiaries. Metanationals view the world as a global canvas dotted with pockets of technology, market knowledge, and capabilities. They build their strategic innovations from these pockets of specialist knowledge scattered around the world.

us, and as researchers we must be careful: tomorrow's global companies may not resemble yesterday's, they may not follow the same internationalization path, nor may they face a similar environment.

Turning history into theory may also hide the fact that most companies fail to exploit the vast potential of distributed innovation. Adopting projection, they ignore innovations from their periphery – even if they vow to 'think global, act local'. First, the knowledge on which to deploy innovations from the periphery is seldom even transferred back to the centre. Many opportunities are missed and good ideas are abandoned. As an illustration, let's consider the factors that led Unilever to introduce *Ala*, a low end detergent, to the Brazilian market. Years earlier, Unilever introduced a low end detergent to the Indian market in response to a low cost competitor, *Nirma*. By complete coincidence, a junior manager from Brazil, on secondment within Unilever to Pakistan (not even India), heard about the product and saw an opportunity to release a similar product in Brazil. Back home, in Sao Paolo, he approached the market research experts who explained that the product had been tried three times before – two, five and 10 years ago – and it had never worked so he should forget the idea. Fortunately for Unilever, this Brazilian manager was tenacious and would not be discouraged. He mobilized four of his colleagues who went to the Nordeste and Amazon regions, stayed among the poor villagers, and discovered that they cared more about cleanliness than did the affluent, if only they could afford it. His conviction confirmed by his team's observations, the young manager created a market – reinventing the product, its manufacturing, packaging and distribution in the process – making low cost detergents a very successful product for Unilever in Brazil. By the late 1990s, India and Brazil were the two most profitable subsidiaries for Unilever, worldwide.

Behind this success story, a nagging question remains: should MNCs like Unilever depend on the happenstance of the right manager being in the right place or can they build a managerial process that systematically moves knowledge for innovation? In a similar vein, IBM failed to capture the benefits of innovation when it turned down the ideas of its own employees in Germany who subsquently left and set up a separate company, SAP, that went on to become a great success. How many ideas end up being abandoned in the complex of the multinational company that is unwilling or unable to leverage knowledge from its geographical periphery?

Second, at even greater cost than ignoring innovations from the periphery, the traditional models of internationalization also lead companies to fail to combine knowledge from multiple sources around the world. When mobile telephony started to bloom, who would have bet that a little-known upstart from the Arctic Circle called Nokia would overtake the American leader, Motorola? Cellular telephony was invented in the US, and Motorola was the first to mass-produce mobile phones; its engineering, supplier, and marketing networks were deep and sophisticated. Nokia's ace was its ability to prospect technologies and learn from customers around the world. Observing trendy customers in Asia and Los Angeles, it saw the potential for mobile phones as fashion accessories. Different user segments first emerged in Europe, and they needed customized handsets. Observation of pilot users across Scandinavia suggested that digital technology could dramatically improve functionality. In China and India, Nokia realized that mobile phones might substitute for a fixed-line network. Meanwhile, Motorola continued to develop its products for the US market and environment. It thus missed the chance to be first in turning mobile phones into fashion statements, to develop digital mobile telephony, or to grasp the diversity and depth of new uses for the product. Its failure to engage with the world as a source of innovative ideas, and not just as a (secondary) market, cost it dearly.

Failing to widen and renew the knowledge pool they fish from, many traditional multinationals drift from true innovation to more incremental learning. The global learning activities of the MNC are in danger of being reduced to process engineering, efficiency improvement and the sharing of best practice. All of this is clearly required, as table stakes, but is no longer sufficient for winning. Competitors are increasingly well matched in the deployment of their resources and in the mastery of basic process discipline such as TQM. With the goal of helping firms develop sustainable competitive advantage we try to understand untapped innovation opportunities in the context of the knowledge economy, an economy where knowledge is becoming the key to sustainable advantage and where sources of useful knowledge are increasingly dispersed around the world.

Revisiting the Multinational: A Knowledge Based Perspective

The prevailing explanation of the structure and conduct of multinational companies can be summarized in a set of four models (or 'strategies') that MNEs adopt: international, multidomestic, global, and transnational. These models are effective as vehicles for describing how MNEs exploit around the world the products, processes and business models that they have innovated and perfected initially in their home base. When expanding its business overseas, the prospective MNE can either (Bartlett and Ghoshal, 1989): exploit a unitary world market with a standard product offering and with centralized global-scale operations (the 'global' model); be sensitive to the different national environments and let each country subsidiary adapt and develop its business model to the respective market in an autonomous fashion (the 'multidomestic' model); diffuse the parent unit capabilities by replicating its business model around the world, while keeping a high degree of central control (the 'international' model); or it can achieve global integration of its worldwide operations, keeping its country subsidiaries responsive, and even learning from certain subsidiaries (the 'transnational' model).

It is possible to re-interpret these four MNE models from a knowledge perspective, starting with the proposition that MNEs exist because they can transfer complex knowledge across borders – something that markets are unable to do effectively. If all knowledge were explicit, the world could do without MNEs. Complex knowledge is largely messy and hard to articulate (tacit knowledge) and sticky to its original context because it is easily misinterpreted or misapplied when transferred into another context (context-specific knowledge).

Under the common assumption of projection that underlies the four models described above, what the MNE transfers across borders is knowledge that the firm learned in its home base. Such a knowledge set includes items of *market knowledge* (such as how to serve consumers that behave in a certain way, or what consumers value in a product) and items of *technical knowledge* (such as the technologies used in the production of a product, or how to recruit, train, and motivate its salespeople). The firm obtained the various items of knowledge at home and melded them into some strategic innovation that made it distinctive. It is this distinctiveness that lies at the heart of the firm's superior performance even outside its home borders: the competitive edge that comes from a new product, for example, that satisfies consumers in the home market and elsewhere. Such strategic innovation is the embodiment of a knowledge set that the firm created 'at home' and this knowledge set is refined over time as the firm learns 'by doing' in the course of conducting its business as a domestic firm in its original setting. As the firm becomes multinational it will transfer its knowledge abroad – and, in so doing, it 'teaches the world'. It is exactly this sequence, first creating a knowledge set in its home country and then becoming a MNE by exploiting it around the world, that we call 'projection'.

The MNC can choose to accomplish the necessary transfer of knowledge in one of four modes. First, it can choose to replicate its home base business and operations in each host country (by transferring the whole of its knowledge set) or to extend its home base operations by having a limited functionality in the operations of each host country (by transferring only a part of its knowledge set). Second, it can choose whether or not to treat its knowledge set as peculiar to a particular national context (context specific) or to behave as if its knowledge was universal (context free).

Projecting the Whole Knowledge Set

Suppose the firm chooses to transfer to a foreign country the whole of its knowledge set as if it were all context-free. The transfer process will involve the codification of those items of knowledge that can be articulated. The more tacit knowledge will be carried abroad by trusted expatriates or by bringing overseas employees for 'immersion' training at the MNE's home base. Because the items of knowledge that are transferred to other countries are treated as being universal, they will be applied there exactly as in the original context. The visible result will be a firm whose offerings abroad are standard: undifferentiated from country to country. Because the host country will now have the whole knowledge set, it constitutes a stand-alone copy of the home base unit. Indeed, what is transferred is not only the operational knowledge, but also the knowledge required to develop the business locally: P&G would transfer not only the specifications of its products, or production and selling routines, but also the 'P&G way' – the strategic piece that allows each local unit to grow. In this mode, each host country unit does business in a quasi-autonomous way: it depends formally on the home base unit that maintains the uniform behaviour of its units abroad. This MNE strategy of projecting the whole knowledge set is the knowledge analogue of the 'international' model.

Another possibility is that the firm behaves as if its knowledge set contains items that are context-specific. The firm may recognize, for example, that a pricing model or an incentive system is effective in the home country but may be dysfunctional if replicated in other countries. Whether the firm recognizes the process or not, it is a fact that when context-specific knowledge is transferred, it will be re-contextualized in each host country and acquire a different meaning there (Brannen and Wilson, 1996). To prevent such re-contextualization from becoming dysfunctional, the firm must add one new step to the knowledge projection process: its knowledge will need to be *de*-contextualized at home. De-contextualization involves converting each knowledge item in such a way that its home-specific nature is neutralized. For example, instead of transferring a routine (such as 'give a silver commemorative plaque to the employee that delivers the best suggestion each year, during the annual Christmas party') the firm transfers a generic principle (such as 'give non-monetary rewards according to local traditions').

The outcome is a knowledge set in each host that is different from the original one: it has been 'localized'. The adapted knowledge set is complete and host-country specific. This set of choices about how to transfer knowledge results in the 'multi-domestic' MNE.

Projecting Part of the Knowledge Set

The firm may recognize that part of its knowledge set is context-specific and choose to transfer abroad only that sub-set of its home-base knowledge that is context-free. Only that sub-set will be transferred abroad. Again, the transfer will involve such carriers as manuals or blueprints, for the explicit items, and experienced personnel for those items of knowledge that are experiential and/or tacit. The items of knowledge that are transferred to other countries will be learned and applied exactly as in the original context. As in the 'international' model, the visible result will be offerings abroad that are standard, undifferentiated from county to country. But because not all the home-base knowledge set has been transferred, the overseas unit won't undertake the complete set of activities required to support the value chain. IKEA, for example, leaves its design function at home as its interpretation of 'Scandinavian minimalism' is deeply cultural. Because each country unit has only a part of the knowledge set and thus can conduct only a partial set of value chain activities, it will remain an extension of the home country operation and the activities of the MNE will necessarily be globally integrated. The outcome of projecting only the universal sub-set of the home knowledge set results in what has been termed the 'global' model of the MNE.

Finally, the MNE may recognize that its original knowledge set has context-specific items that can be successfully transferred to some contexts, but not to others. It may therefore choose to transfer a different part of its complete knowledge set to each host country. The choice of which sub-set of the knowledge bundle to transfer will be determined according to the particular context in each host country. For example, an American MNE may transfer its R&D knowledge to large, developed countries such as Japan or Germany – but not to the smaller, less developed markets. Such a projection mode requires the firm to identify the context in each country and then decide which parts of the knowledge set it makes sense to transfer to each one. In order to achieve this, the MNE must perform the de-contextualization and transfer of knowledge described in the multidomestic case, but it must also receive and act on knowledge about the host's context. This requires the *host unit* to first de-contextualize its unique knowledge and convey the resulting representation of this knowledge to the parent. The parent will then need to meld this knowledge with its own to create a new knowledge set. Next, the parent must decide which part of the new knowledge set to project back to the host.

As a result of this process, the various units will each receive a different knowledge set. Because each host receives a different set of knowledge from the parent and then re-contextualizes it locally, each host will end up with a unique, but incomplete, set of knowledge assets. The various units are, therefore, interdependent. Pieces of knowledge will therefore move laterally between country units (as in the transfer of best practices). A particularly favourable location may even be selected to replace the home location and to become a 'strategic leader' or a 'centre of excellence' for a particular function or product.

The result of this approach to knowledge transfer is a 'transnational' organization, able to respond locally and be globally integrated, as well as capable of using a process of worldwide learning to refine the original innovation projected from the original home country. An exemplar case of a transnational innovation, reported by Bartlett and Ghoshal (1989, p. 120), is the development of liquid detergent by P&G. Though P&G European and Japanese units were the outcome of initial projection from P&G US, these units were able to make inroads in their own laboratories to improve drastically on what their US parent had developed in response to Unilever's earlier success in the heavy-duty liquid detergents. Eventually, the developments of P&G US, Europe, and Japan – created in response to local needs – were incorporated in new and much improved P&G liquid detergents in each region. This transnational mode is the most intricate of all modes of projection – and this may explain why its execution is so rare.

These four models of how MNEs can choose to project their knowledge across borders are summarized in Figure 12.1.

The Metanational

What we have sketched in the previous section is a theory of the MNE derived from the economics of knowledge transfer, not from an interpretation of the history of MNEs. But unlike the the traditional integration–responsiveness formulation, the knowledge-based perspective also suggests that the received set of options open to an MNE is incomplete. It alerts us to a totally different kind of MNE that has been ignored by extant theory: that the original knowledge set (embodied in the strategic innovation that gives the firm its uniqueness and cross-border value) can be the result of melding pieces of complex knowledge drawn from different countries – i.e. from dispersed knowledge – rather than knowledge coming from the home base or a single unit chosen as a centre of excellence.

The idea that an MNE's competitive advantage could be based on melding knowledge that is dispersed around the world does not fit within the four traditional models. But, in fact, building advantage by drawing knowledge from multiple sources

	Projection of knowledge as context-free	Projection of knowledge as context-specific
Projection of part of the knowledge set	**Global** - Strategic innovation (knowledge set creation) at home - Identifying context-free part at home - Articulating knowledge at home - Transfer of tacit knowledge to host	**Transnational** - Strategic innovation (knowledge set creation) at home - Identifying context-free part at home - Articulating knowledge at home - Transfer of tacit knowledge to host - De-contextualization at host - Melding at host - De-contextualization at home - Pooled melding at home - Lateral sharing by hosts
Projection of the whole knowledge set	**International** - Strategic innovation (knowledge set creation) at home - Articulating knowledge at home - Transfer of tacit knowledge to host	**Multidomestic** - Strategic innovation (knowledge set creation) at home - Articulating knowledge at home - Transfer of tacit knowledge to host - De-contextualization at home - Melding at host

Figure 12.1—A knowledge-based view of the traditional MNE models.

is a feat that would be especially difficult for a market to orchestrate. It is therefore a potentially strong source of advantage for the MNE organizational form. At the same time, the knowledge processes involved go well beyond those in the transnational, because they demand the added ability to discover and access new pieces of knowledge located around the world (and even outside existing subsidiaries) and to perform the combination of complex knowledge in virtual space.

We call this model the 'metanational' because it describes a multinational that truly transcends countries. The raison d'être of the metanational is not the absolute advantage of a home-base or leading unit location, nor the transfer of best practices from one subsidiary to another. Instead, the metanational draws its strength from its ability to *first* learn from the world and strategically innovate by melding pieces of market knowledge and technical knowledge embedded in dispersed locations around the world – and *then* exploit its knowledge set wherever it may be valuable (which may be just a few global customers or even a single national market).

The Metanational in Practice

In our research (Doz et al., 2001) we studied conventional multinational companies and found little evidence that they were exploiting their potential for innovation advantage by melding dispersed knowledge – a capability which, at least theoretically, they should be uniquely well placed to develop. They did not depart from conventional wisdom, except by accident, in cases like that of Unilever discussed above. On the other hand, there were a number of innovative companies we identified, which did not come from the main knowledge cluster of their industry, or put differently, which were 'born in the wrong place'. According to the conventional wisdom of internationalization, these companies should not have succeeded. For instance, Shizeido, which comes from Japan where there is no domestic market for fragrance except as a collector's item, built an unprecedented success in perfumes by learning from France (Asakawa and Doz, 2001). STMicroelectronics, one of the most successful semiconductor companies over the last decade, was based in Milan and Paris, where there are no significant domestic markets for microelectronics and where Europe had been discounted in the industry (Santos, forthcoming). Egmont, a Danish publisher of comic magazines, used licences from the US and France, story writers from the UK, and graphic artists from Spain; its market is not home nor neighbouring Germany but China, using a very innovative distribution alliance with the Chinese post office. ARM, a start-up in the UK, recognized that its original country 'would never get us off the ground'. It created a web of partners around the world and an original licensing agreement that allowed it to fish for new knowledge about technologies and applications everywhere – to become a world leader in RISC chips (Williamson, 2002). In all of these situations, we were looking at companies which are tapping the world for pockets of unexploited, underleveraged knowledge and competencies, and whose lead markets are elsewhere.

We also researched how these companies that were born in the wrong place became metanationals. No matter their exact starting point, or the precise path each followed, all violated the key assumption that multinationals succeed through projection from their home base.

Competing on Three Planes

In gaining innovation advantage from knowledge dispersed around the world, the budding metanationals we identified competed on the three distinct planes illustrated in Figure 12.2.

The first level of competition was their race to identify and access new and relevant technologies, competencies, and knowledge of lead markets emerging in locations dotted around the world. Identifying where, for example, the next advance in biotechnology is being hatched. Where are consumers experimenting with new uses for mobile phones?

The second level of competition was in the effectiveness and speed with which they were able to connect these globally scattered pieces of knowledge and use them to create innovative products, services and processes. How effectively, for example, could STMicroelectronics marshal technologies scattered around the world to serve a customer need emerging elsewhere, thus creating a radically new 'system-on-a-chip'?

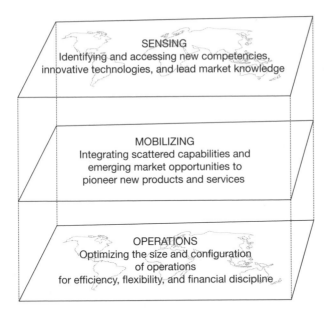

Figure 12.2—The three levels of competition in the global knowledge economy.

The third level on which they competed was in trying to optimize the efficiency of their global sales, distribution, marketing and supply chain to deliver these innovations across global markets rapidly and cost effectively. How efficiently could STMicroelectronics, for example, adapt, produce and sell its new chip to customers around the world?

To succeed on these three planes, the pioneering metanationals needed to build three corresponding sets of capabilities for sensing, mobilizing, and delivering.

Building Sensing Capabilities

They first had to learn how to sense and process complex knowledge scattered around the world into a form that they could use efficiently. Sensing is much more than market research or information gathering, it involves accessing complex knowledge that is often tacit and deeply embedded in a local context. But identifying and accessing knowledge that rivals had already mastered would only bring competitive parity. Building a new source of innovation advantage required a *sensing network* that could identify innovative technologies or emerging customer needs that competitors had overlooked – a network that pre-empted global sources of new knowledge. Effective sensing involved the following.

- The capacity to identify a *sensing need*. A goal, even if broadly defined, is essential to move from aimless exploration to purposeful reconnaissance work.

- The capability to *prospect* the world for sources of relevant knowledge, unearthing new pockets of knowledge ahead of competitors.
- The capacity to *access* new knowledge once its location is identified – not a trivial task when the required knowledge is complex or when it needs to be pried loose from a tight-knit local club.

Sensing networks may be comprised of the following.

- Alliances with lead customers, suppliers, other partners, or even competitors who can provide access to new market or technical knowledge.
- Targeted acquisitions to access specialist know-how.
- Links with venture capital funds to intercept promising new technologies or ideas at an early stage.
- Cooperation with universities or research institutes in various parts of the world.
- 'Roving reporters' charged with identifying and assessing pockets of emerging technologies or new customer applications.
- Existing subsidiaries and sites as they generate new knowledge in the course of adapting products and services to local markets.

Building Mobilization Capabilities

To create a strategic innovation that would provide competitive advantage, it was clearly not enough for a company to amass a rich hoard of knowledge from around the world. Stopping there risked becoming exceptionally well informed, but impotent. The metanational would not only have to access dispersed knowledge, but also mobilize it to create innovative products, services, processes, and business models.

This required building a set of structures (which may be virtual, temporary, or both) to translate new knowledge into innovative products or specific market opportunities. These new structures (the evidence suggests that existing operating units and systems will seldom do the job) need to mobilize knowledge that is scattered in pockets around the corporation and use it to pioneer new products and services, sometimes with the help of lead customers. The record company Polygram (now part of Vivendi Universal) created such a structure – the international repertoire network – for unlocking the potential appeal of unknown global artists. This new structure enabled Polygram to connect and mobilize a complex bundle of dispersed knowledge about new acts, international markets, and local capabilities to create international hits. STMicroelectronics used projects with Seagate to replace the motherboards in hard disk drive conrollers with a 'system chip' set as the way to mobilize complex knowledge scattered around its own global network and that of a lead customer and bring it together to create an innovative solution.

We called these structures 'magnets'. They may take the form of a project to develop a new solution for a lead customer, to design a global product or service platform, or units such as Polygram's International Repertoire Centres staffed by people dedicated to mobilizing and leveraging knowledge that is scattered around the world. Whatever their organizational form, these magnets attract dispersed, potentially relevant knowledge and use it to create innovative products, services, or processes, and they then facilitate the transfer of these innovations into the network of day-to-day operations. The challenge is to build the capabilities to design and operate a better set of magnets than competitors.

Building Delivery Capabilities

Once a new product, service, or business model has been pioneered, its profit potential must be realized. This means scaling up the supply chain, improving efficiencies, making incremental improvements, and engineering local adaptations. Most multinationals are already proficient in this arena.

As multinationals evolve to become metanationals, therefore, the ability to produce, market, distribute and sell products and services around the globe will be critical. But the ability to reap the benefits of global leverage and local adaptation will be taken for granted among premier league companies. What will distinguish the leaders from the followers will be the capability to access, mobilize and leverage the global knowledge pool to come up with innovations that open up 'clear blue water' between them and their competitors. The interaction of these activities to form the metanational innovation process is illustrated in Figure 12.3.

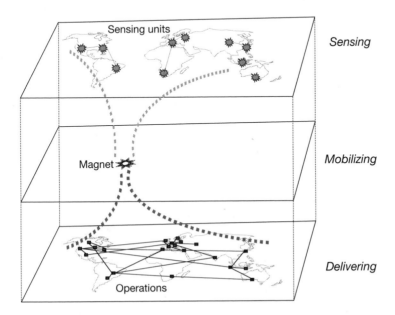

Figure 12.3—The metanational innovation process.

Two Traps on the Evolutionary Path to the Metanational

As companies tried to move beyond traditional multinational organizational forms and build metanational capabilities, we observed a risk of them falling into two traps: the trap of trying to 'shoehorn' the new capabilities into an existing organization, and the trap of investing in costly communications channels between existing units only to end up with a 'global debating society' instead of a powerful new innovation engine.

The shoehorning trap arose from the instinctive response of most multinational companies on recognizing the need to create a new source of advantage through metanational innovation: start from their existing multinational structure and adjust it to accommodate the new objective. The evidence of this strategy is all around us. Companies spend millions on information technology and communications systems to share knowledge among existing subsidiaries. They appoint Chief Knowledge Officers. They establish centres of excellence and business unit headquarters around the world with responsibility for innovation in particular products or processes.

From the discussion in this chapter it should be clear why all of these worthy initiatives, while in some cases necessary, will not provide multinationals with the new sources of competitive advantage they are trying to create. The traditional multinational was designed to leverage innovation from home base across the world. Its beliefs, performance measures, incentive systems, decision-making processes, organization structures, information systems, and financial controls were all designed to achieve these objectives. And for the most part, the multinational systems and structures achieved these operating goals extremely well.

But ask the traditional multinational organization to create its next strategic innovation from new capabilities, technologies, know-how and understanding of lead customers, where all of these different and specialized inputs are dispersed around the world – often on the periphery of the company's transnational network – and it will come to a creaking halt. Overhead and costs of coordination will rise, and the organization will become paralysed with ambiguity.

The second, 'global debating society trap', arose from attempts to build a highly interdependent organization thought necessary to share dispersed knowledge. But this does not mean simply trying to 'connect everyone to everyone else' in a massive internal market for knowledge and resources – such an organization would simply drown in its own overhead. Building an effective metanational requires management to put in place a limited number of carefully selected connections and communication channels between specific sites, units, teams, partners and customers – not just between national subsidiaries or global business units. The key roles within this network are no longer automatically allocated to the most important national subsidiaries or the units with the most resources, people or even experience. In fact, in a metanational, innovation and leadership are just as likely to come from the periphery of the organization as they are from headquarters, from large and powerful subsidiaries or even from designated centres of excellence.

In a worst-case scenario, trying to force fit an existing multinational organization and its people into a metanational mould will undermine its operational excellence and could imperil the company's very survival. Rather than delivering innovation by tapping into, and mobilizing, pockets of knowledge scattered around the world, the traditional multinational organization will end up:

- becoming a 'global debating society' where unguided networking and consultation undermine efficiency and rapid decision making;
- giving managers and staff ulcers and sleepless nights as they juggle a raft of new responsibilities on top of their operational 'day jobs';
- drowning in complexity and increased overhead.

To move successfully from a traditional multinational to a metanational, companies must fundamentally augment their existing organizations, or build new ones that are much more than simply clones of today's multinationals.

A New Breed of Company: Born Metanational

For today's budding multinationals and new economy companies our findings underline the need to leapfrog their older cousins to build 'metanational' companies, rather than emulating the internationalization strategies of the past. This means:

- avoiding the creation of a senior management ghetto in a single location;
- seeking out and leveraging global diversity – recruit people from multiple nationalities and backgrounds from the start; look for unity in a common corporate culture and value system, rather than shared nationality or business experience;
- assessing each international foray according to the ratio of learning over investment;
- leveraging partners that can provide elements of the delivery plane to make the company 'instantly global'.

The goal is to create a metanational company that will be tuned to harness and exploit this hidden strategic innovation potential by harnessing knowledge scattered around the globe. This requires the building of new structures, teams, and processes to achieve sensing and mobilization around global lead customers, global platforms, and global activities. These structures will form a new sub-organization dedicated to entrepreneurship and innovation, with a unique set of roles, responsibilities, culture, and incentives. A flexible, efficient delivery network, augmented by the capabilities of suppliers, subcontractors, and alliance partners, will turn these metanational innovations into global profits and shareholder value.

Conclusion

The logical next step in the evolution of the multinational company is not about choosing between innovation and operating efficiency, or between exploitation and entrepreneurship. It is about winning a global tournament played at three different levels: the race to identify and access new technologies and market trends ahead of the competition, the race to turn this dispersed knowledge into innovative products and services, and the race to scale and deliver these innovations to markets around the world. A prerequisite to taking this next step will be to abandon the deeply rooted and often implicit assumption that the advantage of multinationals is their efficiency in projecting their advantages perfected in their home base around the world. This will require a new organizational form that breaks free from the assumption that multinationals thrive because they overcome market failure in projecting advantages perfected in their home base around the world. This new, metanational organization will have a clear focus on building and exploiting the unique potential of multinational companies to innovate by melding knowledge that is scattered in isolated pockets around the world.

Section 3

REJUVENATING THE MATURE BUSINESS

13 The Critical Role of Sense-making in *Rejuvenating the Mature Business*

John Stopford[1] and Charles Baden-Fuller[2]

[1]*London Business School and* [2]*City University Business School*

During the 1980s we became intrigued by the fact that some individual firms were achieving persistently spectacular results despite being in the so-called mature industries. By outperforming their industry averages for many years they seemed to challenge the central tenet of industrial organization theory, that industry structure is the primary determinant of performance. Closer examination revealed a greater curiosity. A few of these high performers had been declared 'dead' by the supposedly efficient capital market but had popped out of the coffin to reach new heights of excellence. Were such extraordinary feats merely aberrations or did they represent a category of management that deserved close study? We chose the latter proposition.

In our book (especially in the second edition in 1994) we focused on the actions of individual managers and firms and tried to model them. These managers were pioneers, charting ways to break the mould of pre-existing industry conventions. Looking back now, nearly 10 years after the original work, we realize we underestimated the significance of their innovative behaviour. They were, in part, following their intuition as they sensed, but could not initially prove, the case for change. We now believe that probing and sensing, in both a collective and individualistic form, was one of the driving engines behind the renewal processes we observed. Although we discussed this behaviour in Chapter 5 on Corporate Entrepreneurship and in every section describing the renewal process, we did not explore it enough. The symposium provided us with a welcome chance to revisit and elaborate the theme.

In this chapter, we begin by summarizing our rejuvenation model, highlighting the role of 'sense-making'. Then we explore why sense-making is such an important driver of renewal and why it reveals rejuvenation as an effective and proper use of management talent. Finally we speculate on why maintaining the momentum of success is so difficult.

The Crescendo Model

Our book focused on the activities within 10 firms that had made great progress in throwing off the shackles of operating in low-growth environments, typically 'rust-bowl' industries. However, to provide a consistent context for interpreting the implications of their actions and also to make our study academically credible, we examined many of their direct competitors. We chose four industries where international competition was strong, and examined the performance of 50 firms over a period of more than 10 years. By the mid-1980s, most of these 50 firms were in competitive difficulties. We were very fortunate that our research funding allowed us to watch events as they unfolded and so avoid the dangers of exclusive reliance on retrospective reconstruction.

The 10 firms we examined in greatest detail all had remarkable journeys out of the pitfalls of maturity and stasis. They took many similar actions, which we simplified into a 2x2 matrix. On the *x*-axis is the managerial 'agenda', which was either narrow or broad. What we mean by agenda are such typical complexity issues as the extent of product diversity. In addition, the agenda encompasses a notional measure of the scope of the activity of top management, including the number of fires the board is trying to put out at the same time. On the *y*-axis is shorthand for various properties of the organization, which we termed 'static' or 'dynamic'. We called the resulting model a crescendo to capture the sense that the size of the investment bets and the attendant risks rose over time. The model is shown in Figure 13.1, in slightly modified form.

We realized subsequently that we had omitted a crucial part of the story. The majority (about 30) of the 50 failing firms we studied took little or no action to

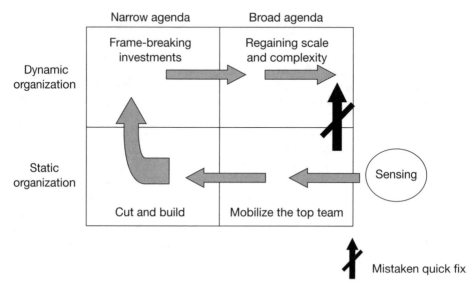

Figure 13.1—The crescendo model: the critical path for corporate renewal (adapted with permission from Baden-Fuller and Stopford, 1994, p. 171).

change how they worked. They failed or were acquired, leaving to others the task of recovery. They did not adequately 'sense' the possibilities that some competitors, with similar resources, both understood and acted on. While we did study these failed firms, we did not comment on them extensively. Now we recognize that the distinguishing mark between success and failure of our firms was that the successful were committed to, and better at, sensing.

We obviously differ from many writers on renewal who assume that management has already got a clear idea of what to do but needs to work out how to do it. Such writers typically talk of individuals taking actions, of the use of consultants for implementation, and of the kinds of projects required for renewal. But our research suggested that getting to the first step of knowing what is there and what to do is a far more difficult task than many realize. Most of our organizations were unable to get to this point. They did not map territories and explore possibilities. Rather they rushed headlong in one direction then another or became paralysed into what we now call 'active inertia'. By contrast, those that escaped the trap of maturity probed the context, initiated experiments, and learned from these programmes, and, indeed, often learned from failure.

The dynamics of the processes that achieved this initial sense-making fell into four broad stages, each of which turn involved yet more sensing and sense-making.

The early processes in the managerial agenda focused on *galvanizing the top team*. Typically, if a company is in a recovery programme, all it does is cut. One does not need a galvanized team to cut and some firms fell into this trap. Managers in our more successful firms asked themselves: if you just cut, what hope are you giving the organization? What experiments are you conducting to try to find the future?

How to recover was not obvious – if it were, our companies would not have reached this state. We did not find stupid managers, rather many that were confused. The real challenge to management was to realize that wholesale change was essential and that the change would be a collective exploration. For that to happen, galvanizing the top team into action on a shared agenda appeared as critical.

The *cut-and-build* stage requires a myriad of actions, some coordinated, some independent experiments within the functions. There was a lot of iterative work as experiments failed and double-loop learning was carried out. We found that this was one of the absolutely crucial transitions in the rejuvenation process. It began changing the base of the organization and making it sufficiently simple so that managers could 'get their arms around' the problems. We found that only 10 firms really mastered this agenda, about half of those that had some 'sense' of possibility.

These first two steps are essentially those of securing a robust platform for catching up with good practice. Typically, firms are building capabilities and cost structures that are equivalent to their competitors. But they are doing more: they are creating an organizational climate that makes it easier to move further forward.

We labelled our third stage *frame-breaking investments*. It is important to note that none of the firms we studied knew in advance what would be a successful frame-breaking investment. But they wanted to make such an investment, and sensing and probing never left their agenda. At this stage, our companies were aware they had to change how the whole organization worked, coordinating across functions. Experiments became embedded in processes and moved from being concerned with small groups (for example, within the sales function) to gaining leverage across the organization. These investments began to create new competencies that had an impact on the industry as a whole.

Figure 13.2 illustrates the progress that can be achieved by scattering experiments across a company – resources become assembled into investments that then begin to challenge industry norms and practices. We found that competitors noticed that there was real life inside an organization when it initiated frame-breaking investments and began to change the industry rules.

In the final stage (the upper-right quadrant of the model in Figure 13.1), we found some firms trying to leverage their advantages across a broad set of markets and customers. These firms started re-complicating their organization, moving back into some of the technologies, functions, products, or territories they had earlier cut out. We found that only four out of the 50 companies sampled reached this stage of aiming for world leadership. We also realized that at this stage we had come to the limits of what we could infer from our data. So few firms were in this box that generalizations were risky, though it was quite possible that others would reach the same stage later – as indeed has proved to be the case.

When we tried to map the path of progress we obtained messy, iterative curves (represented in Figure 13.3). Progress is never linear. Inside our firms, the messiness of the changes made it extremely difficult to control the pace and sequence of specific actions; leadership becomes a key resource. All our stories emphasize exceptional personal leadership. This really did make a difference.

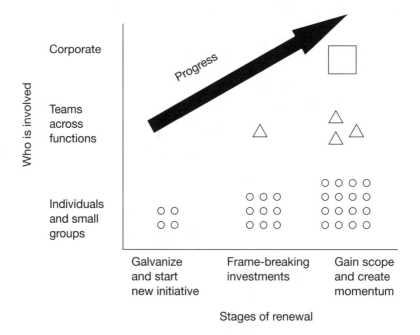

Figure 13.2—The locus of activity in different stages of rejuvenation (adapted with permission from Baden-Fuller and Stopford, 1994, p. 18).

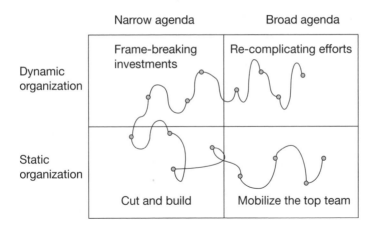

Narrow agenda   Broad agenda

Dynamic
organization

Static
organization

Frame-breaking investments

Re-complicating efforts

Cut and build

Mobilize the top team

Figure 13.3—Maintaining continuous renewal (adapted with permission from Baden-Fuller and Stopford, 1994, p. 171).

Sense-making

In the above paragraphs we have stressed the role of perceptions and sensing in driving successful renewal in established organizations, a process undertaken by both top and middle levels of management. It is a process that does not assign particular roles to particular participants but one that puts management at centre stage.

Let us put our model into the language of the evolutionary literature. We now have a better understanding of the processes of variation–selection–retention in organizations. We know they are co-evolutionary and integrate both market and organizational perspectives. The initial work of population ecologists seemed to echo the views of the extreme neoclassical economists: management may matter but it does not matter very much. They argued that the best form of variation is new entry and the best form of selection is the market.

However, co-evolutionary research that looks more closely at the processes of variation–selection–retention shows how new entry is not necessarily best at variation and that the market is not necessarily best at selection. It appears that we have multiple, co-existing methods of creating variation and of organizing selection. The co-evolutionary view is that processes of management sit alongside market processes and that the two operate together rather than in opposition, a point made in exemplary fashion in Burgelman's 1994 study of Intel's investment behaviour.

For top management, the belief is not in concepts such as 'the market knows best' or in elitist views expressed as 'take control' but in a much more democratic sense of 'total involvement of all in the challenge'.

Our stories were full of evidence of collective sense-making and subsequent observation of other firms' rejuvenation experience shows the same characteristic. Moreover, it was not a case of variation and selection being separated by hierarchical level or time. Teams cut across levels to integrate their work and to ensure iterative learning over time. The mobilization of the energies of many managers created 'engines' that ran in cyclical journeys. During the unfreezing stage, old ideas are discarded in order to make way for new understandings. Once old beliefs are unlearned, new understanding can be achieved. In the final stage, changes in strategic thinking may perhaps be solidified.

The journey of renewal is transparent when applied to the very small unit. There, a single entrepreneur has to be the driving force of the innovation process. Typically, he or she imbues a spirit in the whole enterprise, collecting and motivating like-minded individuals. For such small entrepreneurial units, there is typically a dynamic alternation between exploitation and exploration because of the rise and fall in the energy levels of the founders. Variation and selection take place together, perhaps in the same individual. The lack of tight commitments and relatively low sunk costs enables these smaller start-ups to change radically and easily.

In the larger, mature firm, shared strategic concepts and thinking are more diffi-cult to change. It is important to understand that such a strategic schema is not purely a system of beliefs and assumptions but that it is preserved and legitimized in a 'cultural web' of organizational actions in terms of myths, rituals, and symbols.

To speak of rejuvenation as a series of individual actions by top management or by any other set of actors is to miss this important point. Our work shows that the underlying cognitive changes begin with incremental changes in causal concepts and linkages then exhibit a more significant and dramatic change, followed by incremental adjustments that further specify the new interpretation.

In our model, collective sense-making drives both variation and selection and is the result of participation of all levels. In this process, the chief executive is much more than an administrator. He or she must be a transformational leader who drives the process from the front but involves others and brings them along.

Collective sense-making is also an important requirement for knowledge integra-tion processes. Collective sense-making is a key component of the integrative processes that seek to maximize organization learning. Of course, top managers do have a special role. As a group, they are primarily involved in the promotion and protection of values and have variously been described as institutional leaders, heroes, change masters, and purposing leaders.

Our empirical work confirms the importance of this kind of behaviour in co-evolutionary processes. We give instances of mature firms renewing to achieve not only radical change for themselves but also change for their sectors, thus linking corporate renewal to industry renewal. Our examples of Richardson in knives and Edwards in high-vacuum pumps show that although triggers for change may have come from many quarters and may take time to gather speed, in the end the whole industry can change from maturity to dynamism.

Using Resources Effectively

The work we undertook shows that rejuvenation is possible and the passages above show that collective sense-making across managerial levels can provide a well-defined engine for replication. However, is attempting rejuvenation an advantageous use of resources for the firm, its managers, and its stakeholders? The question is important because the odds against successful rejuvenation are long and valuable resources can easily be wasted.

Our data showed that only four out of 50 firms in trouble recovered and gained industry leadership. However, about 20 out of 50 made at least a good fist at recovery and 10 out of 50 got to the transformation stage. These are rather better odds than those usually considered normal for the new product development process and certainly much better than those achieved in newly emerging industries such as biotechnology. However, such arguments only go part way to answering the question.

The standard view of economists and financial analysts is that if the market thinks the firm is worth very little, it is a waste of resources for management to make the effort But market tests of efficiency, while important, are neither best nor singular. They are not necessarily best because information is not well distributed.

In the case of Rolls-Royce, the market (evidenced by stock prices and analysts' statements) believed in the early 1970s that the RB111 had no future as an aero engine. The government and management thought otherwise. With the benefit of hindsight, one knows the market was wrong. Our research signalled that the RB111 was not an isolated instance. Market signals are inevitably based on limited knowledge and seldom provide early warning of the possible disruptive changes of management-inspired rejuvenation.

Our research showed that in many cases top management was poorly informed about the firm's costs and market positions because information systems were out of date and giving wrong signals. All too often, the information system in place when rejuvenation was initiated had been designed to support the strategy that had failed.

Because they lacked data to support the case for renewal, managers had perforce to rely on their belief in the possibility of recovery – hence our insistence on the crucial role of *sensing*. Our research also showed that outsiders (parent companies and the stock market) were no better placed. No wonder so many of the firms failed to perceive or act on the signals for change.

This is different from the situation often claimed by economists that management does not see that resources would be better used elsewhere. Since we wrote about this, the knowledge management literature has made enormous leaps forward to tell us our view is correct. The knowledge literature stresses that much of the valuable stocks of knowledge in organizations may be tacit and held in a variety of places. Even formal routines may be hidden and the sources of advantage may be causally ambiguous.

In this context, our recipe for action is simply one of taking a proper inventory in an effective managerial fashion. Rob Grant, who has researched extensively on knowledge, has pointed out that there is a big asymmetry in organizational knowledge stocks – they take years to build up yet can be destroyed quite quickly.

Can Momentum Be Maintained?

Does the sense-making model of rejuvenation guarantee sustained success? We did not address this question in the book because we wanted to explore the optimistic theme that rejuvenation is possible, often in seemingly unpromising circumstances.

If rejuvenation is about making the sinews of the organization suppler, then time acts to harden the arteries.

In our model, industry leadership requires people at every level of an organization working together continuously to sustain the competitive edge. But the more people that are involved, the greater are the chances that suppleness will eventually be replaced by the increasingly inflexible routines often required to ensure discipline and conformance to standards. This is the problem of 'active inertia'. Managers may respond to the challenges of leadership by trying harder to implement yesterday's recipes rather than continuing to search for tomorrow. (In the book, we talked about such managers as being like rabbits frozen in the headlights of an oncoming vehicle of change. We were wrong; we should have talked about managers as hamsters, running faster on the treadmill and staying still.)

The theory-based literature suggests that this intuition is correct. It points to cognitive changes giving rise to cyclical renewal journeys alternating between change and preservation. It is typically a tenet that radical change paths (such as our rejuvenation) will alternate with incremental change paths. Radical ways of thinking and new mindsets will not be sustained. Changes in corporate culture have limited capacities.

Looking back, we should have anticipated the gloomy supposition that sustained success may require continuous oscillation. Over the last 12 years, for example, Unilever has seen three periods of sharp upheaval followed by periods of comparative stability that have foretold of relative decline. All of our successful firms that we valued for their rejuvenation have had to undergo further shocks to stay competitive. There seem to be some natural limits to 'smooth' evolution.

Paradoxically, of our four successful rejuvenators one firm, Edwards High Vacuum (EHV), that succeeded in maintaining industry leadership did so by progressively *imitating* others' experiments. Sixteen new Japanese entrants challenged EHV in one year during the early 1990s. It responded by reverse-engineering all the new competing machines and found that the Japanese had solved a number of its own technical problems. EHV then imitated these innovations, doubling its world market share and reinforcing the competitiveness born of supple processes and multi-skilled workforces. But imitation brings in its train the routines of cost control and consistency. Even EHV has found it imperative to repeat the cycle.

There is a further reason to suppose that oscillation is likely. As Doz, Santos, and Williamson show in their metanational model earlier in this volume, the imperative for successful firms is the melding of knowledge from all over the world. But knowledge does not travel easily and tends to follow established, socially defined tracks. Distributed knowledge structures have in-built inflexibility.

It seems that firms are destined to repeat the cycle of rejuvenation and, in the knowledge economy, this seems to be required at ever-shorter intervals. Some of the high-technology darlings of the 1990s are already showing all the signs of mental maturity we examined in older industries. If that is indeed so, then we can mitigate the pain of repeating the cycle by developing early-warning systems that signal the need for change before the inertia becomes endemic. Quite how to do that effectively requires another cycle of research.

14 The Invisible Underpinnings of Corporate Rejuvenation: Purposeful Action Taking by Individuals

Sumantra Ghoshal[1] and Heike Bruch[2]

[1]*London Business School and* [2]*University of St Gallen*

'Can a mature business turn itself into a successful one?' Charles Baden-Fuller and John Stopford asked in the first chapter of their 1994 book *Rejuvenating the Mature Business*. The answer, obvious from the title, was a resounding yes. 'It is amazing that a caterpillar can turn into a butterfly. The caterpillar creeps along the ground, has limited horizons, and is unable to move quickly. Yet, that small furry larva can become one of nature's most graceful creatures, able to fly and traverse a much wider terrain. Naturally, one might doubt that a mature firm could become dynamic and entrepreneurial, yet such a metamorphosis is possible.'

Having started with this bold assertion, Baden-Fuller and Stopford presented a compelling case with some rigorously researched illustrations of how such a change could be achieved. Their 'crescendo' model, suggesting a step-by-step approach to revitalizing companies, has since been widely acknowledged as a powerful framework for driving corporate transformation.

In management research, there is always the intrigue of the ultimate cause. Explanations of all organizational outcomes resemble an onion – there are always layers under each layer, always an underlying causation, typically at a lower level of analysis, of a phenomenon observed at a higher level of analysis.

Baden-Fuller and Stopford's analysis of corporate rejuvenation focused on the strategic and the organizational levels of a company. They demonstrated how Edwards High Vacuum, Richardson Sheffield, Hotpoint, and a number of other companies moved up the strategic staircase, building layers of capabilities to shape dynamic organizations.

But this poses the next question: ultimately, what served as the engine of each company's ability to do these things? Why were they able to take these actions while others could not or did not?

Anything that happens in a company is a result of one or more individuals doing something. Several scholars have recently emphasized the important role of individual action taking in explaining strategic and organizational outcomes and have argued for refocusing academic work on management at this level of analysis. In no area of research is this need more important than in the analysis of corporate change.

Our goal here is to build on the arguments that Baden-Fuller and Stopford presented in *Rejuvenating the Mature Business* by looking at the underlying individual-level action taking that leads to corporate rejuvenation. We can do that because of the rich research cases that they wrote on some of the companies they studied – for example Stopford's case Rejuvenation of Edwards High Vacuum', (London Business School, 1989), because others have written cases on the same companies covering the same issues (for example Chris Bartlett and Ashish Nanda's case Richardson Sheffield, Harvard Business School, 1992), and because of our own personal familiarity with some of the key managers such as Danny Rosenkranz, who masterminded the turnaround of Edwards and then went on to become the CEO of BOC, the parent company.

Individual-level Drivers of Organizational Outcomes: Looking Again at Richardson Sheffield

To establish the basic premises of our argument, let us start by looking at one of the companies that played a key role in shaping Baden-Fuller and Stopford's views on the crescendo model of rejuvenation: Richardson Sheffield.

The model suggests four sequential steps in the rejuvenation process: galvanizing the top team; simplifying the tasks; building capabilities; and leveraging those capabilities (see Figure 14.1). Let us explore beyond these 'what to dos' to the 'how tos': how were these organization-level outcomes brought about at Richardson Sheffield?

As Baden-Fuller and Stopford themselves point out, the real process of galvanizing the top team started at Richardson Sheffield after Bryan Upton, the new CEO, visited Japan and recognized how much improvement was possible in the company's manufacturing practices. But what was it about Upton that allowed him to transform the basic thinking of his managers in so radical a way?

To answer this question we need to look deeper into the individual and for that we can seek guidance from the Bartlett and Nanda case on the company. As they described him, Upton was a man 'who never says no to an order, and never takes no for an answer'. In Upton's own words: 'I am not an easy person to get along with. But I am not difficult. I'm just demanding. I will unload lorries on the dock, if need be. I'm the first in, and the last out. I believe in leadership by example.'

Bartlett and Nanda also provide a specific illustration that brings the personality of Upton to life: 'For example, on one of his frequent shop floor rounds, he saw knife blades that had been dropped near a machine. He took some 10 pence coins from his pocket, threw them on the floor and, in full hearing of the workers, asked the supervisor, "would you leave these coins lying on the floor? Well, those blades are worth much more."'

It was this demanding, direct, and forceful individual who converted Richardson's managers like Kathy Sanchez, Bob Russel, Tony Seagrave, and Denise Ogden into passionate, determined, and persistent action takers. 'Galvanizing the top team' is, therefore, the concrete outcome of the behaviours of senior managers, of specific

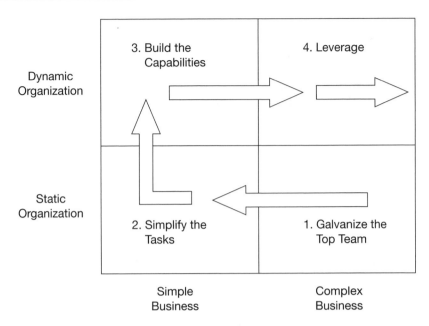

Figure 14.1—The crescendo model (reproduced with permission from Baden-Fuller and Stopford, 1992, p. 153).

and persistent actions taken by the leader. Bartlett and Nanda capture this under-lying individual-level stimulus of galvanization very accurately in the following quote from one of the company's managers:

> 'Bryan personalizes the culture of our company. In order to survive here, you have got to be very open and have a sunny personality, yet be able to work under pressure and give and take with Bryan and others. Those who are quiet or sensitive are so unhappy that they have to leave. And yet, we have built a great team here. Many in the company would walk through fire for Bryan. He is very enthusiastic and his enjoyment of what he is doing is very infectious.'

It is the same high-energy action taking by Upton that leads to the 'simplifying the tasks' step. He closes down knife assembly to focus the entire organization on blade production. His clarity about the future of Richardson and his obsession with improving productivity was behind this step, which, without that clarity, obsession, and self-confidence, would appear to be highly counter-intuitive at best or completely misguided at worst.

However, the story of Richardson is not merely the story of determined action taking by one individual. It is the story of purposive action taking by many. What Baden-Fuller and Stopford describe as 'building the capabilities' is nothing other than individuals like Sanchez, the then customer liaison manager, taking persis-tent, determined action to build up the company's marketing capabilities, and Bob Russel, David Williams, and Gordon Bridge, the company's manufacturing man-agers, developing new manufacturing capabilities. If a key element of Richardson's rejuvenation was the dramatic improvement in its productivity – reflected, for example, in cutting down the blade-grinding operation from a 35-second manual job to a five-second automatic cycle – it came about through the determined action taking of these individuals.

The same is true for the step that Baden-Fuller and Stopford describe as 'leverage'. Richardson's market expansion into Europe was not the outcome of some abstract force – it was the result of Sanchez's relentless efforts to develop these markets. To quote her, from the Bartlett and Nanda case: 'I began doing some simple, basic things, like corresponding in German with German agents. After a visit to the Cologne trade fair in 1976, I became convinced that we could do very well and Bryan supported my initiatives. I looked up the business directory, and wrote personal letters to 300 traders all over the world, enclosing our prices and catalogue. Our export sales rose dramatically, and we won the Queen's award for export achievement in 1986. Today, 60 % of our sales are overseas.'

This is our case: the process of rejuvenation that Baden-Fuller and Stopford described is driven, ultimately, by the action taking of individual managers. To understand rejuvenation, one has to understand that action-taking process. What is it about people like Upton and Sanchez that allows them to accomplish the tasks that underlie the different stages in the crescendo model?

In terms of both management theory and practice, this question is interesting if only because such purposeful action taking by individuals is so rare in companies. Most managers know what they need to do, at least roughly. The problem is that, knowing what they should do, few managers actually do it. At the level of senior managers, this 'action gap' has its effects not so much in day-to-day routine activities but in the area of strategic actions that are vital for leading change and renewal.

Over the last five years, our own research has primarily focused on the issue of individual-level action taking that underlies corporate rejuvenation. While the overall research project has included interview-based case research as well as empirical surveys in several companies, we will focus here on our learnings from one company, the German airline Lufthansa.

Over the last five years, we have followed this company closely, observing at first hand its experiments and experiences with managing change and renewal. Over this period, the company has changed completely – from near-bankruptcy and a DM 730 million loss in 1991 to a record profit of DM 2.5 billion in 2000 and global leadership in most of its business areas. While led firmly from the top by CEO Jürgen Weber, this widely acclaimed transformation of Lufthansa was the product of more than a hundred projects initiated and executed by middle-level managers in different parts of the company. We have followed several of these projects, some extremely effective and others less so, and observed action and non-action on the part of the managers responsible for them.

These observations have revealed certain typical behavioural patterns of managers and some insights into why some managers take purposeful action – as did those in Baden-Fuller and Stopford's cases of rejuvenation – while others do not. We have distilled these learnings into a simple framework that we present in the following pages. The framework shows the different pathologies that lead to non-action of different kinds and also the individual-level requirements for purposeful action taking. Having presented the framework, we then explore its implications in terms of both what individual managers can do to enhance their own action-taking capabilities and what corporate leaders can do to create an organizational context that facilitates rejuvenation by engaging the action-taking abilities of people.

The Drivers of Purposeful Action

One of the central traps of management is that 'being active' is confused with action. Most managers are not passive. On the contrary, as Henry Mintzberg documented in his groundbreaking book *The Nature of Managerial Work*, a manager's day is usually busy and there is seldom any relief from the workload. There is practically no interruption in 'doing' – attending meetings, talking, writing letters, and so on. During a typical day, managers face a constant stream of demands for their time and attention. Usually, more problems arise than they can deal with.

However, the strategic importance of a problem is rarely the basis of priority of response. Rather, managers tend to ignore or postpone problems that require reflection, systematic planning, or creative thinking, and for which there is no external pressure for immediate action.

Fuzzy, complex problems, or those that require additional resources, large blocks of time, or support are squeezed out by coping with immediate operational issues. The capacities of many managers get absorbed in daily routines, superficial behavioural patterns, and poorly prioritized or unfocused activities – briefly, in 'active non-action'. Active non-action is, according to our observations, a central behavioural hazard of managers.

This lack of purposive action is not because managers can't act. As all the examples in *Rejuvenating the Mature Business* illustrate, managers *can* act. As a rule, their jobs provide sufficient scope and freedom, and yet relatively few managers actually make deliberate use of their action-taking opportunities. Most, in contrast,

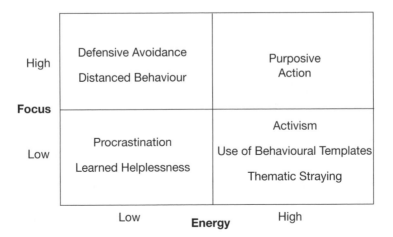

Figure 14.2—Purposeful action vs active non-action.

get lost in the stream of their own activities. They spend their time making the inevitable happen instead of purposively making happen what otherwise would not happen.

What is the difference between 'being active' and taking purposive action? Our observations in Lufthansa and other companies suggest that purposeful action taking has two key drivers – energy and focus (see Figure 14.2) – and that the pathologies of active non-action arise from the lack of either one or both of these drivers.

Low Energy

Action demands energy. The preceding discussion on the Richardson Sheffield case clearly shows the enormous amount of energy that managers like Upton and Sanchez brought to their action taking. Similarly, the one defining characteristic of Rosenkranz, the key actor in Baden-Fuller and Stopford's story of Edwards High Vacuum, was his boundless energy.

In contrast to these action takers, some managers we studied at Lufthansa failed to take purposive action simply because they lacked the energy – at least for the activities necessary to drive radical change. Some of them were exhausted or burnt out from stress and did not have the inner resources to re-energize themselves for the required change. For others, the lack of energy was relevant to the specific projects, which somehow were not meaningful to them.

In all cases the managers concerned continued to perform their routine tasks – attending meetings, writing notes, making phone calls, and so on. But they were unable to marshal self-initiated and self-driven energy for the non-routine tasks of their projects. This lack of energy manifested itself in a variety of ways.

Instead of acknowledging the need for change, some practised 'defensive avoidance', allowing themselves to perpetuate their accustomed patterns of thinking and acting that had been continuously reinforced and refined over long periods of time. Indeed, as Stopford's case on the company makes clear, this is precisely what the predecessors of Rosenkranz did at Edwards. Instead of actively coping with problems, they refused to put any energy into thinking about the need for change and even less into doing something about it. On the contrary, they were investing their energies into legitimizing their unwillingness to confront reality and their avoidance of the need to act.

Defensive avoidance was indeed the central reason for the 'late awakening' of Lufthansa when it was on the brink of bankruptcy in 1991. Although the entire industry faced a severe market downturn and the need for fundamental change was obvious, the company realized the need to act far later than many other airlines. Engaged in an expansionary strategy grounded in the belief that in the airline industry only the biggest would survive, most managers continued to ignore or reinterpret market signals, convincing themselves that there was no internal problem and that their planned course of action was right.

Although an awareness of a serious crisis began to spread in early 1992, most Lufthansa managers were so programmed on growth and success that employment continued to rise over the first six months of the year despite massive operating losses. It needed a deep emotional shock to unleash the energies for action that had been blocked in defensive avoidance until the middle of 1992.

Even after the turnaround had started, several managers considered the change to be 'not that important'. 'Lufthansa – the German airline – could never die' was their ultimate refuge. Others distanced themselves personally from their roles in the transformation, having problems, for example, with reducing the work force. Still others were frustrated about the poor situation, expected the change efforts not to be successful, or did not see how their activities contributed to the overall transformation process and therefore only half-heartedly engaged in the change. All of them practised what we have labelled as 'distanced behaviour'.

In all cases, distanced behaviour stemmed from a feeling of being forced to do something that lacked personal meaning. Since they did not fully believe in what they were doing these managers performed with little energy. In consequence, their activities lacked drive and were in most cases ineffective. Due to their inner reservations, they refused to take initiatives.

Paradoxically, such half-hearted action was more exhausting than highly energetic behaviour. Being mostly reactive, their distanced behaviour involved little foresight so that most incidents occurred unexpectedly. This, in turn, created emotional and cognitive overload and managers who engaged in distanced behaviour suffered far more from stress or burnout than their more energetic colleagues. Furthermore, they were also exhausted from the emotional costs of not being involved – they were expending energy to justify and protect their inner distance.

Low Focus

Lack of focus in managerial activity is even more common and more critical than lack of energy. Particularly for motivated managers, energetic but unfocused behaviour is probably the most dangerously seductive non-action.

Faced with a high need for action, especially in combination with time pressure, some Lufthansa managers tended to 'activism' – highly energetic behaviour that was superficially or insufficiently planned, not consciously chosen, and not geared to specific goals. As one of the project leaders told us: 'Everybody knew and felt that we had to do everything possible to reduce costs . . . so I started trying to make savings in my area and – I have to admit – not always using my brain. It's only human that in such situations you are dominated by the feeling that something has to happen quickly and you just can't think. In that process, I made major mistakes, which we had to later correct at considerable cost. Afterwards it was clear to me, but not at that moment.'

Managers are more likely to fall victim to activism in a crisis. However, our observations reveal that almost every manager has a weakness for the 'doer tendency' that is typical of activism. Even in routine business situations, many managers create a quasi-crisis, driving themselves and others into a state of frenzy – for no objective reason. Their doer tendency shows up as an increased readiness to react rashly or on impulse and deal with immediate problems while neglecting long-term issues, resulting in short-sighted strategies.

For some other Lufthansa managers, a lack of focus showed up in the use of established 'behavioural templates'. Faced with a crisis, they continued to do what they used to do, only with greater vigour. Essentially, instead of generating new and more appropriate strategies they practised their outdated behaviour more intensively. On the other hand, some managers developed new behavioural strategies but they did so without real thought. Because they had not really understood why they should give up their former habits, they fell back on outdated patterns of behaviour and ingrained ways of doing things. Some gave way to negative emotions such as anger, depression, or anxiety and resorted to displacement activities or extensive and uncontrolled trial and error.

A third kind of non-action and a particularly seductive one – indeed, we observed several managers actually enjoying it – is 'thematic straying'. In the excitement of the moment a number of Lufthansa managers became involved in several different projects at once. But, initially euphoric, they soon lost interest in the projects, had difficulty concentrating on one thing, or were overwhelmed by the extent and diversity of demands resulting from the projects. Many ended up simply fire fighting while others abandoned their projects.

These managers pursued a number of different objectives without having a clear idea of priorities. Because they gave the same level of importance to many different goals, they could not commit to a particular project. They failed not because they tried to do too little but because they tried to do too much.

Low Energy and Low Focus

A number of managers agonized about why their projects did not succeed: 'I could have done it but, for God knows what reason, I hesitated and postponed – I somehow could not get started.'

Such procrastination is a very common form of human behaviour and is typically a result of both low energy and low focus. Managers often fall victim to procrastination in the face of deadlines or high-profile projects. They know what they have to do, are motivated to do it, and yet do not do it. Instead they postpone, prevaricate, and engage in displacement activities.

Why did some Lufthansa managers procrastinate? One group tried to avoid activity because of negative energy. Some of them took the task too seriously, were insecure, overexcited, or anxious about failure. Others felt uncomfortable with the task and expected not to enjoy doing it. A few were insufficiently involved and had no commitment to the project. They exhibited exaggerated sensation seeking, showed a low degree of discipline, and evaded serious engagement.

Though they had agreed to the projects they were not really personally involved in them – perhaps because the tasks were not challenging enough, the cost of *not* getting them done was not high, or the purpose of the projects was not really exciting – all of them lacked energy as well as focus.

While almost every manager tended to procrastinate in certain situations, some managers suffered from a persistent deficiency of energy and focus. They coasted along in a state that has been described as 'learned helplessness'.

After repeatedly experiencing that 'making an effort' did not make a difference, they drew the conclusion that taking action was not worth the trouble. As a consequence, they simply gave up because 'it was hopeless to try to achieve anything, anyway'.

Middle managers are particularly prone to learned helplessness because they feel they are not in charge, they are 'externally controlled'.

Even in managers who have accepted change, this can happen when circumstances revert to normal.

During Lufthansa's change project, most managers' jobs were unstructured and involved a high degree of complexity and uncertainty. Counter-intuitively, this complexity and lack of clarity actually had the effect on some people of making them feel free to take action on their own account.

After the turnaround, circumstances became relatively more normal and bureaucracy and formal procedures began to grow again, creating administrative constraints for middle managers. Managers who had become used to being in control had problems dealing with their growing lack of autonomy. Feeling unable actively to affect their environments, several managers 'learned' that it was not worth taking initiatives any more, withdrew their energy, and switched to a passive mode.

A key issue with learned helplessness is that – as opposed to most of the other forms of non-action – it describes a relatively stable behavioural tendency. It is based on a deeply internalized perception of lack of control coupled with a highly passive self-understanding. As a consequence, it is one of the most common and debilitating causes of active non-action in companies.

Strategies for Action Taking

The changes at Lufthansa came about because of managerial action. When we observed how the behaviour of managers actively dealing with change problems differed from those who struggled, we found a combination of two dimensions, precisely the same that the rejuvenation leaders demonstrated in Baden-Fuller and Stopford's work.

First, acting managers' behaviours were highly energetic and involved an exertion significantly exceeding the effort made in routine activities. Nobody had forced them to this degree of effort. Their engagement and drive came purely from within themselves – fuelled by a personal commitment to doing the right thing. Overall, their behaviour was characterized by a higher form of personal involvement that distinguished action from 'just doing something'.

Second, their behaviour was clearly focused. Action-taking managers distinguished themselves from those who showed blind activism, used certain behavioural templates, or dissipated their energies. They consciously concentrated their energies and channelled them towards specific projects or goals.

What enabled them to maintain high levels of both personal energy and focus throughout the execution of their projects? We found that they adopted one or more of three key strategies for overcoming the traps of non-action.

Building Personal Volition

While others had difficulties in articulating their goals, action-taking managers in Lufthansa, like Sanchez at Richardson, had a clear notion of what they were doing and why. This does not mean that every step of their action was strictly defined. Some, particularly those responsible for projects involving high levels of complexity and uncertainty, could plan their activities only roughly. Action was sometimes the result of a rather spontaneous or volatile planning process. However, their behaviour never emerged 'by chance'. It always involved a certain degree of awareness of and reflection on the purpose of their actions.

Indeed, all the action-taking managers were not only aware of the purpose of what they were doing but also attached high significance to it. They were personally convinced that their activities served certain higher needs, contributed to something bigger, and were important for the organization. Managers who were involved in the turnaround explained, for example, that their engagement was needed to save Lufthansa. As several of them emphasized, their initiatives directly supported the 'fight for survival', 'staunching the loss of blood', or provided 'first aid' to the corporation.

In all cases, a personal conviction of 'doing the right thing' was accompanied by a high emotional arousal and a feeling of strong personal responsibility for their actions.

This strong sense of ownership was without exception the product of a commitment that was both initiated and driven from within. Managers who acted developed goals beyond what might be expected in their positions and responded to problems proactively rather than waiting to be told what to do or being forced to react.

For Lufthansa's managers, the turnaround involved a large number of unplanned and unexpected events. Those who acted actually enjoyed this situation. As opposed to those who felt threatened or left helpless by the increased uncertainty, they perceived it as an opportunity allowing them to take initiatives, to use creativity, and to quickly push their projects forward. For example, one manager told us: 'I took advantage of the irregular situation – I developed the philosophy that when nobody is responsible, I am responsible. I can own that issue and do what I think is necessary. And I acted accordingly – unless and until Jürgen Weber (Lufthansa's CEO) pulled me back.'

Interestingly, most of these managers did not throttle back their self-driven behaviour when the turbulence of the transformation had eased. On the contrary, although the immediate demands had disappeared and there was no external pressure to do something, acting managers did not lose momentum.

All these managers had gone through a difficult inner process. Some of them described their commitment as being the result of an inner conflict. As one of them, who had taken up a particularly difficult role in the operations team that was put in place to ensure implementation of all the projects, told us: 'I was fully committed. One central moment was in the beginning when a board member asked me: "Do you really want to do this? You may upset everybody during the process and may have to leave the company afterwards. Do you have a problem with that? Do you really want to do this job – think about it". I really struggled for a couple of days. Afterwards I was sure: I really wanted to do it.'

Most reported similar experiences. At first they had reservations, inner conflicts, or doubts. They took time for intensive inner questioning until they were sure what they wanted. Thereafter, they were rarely bothered by reservations. Most of the managers explained that from a certain point on they knew that they would do everything to lead their projects to success.

In contrast, managers who had made spontaneous or ill-considered commitments faced difficulties staying focused on their projects. Typically, they had agreed on a project in a moment of euphoria, often in the process of an emotionally charged group meeting. Or they had assumed that others – their bosses, colleagues, or followers – expected them to engage and did not want to disappoint them. They did not ask themselves what the task meant for them and whether they really wanted to do it.

External forces rather than their own free will had driven them into their projects. In turn, they showed pseudo-commitment or superficial compliance but not a real inner commitment. Having not, like the successful managers, conducted and won their own inner battle earlier, they were constantly struggling with 'inner noise' – reservations, dissonance, the question 'why?' – in the later phases of their projects.

Shaping an Action Context

Managerial work is essentially discretionary in nature and all managers influence their own work environments, whether knowingly or not. Unfortunately, only a few make use of this opportunity to actively shape their own contexts for action.

A second key strategy adopted by those in Lufthansa who were able to take purposive action was to consciously create contextual conditions that allowed them to act. Action-taking managers had a high sensitivity for their job environment. They knew about the hazards of losing focus. They were aware of potential drains on their energy and they were also conscious of constraints and the expectations of others. They used this understanding to reshape their work environments, making them more conducive to purposeful action taking.

They did this in various ways. Some altered the nature of their work to reduce fragmentation, refusing to respond to emails, phone calls, or visitors outside certain periods. Others reserved specific time windows for reflection. Some even concentrated their working relationships on selected core partnerships while minimizing contact with others.

Some deliberately took 'time off' in order not to lose sight of strategic issues. One manager explained to us: 'The processes are so turbulent that I am constantly facing the hazard of getting overwhelmed by the vehemence of all the different forces – expectations, meetings, people, not enough time . . . At times everything starts turning in my head – I am almost not master of what I am doing any more. Just in those moments I slow down and take time off to reflect on what I actually want to achieve. I kind of clean up my head to get a clear picture again of what matters and what is irrelevant "noise". And then I force myself to do what is most important. You can actually leave many things out if you develop the discipline to. Otherwise you plan to do certain things in the morning and when you leave in the evening you haven't done a single piece of what you intended to do.'

Another way of building an action context lies in broadening the scope of discretionary behaviour. A major drain on managers' energy is the perception of having limited influence. It nurtures the feeling of being externally driven, leads to distancing behaviour, and undermines identification with the work. As a rule managerial jobs include choices. However, they are usually insufficiently perceived and exploited. Managers who took strategic action were often not only more aware of their choices and made conscious use of them, they also systematically extended their freedom to act – in particular by making themselves less reactive and dependent on the demands of others. They managed the expectations of their superiors, found ways of independently accessing resources, developed strong network relationships with influential people within the organization, and built specific competencies or a high standing that contributed to broadening their personal space for action and gave them a 'strategic voice'.

One of the consequences of being able to shape their action context was that these managers were also able to operate with a long-term focus. The combination of discipline, broadened personal space for action, and strategic voice allowed them to resist the pressure for quick results and to engage in issues of long-term strategic priority, even during the initial turnaround phase when an intense short-term orientation dominated the psyche of the organization.

For action-taking managers, the basis of their long-term orientation was a behaviour that involved significantly more preparation as well as a better understanding of processes and potential action-taking strategies. The strategic perspective of their activities allowed them to maintain control over their activities. Reactive or impulsive behavioural patterns, in contrast, implied little foresight, forcing managers to react to, and being constrained by, the immediate needs of the moment.

Maintaining Emotional Force

Energetic and focused action taking needs a great deal of emotional force. Yet, managers' jobs in general, and crisis situations in particular, are often highly stressful and involve many calls on their energy. While positive emotions are the fuel for action taking, one of the key energy depleters is emotional stress.

At Lufthansa, every manager was confronted with carrying out painful tasks under difficult circumstances. Most of them not only experienced a substantially increased workload and long-term strain but also a very high level of emotional tension and pressure. As one of these managers explained to us: 'Doing this project pushed me to my limits. Apart from the crushing workload, it was the persistence required that was an enormous strain – overcoming obstacles, solving all different kinds of new problems, dealing with people's emotions and my own . . . all that required my entire force.'

Under these circumstances, only those who were able to re-energize themselves continuously could keep pursuing their projects. Others fell victim to a gradual but inevitable erosion of their emotional energy.

Active non-actors and purposive action takers dealt very differently with these energy-sapping demands of their jobs. The active non-actors were victims of their negative emotions. They were literally consumed by their frustration, paralysed by anxiety, or dominated by negative stress amounting, in some cases, to complete emotional exhaustion and burnout. Action takers, in contrast, actively managed their emotions. They sustained their emotional force by two simple but effective mechanisms.

First, they appeared able to regulate the flow of emotions. They knew exactly how to get rid of negative emotions and inner tensions. Sports helped some let off emotional steam. Others relieved themselves with the help of a personal 'crying wall' – their partner, a good friend, a colleague with whom they could share their fears, frustrations or inner burdens. Most of them could name certain locations or activities that helped them dispose of their negative emotions. For example, one manager told us about his garden, which had a strong stabilizing effect on him. In difficult periods he spent long hours there, often talking to himself about what bothered him. He knew that this would give him back the inner balance needed for moving on to the next step.

Second, most of them had a 'personal well' – a distinct source of positive energy. These wells differed in form. Some managers were active in clubs, others had enriching times with close friends, some loved doing certain things with their partners, and others regularly spent time in certain places, which they particularly enjoyed. In some cases, the crying wall and the personal well were the same people or places but often they were not. What mattered was that those who had a personal well knew what their well meant for them and how to use it.

Creating a 'Desire for the Sea'

What can top managers do to foster purposive action in their organizations? Based on our experience and observations we conclude that there are no levers that allow them to directly create energy and focus in others. Motivating people or telling them what they should do does not go very far. At times, it leads to the exactly opposite result. Top managers feel obliged to provide solutions, make the life of middle managers comfortable, motivate them to carry out certain activities, and so on. These well-intentioned interventions often lead to distancing behaviour, feelings of being externally controlled, and lack of space that destroys positive emotions.

So is there anything that top managers can do? Yes there is. They must stop providing solutions and raise questions instead – and show why solutions are worth finding. They must change the orientation of people away from talking about doing something to consciously committing attention and energy to achieving something.

The French pilot and writer Antoine de Saint-Exupéry coined a striking metaphor: 'If you want to build a ship, don't drum up the men to go to the forest to gather wood, saw it, and nail the planks together. Instead, teach them the desire for the sea.' Herein lies the leadership challenge of creating a propensity for purposive action.

To illustrate what a desire for the sea looks like, let us recall an event that was the starting point of Lufthansa's turnaround. On a weekend in June 1992, Jürgen Weber invited about 20 senior managers to the company's training centre at Seeheim for a meeting that was originally entitled 'Mental Change'. It was aimed at building a network of managers who would drive the change process within the company. Shortly before the workshop Weber got a deeper insight into the acuteness of the crisis and changed the title from 'mental change' to 'crisis management meeting'.

The meeting began with Weber presenting the unvarnished figures. The entire Executive Board was present. There was little debate on the need for drastic actions. The facts were too obvious. Weber made very clear that he himself could not provide a solution. He explained that the participating managers had three days to develop ways for saving Lufthansa. If they came to the conclusion that there was no way of saving the company, he would accept it and bankruptcy was assured. Then he and all the other board members left Seeheim for three days.

One of the participants described to us what happened afterwards: 'No one had an idea of the gravity and the brutality of the crisis. After a long phase of denial or "not wanting to believe", there was a next phase of "searching for the guilty people" which was followed by a massive outburst. After the first phase of discomfort we were sure: Lufthansa was worth fighting for. Then it became actually a completely captivating idea: We would save it. After this, everything went very fast. The goals we committed ourselves to at Seeheim were very ambitious and nobody believed that we could ever meet them, but after this process we committed ourselves to them.' Another participant described a similar experience: 'I was deeply moved. During one or two hours a real concern reigned – because we thought "we won't make it". Then slowly we started accepting the situation and started thinking about first steps. (. . .) With the development of projects and solutions, hope and a kind of positive excitement emerged. After this I developed the will to do whatever it took.'

To involve a larger group of managers, Weber repeated the Seeheim workshop with the same design three times with different groups of 50 people. This was done in order to let those people live through the same process, let them feel the threat and the urgency and not just inform them of the facts and the appropriate strategies which they had to implement. After the meetings the majority of senior managers within the company were 'sworn in'. It was not a rational process that created change energy and volition. It was the emotional process they went through. Afterwards it was their change. They were excited about the idea of saving Lufthansa and they had themselves decided to do it.

The output of the Seeheim meetings was a set of 131 projects or key actions concerning drastic cuts in staff numbers (8,000 positions), lower non-personnel costs including downsizing of the fleet (savings of DM 400 million), and increasing revenues (DM 700 million) to respond to the losses of DM 1.3 billion. Seventy per cent of these projects were implemented during the first three years of the transformation.

A desire for the sea tends to be characterized by the following three general attributes.

- Open space. In order to be creative and, even more important, in order to build volition, people must not only have but also feel the freedom to choose.
- A difficult and challenging problem. Easy problems do not seduce. They do not vitalize the will. They do not excite. They neither activate mental capacities nor people's hearts – difficult problems do.

- A meaningful destination. Many corporations set strategic goals that are not seductive. Instead, an exciting destination, painted on a big canvas with bold strokes, is inspiring. It gives the individual an idea of a better future of which he or she can be a part. A desire for the sea is not abstract; it addresses the entire person and activates fantasy.

In every case of corporate rejuvenation described by Baden-Fuller and Stopford, this was the ultimate common characteristic: the ability of a leader to create a desire for the sea. How they created this desire varied, reflecting their different personalities and styles. The reflective, thoughtful and relatively soft-spoken Rosenkranz inspired his people very differently than the aggressive, loud, and gregarious Upton. But in both cases, the leader painted a picture of a future that captivated all employees and engaged not just their minds but also their hearts.

15 Rejuvenation Revisited: Identifying and Managing Strategy Decay and Innovation

Peter J. Williamson
INSEAD

How many corporations have been able to maintain shareholder returns in the same top quartile as their peers each year for an unbroken run of five years or more? Since the early 1990s the answer is less than five per cent (based on total shareholder return calculations for companies in the S&P 500 and FT 100 stock indices). Indeed, over the past few decades the number of firms able to sustain consistently above-average shareholder returns over an extended period has been declining.

These are humbling statistics. They suggest that there are powerful processes at work that undermine the capacity of almost any single business model (a systematic combination of value and cost drivers) to go on creating new value indefinitely. I call this process 'strategy decay'. As we will see below, strategy decay may occur because competitors undermine a business model by imitating it or because changes in technology or customer taste or behaviour render an existing business model obsolete as a way of making money. Competitors emerge with the proverbial 'better mouse trap'. Changes in customer lifestyles eliminate demand for a product or service. Innovative competitors completely transform the economics of the business.

In the face of strategy decay a corporation can only continue generating new wealth for its shareholders (or ultimately survive) if it can go on rejuvenating itself, renewing its business models in such a way as to create new and distinctive sources of competitive advantage.

Strategy innovation makes this rejuvenation and renewal of business models possible. It is not simply about improvements to a product line or service offering or incremental reductions in costs. It is a fundamental innovation, a significant change in the way a company makes money, that opens up new sources of competitive advantage.

Examples of strategy innovation include: Dell Computer's strategy of combining online ordering and specification with the ability to offer the buyer a computer customized to his or her particular needs; Monsanto's introduction of genetically modified seeds that were selectively resistant to its proprietary herbicide (which allowed a change in the proposition to farmers as well as requiring a fundamental shift in the activity chain that necessitated the integration of the seed supply chain with that for herbicides); and Charles Schwab's successive innovations that have taken it from discount broker, through e-Schwab trading and investment portal, to Schwab Access, a mix of transactions account and money market fund that pays much higher interest than a bank.

Below we explore how a company can improve its chances of continually rejuvenating its business model by creating a flow of profitable and opportune strategy innovations. The analysis builds on the seminal work of John Stopford and Charles Baden-Fuller in their book *Rejuvenating the Mature Business*, which introduced what they called the 'crescendo model' of rejuvenation – starting with small-scale experiments and working up to larger investments. This chapter extends their approach, exploring more fully the management of a rejuvenation pipeline from idea to large-scale business. It also seeks to add an element of uncertainty more explicitly into the model, discussing the need to create a portfolio of alternative paths to rejuvenation that provide a set of 'options on the future', each designed to help give the firm a head start in taking advantage of opportunities as an uncertain future unfolds.

Before embarking on heavy investment in rapid rejuvenation, however, many managers ask if the need for rejuvenation is urgent and whether their business really is mature. Stopford and Baden-Fuller rightly point out that 'maturity is a state of mind' but this still leaves the managerial question of how far and how fast a company's established strategy is decaying and therefore how urgently the launch of a strategy innovation is required. This is the question we turn to first.

Measuring Strategy Decay

Most of us put off going to the dentist as long as possible; it's one of those things we never quite get around to. Those well-polished teeth look fine from the outside because the decay is within. When the pain comes, it comes with a 'bang' because that unseen decay is already so well advanced it has hit a sensitive nerve. Strategy decay works much the same way. Traditional measures of performance frequently tell us everything is fine until we hit the nerve and our world starts falling apart. Worse still, even when the decay is already severe, workhorse metrics like ROCE and ROI may be signalling that our strategy is working better than ever.

An important reason that traditional metrics are not good at warning of strategy decay is that when we measure profitability we don't ask whether the profit is the result of creating new value or whether we are just milking the positions we, or our management forebears, have previously put in place. In other words, how much of today's profit is coming from creating new value and how much is really the rents we are collecting on the assets we inherited?

Four Measures of Strategy Decay

If we cannot rely on traditional profit measures to tell us when a strategy is decaying, are there other early warning signs? Four basic measures can be used to help diagnose strategy decay:

- divergence between revenue growth and earnings growth;
- rising ROCE but falling P/E multiple;
- profits highly dependent on rents from declining assets;
- convergence of strategies in the industry.

If a company scores in the danger zone on these measures, especially where several point in the same direction, it should be concerned that its strategy is showing signs of decay.

Divergence Between Revenue Growth and Earnings Growth

For a year or two, maybe even a few more, profits can grow very much faster than revenues. We often see this phenomenon in the turnaround of companies in trouble. The same thing happens when margins rise either through higher prices or squeezing costs. But few companies are in the enviable position of being able to maintain price increases over and above the rate of inflation in their costs year after year for decades.

The fact is that there is a limit to how much profit even the best-managed, most efficient company can squeeze out of any fixed amount of revenue (the well-known law of diminishing returns). As a member of the US Federal Reserve once put it: 'things that cannot go on forever do eventually stop'.

Therefore, if a company's revenue growth has been consistently falling behind its profit growth year after year, it needs to worry that it will soon hit the limit. The capacity of its strategy to generate future profit growth will be in deep decay.

The same holds true if revenue is growing faster than profits year after year. That means the company is working a bigger and bigger operation successively harder for a smaller and smaller increment to the bottom line. Its wheels are spinning. Again, the capacity of its strategy to generate future profit is in decay.

Put the things together and it becomes clear that if the *ratio* of a company's earnings growth to revenue growth diverges a long way from 1 for an extended period (say five or 10 years) then the strategy is probably decaying. Profits growing at a slightly faster rate than revenue is good. But when you see earnings growth or revenue growth outstripping the other year after year that should be a warning sign.

Now, of course, the test 'a long way from 1' is inherently subjective. So to understand how to use the measure in practice, we need to look at some data. Consider the ratio of profit growth to revenue growth over the five years to 1998 for companies like Danone (1.08), Glaxo Wellcome (1.00), L'Oréal (0.94), Nokia (1.14), and Tesco (0.89). Earnings and revenue were pretty much in balance over the medium term (the ratio was close to 1).

But over the same five-year period some companies saw earnings growing tens or even hundreds of times faster than revenues – like Bass (25x), Cadbury Schweppes (17x), GKN (25x), or KLM (38x). Ask yourself how long that can go on. These companies are squeezing dramatically more out of the same revenue base. It looks like they are milking the businesses with a fire hose. This is a warning sign of strategy decay. The capacity of the strategy to generate earnings growth in the future looks extremely doubtful.

At the other end of the spectrum we have companies seeing rapid growth in revenues while profit growth has stalled so that their ratio of earnings growth to revenue growth in the five years to 1998 is well below 1. Examples include British Telecommunications (0.26), Fiat (0.53), and Lafarge (0.39). Just as for those companies for which the ratio was very high, these low statistics are also a sign of strategy decay. The potential of these companies' strategies to create value is just about spent; they can grow revenue but only by practically giving away incremental products and services at close to zero profit.

The bottom line is that if a company's ratio of earnings growth to revenue growth consistently diverges from 1, either above or below, by a large margin (say, over 2 or less than 0.5), then there are probably problems round the corner because its strategy is decaying from within.

Rising ROCE but Falling P/E Multiple

When a company breaks yet another record in the return it delivers on its capital employed (ROCE reaches new heights) the managers may be congratulating themselves. But if, at the same time, its price earnings ratio (P/E) is falling, the market is telling it something: 'You may be earning record profits now, but we are going to mark down your share price because we don't think you can continue to deliver this rate of return long term.' That's another way of saying: 'we believe your strategy is in decay'.

The reason is simple. If a company is delivering strong earnings on its assets today but the multiple of those earnings investors are willing to pay for its shares (which are a claim on future earnings) is going down (a falling P/E), it can only be for one of two reasons. Either investors think the risk associated with those future earnings has increased; or they are expecting future earnings to tail off. In either case, their assessment is that the strategy is in a process of decay.

As shown in Figure 15.1, Bass, Cadbury Schweppes, Bowthorpe, Williams, Cable and Wireless, and Pirelli increased their ROCE consistently between 1993 and 1998 but their P/E ratio fell during the period. What are investors telling these companies? That they may be squeezing more and more profits out of their strategy but are draining blood from their veins. Year on year their strategy is decaying further.

Worse still, of course, is if both ROCE and the P/E are falling. This was the case for companies like Fiat, TI Group, and De La Rue. In this case, investors were not only seeing a decline in earnings today but were telling the company they expected its returns to decline in the future as well.

The message is clear: if a company is earning more on its capital but its P/E has stalled or is declining, that company's strategy is probably decaying. If both ROCE and P/E are falling, its strategy is, well, 'decayed'.

Profits Highly Dependent on Rents from Declining Assets

The third measure of strategy decay is to take a hard look at what proportion of profits represent the rent on assets that have passed their prime. Again, looking at

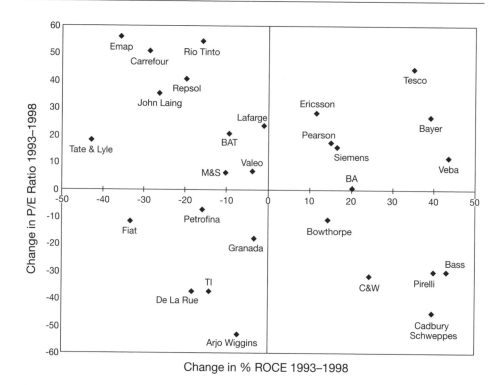

Figure 15.1—ROCE, P/E and strategy decay.

traditional profit measures doesn't give us any answers to this question: to historic cost accounting all sources of economic rents are the same. But from a strategic standpoint the underlying state of the assets (tangible or intangible) that are producing the rents matters a great deal. This is because some assets are sustainable rent producers and others are not.

Rents on a patent, for example, will run out when the patent expires, as will fixed-term concessions for everything from mineral rights to the franchise to operate a toll road or railway. Sustainability can also be greatly affected by whether the asset is being maintained or allowed to wither. Are the profits of the company highly dependent on a brand that is being starved of marketing reinvestment? What proportion of the profits are derived from rents on an installed base of equipment or service agreements where the churn rate is increasing? Unless they are being continually renewed, most strategic assets on which a company collects rents sooner or later begin to depreciate. When this happens, the profit-generating capacity of a strategy that is based on those assets begins to decay. Once the property begins to collapse, so, too, do the rents.

It's not an easy task to judge how much of any year's profit comes from rents on declining assets. But even if this can't be done with pinpoint accuracy, it's a worthwhile discipline. Filling in Table 15.1 is a first step.

Table 15.1—Evaluation of declining assets

Source of rent (strategic asset)	% of current profit
Patents with declining duration	
Installed base showing increased customer churn	
Long-term contracts with declining duration	
Competencies or brands where reinvestment is declining	
Other declining assets	
TOTAL	

If the total number is more than 50 % then the majority of reported profits are rents that depend on declining assets. Nothing wrong with being a good rent collector as long as you are building new strategic assets and creating new value for customers at the same time. If you are not replenishing and extending the asset stock, then you are living off a legacy that, one day, will run out. The higher the percentage gets the more a company needs to worry about how long old strategic assets will go on yielding those rents in the face of depreciation and expiry.

Convergence of Strategies in the Industry

In a survey of more than 500 CEOs sponsored by MCI, a majority said that the strategies of the industry leaders had become more alike rather than more dissimilar over recent years. This should be a warning light. Under economists' notion of 'perfect competition' every business follows an identical strategy. The textbook result is that every company in the industry only makes just enough profit to survive and no more. It is the business equivalent of a subsistence economy.

The final indicator of strategy decay, therefore, is convergence between a company's strategy and those of its main competitors. One ready indicator of convergence is the degree to which the standard deviation in operating margins across competitors is declining.

Two forces are at work to make this happen.

First, competitive imitation means that the major companies end up offering products and services with little differentiation for consumers to choose between. Hence they buy on price, the industry becomes 'commoditized', and margins decline towards a common minimum.

Second, higher-cost, less-competitive firms are either forced out of the business or are acquired so that scale and operating efficiency become prerequisites simply to remain in the business. As costs find a lower floor, there is pressure to cut prices in the quest for volume. Margins are squeezed.

Figure 15.2 presents the data for the computer software and insurance broking industries. In insurance broking the strategies of the main players seem to be converging. Operating margins are becoming more similar and the average margin is falling. By contrast, in computer software, the players appear to be developing innovative strategies that push their operating margins above those of competitors.

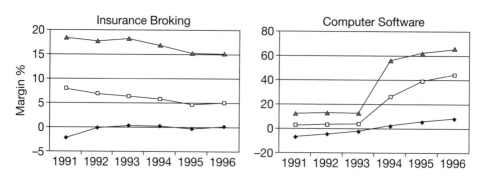

Figure 15.2—Strategy convergence and divergence.

A Composite Measure

If we put these four indicators of strategy decay together, we can make an assessment of a company's Strategy Decay Rate (SDR) – a measure of how fast its strategy is running out of steam. An average score of 'somewhat' or 'yes' puts it in the danger zone (see Table 15.2).

If a company's strategy is decaying, what can it do about it? Even more importantly, what actions can a company take to begin renewing its strategy before strategy decay becomes too advanced? One important answer to these questions is to build and actively manage a rich portfolio of strategic 'options on the future'.

Strategy as Options on the Future

This section begins by illustrating what happens when a company that lacks a sufficient portfolio of strategic options faces strategy decay. It then discusses what a strategy that embodies a coherent portfolio of options for the future might look like and sketches a process managers can use to develop this kind of strategy.

Table 15.2—Assessing strategy decay rates (SDR)

Indicator	No	Somewhat	Yes
Ratio of earnings to revenue growth over five years diverges from one by a wide margin (>2 or <0.5)			
Rising ROCE and falling P/E (or both falling) over last five years			
High percentage of my profits are rents from declining strategic assets			
Standard deviation in margin across competitors in my industry is below average			

Lack of Options as a Powerful Constraint on a Company's Future

Successful companies often get ahead of their competitors by focusing their efforts on a particular segment of customers or geographical market so that they come to know more than anyone else about the behaviour and needs of these potential buyers. They design a profit-generating engine, based on a particular price, margin, and cost structure, that is in turn underpinned by a set of investments in the capability to source, produce, distribute, and support a product or service these customers value. Over time, this profit engine is continually fine-tuned, often reaping economies of scale, scope, and learning along the way.

The history of Woolworth provides a good example of this process. Frank Winfield Woolworth, who founded the company in 1879, pioneered the idea of selling merchandise at no more than five cents. He refined this 'five-and-dime' profit engine to become a finely tuned general merchandising machine. Initial concepts of 'no-frills' service, focus on cheap products, and items that were non-perishable, provided the core. Woolworth subsequently developed its competencies in managing a very wide product range while keeping stock-turn high by carrying only the most popular 'standard' varieties of each product; it added competencies in site selection and development and the logistics to reap economies of scale from a chain of stores.

When he died in 1919, Woolworth had a chain of 1,081 stores with sales of $119 million (an incredible figure for its day). The power of the formula was reflected in the company's headquarters building in New York, which, at 792 feet, was the world's tallest skyscraper until the Chrysler building was completed in 1930. After the second world war the company continued to improve this winning formula, adding new competencies in the management of advertising, consumer credit, and self-service as well as site selection and management in the new retailing environment of American suburbia.

Woolworth's strategy had the advantages of focus. It was able to deepen its existing competencies and incrementally expand both its competency base and its knowledge of different market environments (such as suburban retailing). However, competitors were developing retail formats that required both competencies and market knowledge that were outside the 'box' in which Woolworth was operating. Competitors like Wal-Mart were introducing general merchandise discount super-stores on one flank and speciality 'category killers' (like Toys-R-Us) were attacking on the other.

Despite seeing its overall sales figures declining in real terms year after year (recall our measures of 'strategy decay' above), Woolworth failed to invest in creating the new capabilities or understanding of different market behaviours that would give it options to expand its business into either superstores or speciality retailing.

When, in the late 1980s, Woolworth eventually did try to respond with its own discount and speciality stores, it ran into a hidden constraint. While the strategy made sense, the company had not built the depth of capabilities and market knowledge necessary to gain competitive advantage against determined rivals in these new areas.

Woolworth, in fact, did not have the option to change its strategy quickly because it had not invested in creating new capabilities and knowledge outside its existing formula. Thus, by 1995 it was forced to sell its new speciality stores Kids Mart and Little Folks, established in the early 1990s, because of poor profitability. The company had become a prisoner of its past.

In 1993 Woolworth closed 400 stores in the US and sold its 122 Canadian Woolco stores to Wal-Mart. In 1997 the company closed its last general merchandise store in the US. It had refined and polished its economic engine and deepened its narrow range of competencies into almost perfect extinction. The company had invested in new strategic options too late given the time needed to build the stock of competencies and knowledge of new formats necessary to pursue a new strategy to confront well-established competitors.

In fact, however, Woolworth had invested in one new strategic option that arguably saved the company. In 1974 senior managers had decided to back an experiment in speciality retailing called Footlocker. The pilot lay more or less dormant as a small venture for almost a decade. But when growth in the sports footwear market took off in the wake of growing health consciousness among the American population in the 1980s, Woolworth was able to exercise this option to rapidly build a chain of sports shoes stores, using new retailing capabilities and knowledge of this market segment accumulated in the Footlocker venture. It subsequently introduced new formats, including Lady Footlocker in 1982 and Kids Footlocker in 1987.

Over time, Woolworth opened over 7,100 of these stores and in June 1998 changed its corporate name to Venator Group, reputedly to convey an image of virile sportsmen. In some ways this is an example of successfully repositioning a company whose core business had become obsolete. But, in fact, Woolworth paid a high price for failing to recognize the hidden constraint on its strategy choices and underinvesting in the creation of new strategic options soon enough. It is now a much smaller company, a contraction perhaps best epitomized by the fact that it now occupies only half the floors in that famous New York landmark, which it sold in April 1998.

From the late 1980s, Woolworth had set itself challenging new missions. But in the quest to achieve them, its managers kept bumping up against two important constraints: they did not really understand the different set of customers they would need to attract to achieve a new, broader strategy; nor did they have the capabilities to deliver the advantages necessary to compete with rivals that were already established. They had expanded their ambitions but they had not invested in enough real options, soon enough, to replace their dying profit engine. They were caught in the box depicted in Figure 15.3.

To avoid becoming a prisoner of hidden constraints, a company must maintain a portfolio of new options for its future by building new capabilities and simultaneously expanding its knowledge of new market segments and customer behaviour.

These options on the future may take various forms:

- *an idea* for a new opportunity that has been thought through but not tested;
- *an experiment* or *pilot* that has been conducted to test a new business model or market proposition;

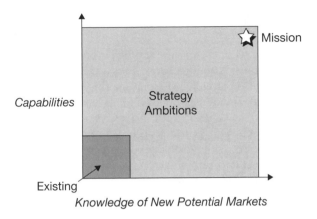

Figure 15.3—The hidden constraints: narrow capabilities and market knowledge.

- *a venture* where the pilot has been launched as a stand-alone business but not yet scaled up or rolled out into a fully-fledged division.

The choice of whether to maintain an option on the future as an idea, as an experiment, or as a venture involves a trade-off between cost and speed. Maintaining the option as an idea minimizes the cost of the option – an idea does not involve much investment. But the speed with which we can exercise that option and its power as a launching pad for a new business is limited by the fact that we have not tested the idea or developed it into a business venture.

By contrast, if we decide to develop every option in our portfolio to the point where it has been launched as a venture, the total investment required could be huge. Developing the option through to the venture stage, however, has the advantage that it will be much quicker to scale up into a fully fledged business when the environment makes it opportune to do so (as Woolworth did when it decided to scale up its Footlocker venture).

As we will see later, it makes sense for a company to maintain a portfolio of options on the future at different stages of development depending on its assessment of the trade-off between investment cost and the likely benefits of positioning itself to react faster than the competition.

Provided the outcome of developments in the market falls within the range of its portfolio of options, a company will be in a position to exercise one or more of the options that turn out to be relevant. Exercising such an option will allow it to reposition its strategy rapidly when changes in the market environment make this necessary. By creating strategic options, some of which (it is hoped) turn out to be relevant to the future, the company will be in a position to out-perform competitors that have not made these investments.

Alternatively it will be in a better position to close the competitive gap with rivals who, for historical reasons, already possess the necessary capabilities and market knowledge (because, for example, they happen to be serving a particular segment of the market that subsequently 'takes off').

Optimizing a Portfolio of Strategic Options

Clearly it will cost money to open up new strategic options. A company must therefore create a finite portfolio of options. How does a manager know if he or she has created the right portfolio of strategic options for the future?

The good news is that this question can be answered without pretending to be able to forecast the exact volume of sales, prices, or input costs five years hence. But traditional spreadsheets with spurious accuracy to two decimal places five years into the future have to be set aside. Instead, to begin creating the right set of options we need to take a view on two sets of factors.

First, broadly what alternative capabilities might be needed to profitably meet probable customer needs in the future (for example, digital or analogue technology, localization or individual customization, high levels of variety, reduced lead times, bundled products and services, and so on)?

Second, which potential future markets (geographical, customer, or non-user segments) or new customer behaviours (such as the impact of the growth of e-commerce) will it be important to start learning about so that we have the option to respond to them in the future?

At this level, far above the detail of unit sales and prices, we can probably forecast with reasonable accuracy. An interesting example is John Naisbitt, who in 1984 analysed 6,000 local newspapers in the US to isolate 10 'megatrends' in his book of the same name.

They were developments such as 'customers would demand a combination of high-tech combined with high-touch'; that 'globalization would mean a combination of more shared production with more cultural assertiveness in individual markets'; and that there would be an 'option explosion' in which customers across more and more industries would demand not just 'chocolate or vanilla' but a huge variety of alternative product or service specifications.

Most of these broad 'predictions' came to pass, largely because they were not predictions at all but trends already underway that simply gathered pace with the passage of time. They are exactly the kinds of views of the future that companies need to know to assess the set of capabilities and market knowledge necessary to generate a sound portfolio of strategic options. Asking, for example, what kind of capabilities are needed to increase options to provide future customers with massively more variety means thinking about what this means for operations, inventory systems, and sales force training. The answers will obviously differ industry by industry and from company to company but we can make a fair 'guestimate' of what they are.

Once a list of alternative new capabilities, market environments, and behaviours that might figure in the future has been accumulated, a table of the main alternatives a company is likely to face can be created. An example of such a table of contingencies identified by Japan's innovative mobile operator, NTT DoCoMo, is illustrated in Figure 15.4.

Once the feasible options have been identified, planners must then decide whether or not to make the investment needed to include a particular option in the company's portfolio. In Figure 15.4, for example, NTT DoCoMo will have to decide whether or not to invest in an option on each of the possible combinations

Market Demand

Technologies	Interactive	Point-to-Point	One-Way	Multipoint
Video	Video conferencing Videophone	Remote medical diagnosis Videomail	Data catalogue shopping Remote education	Mobile TV
Still Image		Web access	Video on demand Digital newspaper Mobile video player	Advanced car navigation
Audio Data			'Karaoke' Mobile audio player	Mobile radio
Text Data	Mobile banking	Email Short message		
Speech	Telephone	Voicemail		

Figure 15.4—Options on the future at NTT DoCoMo.

of technology and market demand ('states of the world') that it has identified. These decisions should be the result of three considerations: the costs of creating and maintaining the option; the estimated probability that the options will be exercised; the probability that creating the option will itself spawn future options, even if it remains unexercised (for example, a company may value an option not for its direct profit-making potential but because of its capacity to open up future options that rely on the technology it relies upon).

When strategy is viewed as the creation of options on the future, minimizing the costs of creating and maintaining options becomes a critical managerial concern. The costs of creating and maintaining options can be reduced by careful design of efficient experiments, test marketing, and prototyping, sharing the costs in partnership with interested customers or suppliers, and by leveraging new information sources, like maverick competitors or innovations taking place on the periphery of the organization.

In attempting to design a company's most effective portfolio of options it is also important for management to make a clear distinction between the cost of investing in the option and the cost of exercising that option (the latter being the costs of scaling up the option into a profit-generating business). Woolworth, for example, had the costs of its initial experiment to establish its first 'Footlocker' store plus the costs of creating an option to move into this type of speciality retailing on a large scale. If this option had been left unexercised, the cost would have amounted to writing off the cost of the experiment. The cost of exercising the option that experiment created included all of the investments required to establish and operate a competitive chain of stores that achieved the minimum efficient scale for the business. This distinction is critical because the decision whether or not to include a particular option in the company's portfolio should be made by comparing the estimated value of that option with the *cost of creating the option*, not with the costs of exercising it.

It is also worth noting that in viewing the first role of strategy as the creation of a portfolio of future options for a company, success does not depend on predicting the continuance of any single trend. Depending on what happens in the future environment, not every option will be exercised. However, those that are discarded are not wasted but will have served to insure against an uncertain future.

Corporate Renewal and the Strategy Innovation Pipeline

The cost of creating and maintaining an option depends on the form in which that option is maintained: as an idea; an experiment; or a venture. A company needs to maintain its portfolio of options in different states of development and to manage the flow of investment into each option depending on the way and speed the environment seems to be moving. As an option becomes more likely to be exercised it pays to invest more in it, moving the option from the idea stage, through experimentation towards a stand-alone venture. Managing a portfolio of options therefore involves actively creating and managing a 'pipeline' of options at different stages of development. Such a pipeline is depicted in Figure 15.5.

Some options will need to be pushed through the pipeline rapidly if the likelihood of exercising them increases. Others may lie dormant for an extended period, possibly indefinitely, if the environment never evolves in a way that justifies exercising them. Each individual option will also need to be managed differently depending on its stage of development.

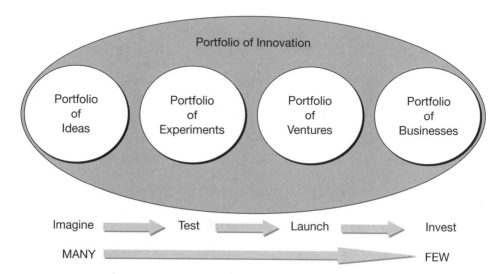

Figure 15.5—The strategy innovation pipeline.

Managing the Strategy Innovation Pipeline

Managing a pipeline of options for strategic innovation and renewal involves four main activities as follows.

- Finding mechanisms to fill the pipeline with different ideas that are possible options on the future.
- Managing sub-portfolios of options at different stages of development: ideas, experiments, ventures and businesses.
- Managing the 'toll gates' and transitions by which an option receives further investment to move through the pipeline.
- Exercising the option by scaling it up into a substantive business within the corporation's portfolio of business activities.

We examine each of these activities below.

Filling the Strategy Innovation Pipeline

A survey of strategy innovation in 25 companies undertaken in 1999 by the author found that in most companies there was no lack of ideas that represented potential innovative options on the future. But most of these ideas were left in 'limbo'; they remained little more than flashes of inspiration in the heads of individuals or small groups because there was no process to develop them. While many companies had suggestion schemes that were effective for small, incremental improvements, they were generally not able to handle ideas for options on the future of a company and its business model. With the backing of a strong entrepreneurial champion, some of these ideas were developed internally. But this was very much a hit or miss process. Others were taken outside the corporation by entrepreneurial former staff.

A few companies, such as Royal Dutch Shell, have developed a more systematic process to collect ideas for options on the future. At Shell this involves inviting individuals to sketch out their idea on a simple one-page form submitted to a 'GameChanger' panel of six peer-group individuals. Members of the GameChanger panel are charged with expanding and nurturing ideas that seemed to have potential, including allocating a small time and cash budget for use by the individual or team to flesh out the idea. Shell also initiated 'just do it' meetings in which individuals or teams with ideas for options for developing Shell's business in a particular area were invited to bring their ideas to a common forum for further development and initial funding.

All ideas submitted were logged by Shell in the portfolio of ideas for options on the future. Some lay dormant while others were pushed forward, allowing the portfolio to be actively managed.

Managing a Portfolio of Ideas

Even with a portfolio of ideas and mechanisms to encourage a continuous flow of new options, ideas must still be managed, evaluated, and developed. But an option in the form of an idea is at an early stage in its gestation. It is inappropriate to apply the same criteria to it as those used to assess an established business. The criteria for assessing the quality of an idea as an option on the future should not be based, for example, on a five-year spreadsheet laying out future forecasts of profitability in existing market conditions. Given the role of an option as a way of dealing with future uncertainty, it is more important that the idea can act as a launching pad into a new technology or market segment that *might* take off rather than its ability to make a return assuming that current trends continue.

Viewed as options on the future, ideas will be valuable if they are:

- capable of dealing with possible discontinuities in technology or consumer behaviour;
- likely to provide new types of customer benefits;
- scalable should the option be exercised.

Given the low cost of maintaining an option as an idea, an optimal portfolio of ideas must be judged by the extent to which it allows a company to 'cover the bases' of alternative scenarios it may face. This judgement can be based on:

- the number of ideas;
- whether they cover the major discontinuities (technological, consumer, competence);
- the likely scalability of the ideas in the portfolio relative to the size of the existing business.

Before an option in the idea portfolio can make the transition to the stage of an experiment (justifying the higher investment required) three conditions must be met:

- the ability to articulate a viable business model around the idea (a value proposition, revenue source, and major cost drivers);
- an experiment to begin to identify the major assumptions that would make the option viable and attractive;
- a team with the right mix of skills to conduct this experiment (either physical or virtual) to test the potential of the idea as an option on the future.

Managing a Portfolio of Experiments

Once it has been decided to develop an option to the stage of experimentation, a new set of criteria become relevant to managing it. These include:

- the ratio of learning over the cost of the experiment;

- how conclusive the results of the experiment are in determining the viability of the option;
- whether the experiment is successful in identifying the critical preconditions under which it would make sense to exercise the option.

Again, the quality of the portfolio of options a company has at the experimental stage will be determined by whether the portfolio covers the major technological or market discontinuities the company could face and whether, taken as a total portfolio, the options are of sufficient potential scale to match the need to grow or replace the corporation's existing business models in the face of strategy decay.

The decision to invest further to push a particular option past the experimental stage and to launch it as a venture, meanwhile, depends on:

- how soon demand is likely to emerge (a proxy for this might be whether a lead customer can be identified for the option);
- demonstrated proof of concept, including a potential revenue stream;
- support of a suitably qualified team.

Managing a Portfolio of Ventures

Once the decision to push an option to the stage of becoming a venture has been taken, the task is to refine and prove the feasibility of exercising the option by scaling it up into a profitable business and to identify under what conditions exercising the option would make sense.

In many cases these assessments of whether the venture represents a viable option for scaling into a significant business cannot be made based on the existing profitability of the venture. It may be, for example, that the venture will never be able to achieve profitability at small scale. Instead the critical criteria for assessing a venture are:

- its potential to create significant value as a new business if the environment moves in a particular direction;
- its potential to act as a profitable alternative to an existing business model should changing conditions accelerate decay of the current profit stream;
- the risks involved in successfully scaling up the venture even if the right constellation of market conditions were to fall into place.

An optimal portfolio of ventures for a company will cover the main technological and market discontinuities it may face (or potentially benefit from) in the future. The strategy innovation pipeline should cover these contingencies so that the maturity of the options in the overall portfolio allows the company to be in a position to exercise each option when required. Technological or customer changes that are likely to evolve only in the longer term should be matched with options at the idea stage in the pipeline. Short-term technological or market contingencies need to be matched with options at the venture stage of maturity so that they can be exercised at short notice as a solid platform to rapidly build or reposition a significant business.

Exercising an Option by Scaling it up to Become a Substantive Business

When a change in the market environment happens the company will have to exercise one or more of the options in its portfolio. This means investing the resources and competencies necessary to scale the option up into a full-fledged business unit. Typically this involves the infusion of:

- cash;
- relevant competencies from the existing businesses (brand-building capabilities, for example);
- operational skills required to drive up efficiency and manage a large scale, possibly complex, business;
- an 'organizational home' within the corporation and associated reporting structure.

Once scaled up, the criteria for evaluation are no longer those used for an option; the business needs to be judged by the traditional measures of an established, ongoing business such as revenue growth, profitability, ROCE, economic value added (EVA), and so on. What was an option has now entered the portfolio of businesses that makes up the corporation's revenue and profit-producing engine. It has cleared the various hurdles described above and reached the end of the pipeline shown in Figure 15.5. This completes the strategy innovation cycle.

In a world that often seems to assume that maximum speed is always the right strategy, it is important to recognize that it may be wrong to push an option through to a full-scale business too early, especially if this means closing off other options.

Monsanto, for example, single-mindedly drove through its strategy for rewriting the role of the herbicide business using genetically modified (GM) seeds to full-scale launch. Rather than retaining a portfolio of options distributed between a portfolio of ideas, experiments, and ventures, it chose a single strategic innovation and simply 'went for it'. When the environment unexpectedly turned increasingly hostile to GM-based products, starting in Europe and spreading back to the US, it was left boxed into a corner. Monsanto had closed off other options too early and driven its concept rapidly through the strategy innovation pipeline before the market was ready. This left the company seriously damaged and looking for a 'rescue partner' with which to merge.

Its competitor, BASF, by contrast, created a new biotechnology division made up of seed companies, biotechnology expertise, and speciality chemicals capabilities. This new division was charged with coming up with a portfolio of options that BASF might exercise in the future to take advantage of emerging biotechnologies. Rather than choosing a single strategic innovation and rapidly scaling it up, it set about building a pipeline of options at different stages of maturity to maximize its readiness to launch successful strategy innovations as the fog of market uncertainty began to clear.

Closing off options too quickly or pushing others to become a full-scale business too quickly can have a downside just as large as developing an option for strategy innovation too slowly and exercising it too late.

16 Racing to be Second: Innovation through Imitation

Constantinos Markides

London Business School

Over the past 10 years, several researchers including Baden-Fuller and Stopford (1992) have developed a wealth of ideas on how firms could *strategically* innovate in their industries. Yet, despite all this advice and good intentions, it is very rare to find a mature, established company among the strategic innovators. All available evidence shows that:

- the majority of strategic innovations are introduced by newcomers in an industry rather than established companies;
- established firms preoccupy themselves with how to respond to the strategic innovations of others (and even then, the limited number of options they consider shows lack of creativity on their part).

It appears that strategic innovation is too big a challenge for most established companies. But why is this the case? Big, established companies have no problem excelling when it comes to *product* or *technological* innovation – why does *strategic* innovation pose such a challenge to them? This chapter seeks to explain this puzzle.

What Exactly Is Strategic Innovation?

To understand why strategic innovation is such a challenge for established corporations, we must first understand exactly what this phenomenon is and what its characteristics are.

Strategic innovation is the discovery of a fundamentally *different* way of competing in an *existing* business. For example, the way Amazon.com competes in the book retailing business is fundamentally different from the way Barnes & Noble plays the game. Similarly, the way Charles Schwab, easyJet, and Dell play the game in their respective industries is substantially different from the way their competitors such as Merrill Lynch, British Airways and Compaq or IBM play it.

A lot has been written on this issue, especially on how established companies could strategically innovate in their industries. The only point that needs to be clarified here is the use of the term 'strategic'. Unlike other researchers, who seem to equate 'strategic innovation' with 'important or really big innovation', we use 'strategic' to mean innovation in one's business model (or strategy). Just as product innovation means the discovery of a new product and technological innovation means the discovery of a new technology, so strategic innovation implies the discovery of a new strategy or way of playing the game.

Unfortunately for established companies, the majority of strategic innovations tend to be disruptive. Disruptive strategic innovation is a specific type of strategic innovation – namely the discovery of a way of playing the game in an industry that is not only *different* but also *conflicts* with the traditional way of doing business. Examples of such disruptive innovations include Internet banking, low-cost flying, direct insurance, online brokerage trading, online distribution of news, and home-delivery grocery services.

Consider, for example, the US retail brokerage industry. Compared to traditional brokerage, online trading represents a fundamentally different way of competing in this business. Whereas full-service brokerage houses rely on an extensive network of brokers and branch offices to build relationships with customers, online traders rely on impersonal transactions to execute trades. And whereas traditional brokerage houses base their fees on the research and advice that they provide to customers, the online traders' value proposition is low price and speed of execution.

Not only is this way of doing business radically different from the traditional way but it also raises thorny issues for any established competitor contemplating adoption of online trading.

A potential problem that a full-service brokerage house might face were it to move to online trading is cannibalization of its existing, full-service customer base. By offering online services, the company risks shifting some of its more independent-minded private investors from high-value, advisory-based activities to low-margin, execution-only services offered through the Internet. These investors might come to consider trade execution as a commodity and might therefore opt to use the company's online site to trade directly rather than use the help and advice of brokers and pay traditional broker commissions.

Furthermore, assume that an established brokerage house decides to embrace the new online trading business, albeit in a limited way. What should the company do with its 'excess' brokers and existing branch network? Should it close certain offices and lay off redundant brokers? Should it divert much needed resources from its traditional business to the online business, thereby undermining the value of its existing distribution channel? The decision is not an easy one.

The very act of setting up an online operation will not only create competition for resources between alternative distribution channels but could also undermine one of the core advantages of full-service firms, namely the broker's role in providing sound advice to clients. This strategy will eventually alienate the firm's brokers.

Thus, by playing an altogether different game, online brokers are challenging the traditional full-service business model and threatening the long-standing competitive positions of incumbent firms in the industry. Their unorthodox tactics make it difficult to find an appropriate response. The underlying trade-offs between the two different ways of competing in the industry add considerably to this difficulty and make the decision on whether or not to offer online trading a major dilemma for established firms.

Characteristics of Disruptive Strategic Innovations

There are certain themes that emerge from the online brokerage example that are actually common to *all* disruptive strategic innovations.

First, note that whereas traditional brokers sell their services on the basis of their research and advice to customers, online brokers sell on the back of a different value proposition, namely price and speed of execution. You see this phenomenon emerging in every disruptive innovation: *innovators tend to emphasize different product or service attributes than traditional technologies or competitors.* As a result, they become attractive to a different customer segment than the one that established companies focus on. This point is made clear in Table 16.1, which, for a number of industries, compares and contrasts the performance attributes emphasized by established firms versus those emphasized by innovators.

It is important to note that since innovators emphasize different dimensions of a product or service, their products or services inevitably become attractive to a *different* customer to the one that likes what traditional companies offer.

Table 16.1—Critical performance attributes emphasized by established firms and innovators.

Industry	Performance Attributes Emphasized by Established Firms	Performance Attributes Emphasized by Strategic Innovators
Banking	Extensive, nationwide branch network and personal service	24-hour access, convenience, price
Insurance	Personal, face-to-face advice through an extensive agent network	Convenience and low commission rates
Airlines	Hub-and-spoke system, premium service, meals, baggage checking	Price, no frills
Brokerage	Research and advice	Speed of execution and price
Photocopying	Speed of copying	Price, size and quality
Watches	Accuracy and functionality	Design
Steel	Quality	Price
Motorcycles	Speed and power	Size and price
Bookstores	Chain of superstores offering nice environment and service	Wide selection, speed, price, convenience
Car Rental	Location (i.e. airports) and quality of cars	Location and price (downtown)
Computer	Speed, memory capacity, power	Design and user-friendliness

This is a point that Clayton Christensen (1997) emphasizes in his own work on disruptive innovation. Based on his research, Christensen suggests that established players in an industry focus on certain product or service attributes that their mainstream customers value. Established players invest aggressively (in both financial and human resources) to improve these performance attributes in order to retain existing customers.

In contrast, new companies enter the industry by emphasizing different product or service attributes. The newcomers bring to the market a very different value proposition than had been available previously. They typically offer different performance attributes from the ones mainstream customers have historically valued and, at least at the outset, they almost always perform far worse along one or two dimensions that are particularly important to those customers. As a result, mainstream customers are usually unwilling to use or purchase these disruptive innovations since they do not meet their current needs.

This means that disruptive innovations tend to be used and valued only in *new* markets or applications and become attractive to a new set of customers. Even though these innovations generally underperform mainstream products or services in the dimensions emphasized by the established players, they have other features and attributes that are superior to those of established firms and that are valued by a certain (and usually new) segment of customers.

In fact, as Bower and Christensen (1995) argue, these innovations generally make possible the emergence of new markets or a new way of doing business in an established industry.

A second characteristic that all disruptive innovations display is that they start out as small, low-margin businesses. Because the innovations are so small relative to the mainstream business as a whole, they are not particularly attractive to big, established companies. Even managers in those companies who want to do something about the new markets find it difficult to justify investment on economic grounds. As long as the incumbents are able to retain their mainstream customers in their existing business, they are unwilling to invest significant resources in the innovation. Not surprisingly, it is rare to find these disruptive innovations originating from big, established companies. It is usually an entrepreneur or a new market entrant that introduces them.

However, it is not long before the innovations start growing into viable businesses. This is the third characteristic common to all disruptive innovations. The way this growth happens is also quite similar across industries and, as Christensen points out, follows a regular pattern.

Once disruptive innovations become established in their new markets, a series of improvements over time raise the performance of the new products or services along the dimensions that mainstream customers value. In fact, these performance attributes improve at such a rapid rate that the developers of disruptive innovation can soon enter the established market and sell their previously inferior product or service to mainstream customers.

This is because they are able to deliver performance that is *good enough* in the old attributes that established competitors emphasize as well as offering *superior* performance in the new attributes. According to Christensen, this happens because companies often give customers more than they need or ultimately are willing to pay for in their efforts to provide better products than their competitors and earn higher prices and margins.

By accumulating experience and relevant expertise in the new market, the innovators can then use that commercial platform to attack the value networks of established firms. In their constant effort to improve their products and services to beat competitors, innovators invest resources to the point where they can address the needs of mainstream customers. This is what ultimately leads to the growth of disruptive innovation into a big business.

For example, consider again the US retail brokerage industry. Online brokers such as Charles Schwab, E*Trade, and DLJdirect are now able to offer high-quality research and financial advice at much lower cost per trade than the established full-service brokerage houses. Online brokers now offer access to real-time personalized market information and financial data, market analysis, and other investment information services previously provided only by traditional full-service companies.

Inevitably, the growth of the disruptive innovation attracts the attention of established players. As more customers (both existing and new ones) embrace the strategic innovation, the new business receives increasing attention from both the media and established players. A point is reached where established players can no longer afford to ignore this new way of doing business and they therefore begin to consider ways to respond to it.

At this stage of deciding how to respond, established firms have to confront the fourth characteristic that all such innovations share. Compared to the traditional business, strategic innovations have different key success factors and, as a result, require a different combination of tailored activities on the part of the firm. These new activities are incompatible with an established company's existing activities because of various trade-offs, or compromises, that exist if it is to undertake two ways of doing business.

Michael Porter (1996) has identified three main reasons that give rise to these trade-offs. First, trade-offs arise from inconsistencies in a company's image or reputation. Firms that simultaneously try to offer two different kinds of value propositions that are not consistent with each other run the risk of jeopardizing their existing image and reputation.

Second, trade-offs occur as a result of the particular set of activities that a company needs to perform in order to compete successfully in its chosen position. A unique strategic position requires a particular set of tailored activities that are different from those needed to compete effectively in other positions in the industry. This set of activities may include different product configurations, different equipment, different employee behaviour and skills, and different management systems. Many trade-offs occur because the tailored activities of a unique strategic position are incompatible with the activities of alternative positions in the industry.

Finally, trade-offs arise due to the limits a firm faces in internally coordinating and controlling incompatible sets of activities. Companies that try to compete in two different strategic positions at the same time find it difficult to set the necessary organizational priorities and clearly communicate them to their employees. They then run the risk of losing focus through adding activities that may confuse their employees. In many cases, the latter are not clear about the overall incentives and priorities and what they need to do to achieve these goals. As a result, they often attempt to make day-to-day operating decisions without a clear framework and direction, which seriously undermines their performance.

The existence of trade-offs makes it extremely difficult for an established firm to respond effectively to disruptive innovation. Because of these trade-offs and conflicts, a company that tries to compete in both positions simultaneously will eventually pay a huge straddling cost and degrade the value of its existing activities. In most cases, this cost far outweighs any potential benefits emerging from the new positioning.

Put a different way, a company cannot compete in both positions simultaneously without experiencing major inefficiencies. Any attempt to manage the innovation by utilizing its existing systems, processes, incentives, and mindsets will only suffocate and kill the new business.

What Should Established Competitors Do?

Given these characteristics, no one should be surprised to learn that most established companies find the whole idea of strategic innovation unappealing. To begin with, these innovations are of no interest to their mainstream customers. To make matters worse, all such innovations start life as small and unprofitable niches. And to top it all off, they have the potential to cannibalize or destroy their existing (profitable) business.

All this means that no matter how much lip service they may pay to strategic innovation, it is highly unlikely that big established companies will embrace this as something good or as a way of moving forward.

This, of course, has not stopped academics or consultants from preaching the virtues of strategic innovation to these firms. But despite the best of intentions and despite all of our advice, it is highly unlikely that established firms will become as innovative as the millions of entrepreneurs out there (simple application of the law of large numbers will tell you this). Nor will our advice ever succeed in converting the big established companies of the 21st century into the small, agile entrepreneurs of Silicon Valley.

The truth of the matter is that start-up firms have certain natural advantages over big established firms when it comes to creativity – trying to convert 'big' firms into 'small' firms (or trying to get big firms to adopt the characteristics of small firms) is an (almost) futile effort.

If this is the case, what advice should we be giving the big established corporations? I believe that future research and advice ought to focus on the question of how established firms should respond to these strategic innovations. Just as small firms have advantages over big firms when it comes to new ideas, so big firms have advantages over small firms when it comes to building new ideas into viable businesses. And successfully converting an idea into a mass market requires as much 'innovation' and 'creativity' as the generation of the idea in the first place.

Therefore, we should stop advising big firms on how to become or behave like small firms. Instead, we should help them understand what their natural advantages are and how they can apply them to out-compete small firms in the game that they know best – scaling up a creative new idea from a niche to a mass market.

The main thesis of this chapter is therefore that established companies should forget about becoming strategic innovators and focus their attention instead on responding to the innovations that are bound to invade their markets.

But how can they 'respond'? Unfortunately, the word respond has become synonymous with 'imitate the innovation'. Whenever you talk to an established company, the question managers always ask is: 'Should we do this (disruptive innovation) – or not? And how can we do it without harming our existing business?'

Thus, the debate within Merrill Lynch has always been, should it get into online brokerage – or not? Similarly, the debate within British Airways has always been should it get into the low-cost, no-frills part of the business – or not? It's as if the only available response to a disruption is either to ignore it or to imitate it.

Needless to say, there are other available responses to a disruptive innovation. In a survey we conducted, we found that established companies considered a variety of response options (Charitou and Markides, 2002).

Of the 98 established companies that completed our survey questionnaire, 30 companies decided not to *embrace* the disruptive innovation – but they did *respond* to it in a number of different ways as described below, proving that 'respond' does not necessarily mean 'adopt'.

The remaining 68 companies decided to respond to the disruptive innovation by adopting it in one way or another. Of these respondents, 42 did so by forming a separate organizational unit while the rest used their existing infrastructure to respond. But again, *how* these established players adopted the innovation proved to be much more complex than simply deciding whether to separate it or not. In what follows, we describe in more detail the different ways that established firms could respond to disruptive strategic innovations.

Response 1: Focus on Our Game and Invest to Make It More Attractive

One of the biggest misconceptions about disruptive strategic innovation is that the new way of doing things will grow and eventually overtake the traditional way of playing the game.

As a result, the story goes, established competitors had better face up to the innovation by embracing it in some form or another. This misconception probably arose from Christensen's research into *technological* innovation, where it was shown that new disruptive technologies completely replaced existing technologies and in the process destroyed the competitors that did not make the jump from the old to the new. This may be true for disruptive technological innovations but is certainly not the case for disruptive *strategic* innovations.

What often happens in strategic innovation is that the new way of competing in the business grows (usually quickly) to a certain percentage of the market but fails to completely overtake the traditional way of competing. For example, Internet banking and Internet brokerage have grown rapidly in the last five years but, at most, have captured only 10 to 20 % of the market. Similarly, budget, no-frills flying as a business has grown phenomenally since 1995 but has captured no more than 20 % of the total market.

In market after market, the new ways of playing the game grow to a respectable size but never really replace the old ways. Nor are these innovations expected to ever grow in the future to 100 % of their markets.

Appreciating that the new way is neither God-given nor 'superior' to the existing way and that it is *not* destined to conquer the whole market opens up alternatives to established players.

What this fact implies is that an established competitor does not necessarily have to adopt the new way. It could 'respond' to the innovation not by adopting it but by investing in its existing business to make the traditional way of competing even more competitive relative to the new way. This might sound like an obvious point but for most established competitors the framing of how to respond to an innovation has almost always been: 'Should we do it – or not? And if we do it, how can we play two conflicting games at the same time?' The option of 'not doing it' but still responding to it is rarely considered.

Yet this is exactly what Gillette did in the face of the disposable razor threat to its business.

Like any disruptive innovation, disposables entered the razor market by emphasizing a different dimension of the product (price and ease of use versus Gillette's closeness of shave) and grew quickly to a large segment of the market. How did Gillette respond to this threat? Rather than go wholeheartedly into this new market, Gillette chose to invest its resources in its traditional business in an effort to improve its competitive standing relative to the new way of doing business.

While producing disposable razors in a defensive way, Gillette focused its energy and resources in its main business and innovated by creating two new products, the Sensor and the Mach-3. Innovation in the traditional business eventually led to the decline of the disposable razor market to about half its 1970s size.

To repeat the main point: established competitors can respond to a disruptive innovation in more ways than by simply adopting the new way. Put another way: the new ways of competing are not destined to win the battle with the established way. Depending on how they respond, established competitors could slow down or even destroy the new innovations.

Response 2: Disrupt the Disruptive Innovation

As indicated earlier, disruptive innovators build their success by emphasizing different product or service attributes to established competitors. Thus, Charles Schwab promotes its low prices and speed of execution against Merrill Lynch's research and advice; Ryanair and easyJet emphasize their low prices and small-city destinations compared to BA's broad service scope and frequent flights to major destinations; and online banks sell their services on convenience and price against the major banks' face-to-face service and advice.

By emphasizing different performance attributes, the innovators originally become attractive to a new customer segment. Over time, as they gradually invest to improve their overall product offering in all performance attributes, the innovators eventually become 'good enough' in the attributes that traditional customers value. That's when they begin to attract not only a different customer segment but also the customers who had originally remained loyal to established companies.

Put in simple language, established players who are good at game A come under attack from companies that play game B. How then could the established companies respond?

Put like this, it should be obvious that one way for established companies to respond is by developing game C, very much in the same way that the innovators developed game B. Armed with game C, which is nothing more than a way of competing that emphasizes a different set of attributes to those promoted by the innovators, established companies could attack the innovators in the same way that the innovators attacked them.

The way the Swiss watch industry responded to the Japanese attack in the late 1970s helps to illustrate this point.

In the early 1960s, the Swiss dominated the global watch industry. They were selling their watches based on Swiss craftsmanship and accuracy of the (mechanical) movement. This dominance all but evaporated in the 1970s when companies such as Seiko (from Japan) and Timex (from the US) introduced a major disruptive innovation in the watch market – cheap watches that used quartz technology and provided added functionality and features. As with every disruptive innovation, the innovators did not attack by trying to become better at the product attributes that the Swiss were emphasizing (quality of the movement and accuracy of the watch). Instead, they focused on different performance attributes – price and functionality.

At first, the new products attracted a totally different customer from the one that valued what the Swiss were offering. It wasn't long, however, before even the customers who valued accuracy were attracted to the new watches. Swiss share of global world production declined from 48 % in 1965 to 15 % by 1980.

The response of the established Swiss watch industry to this disruption should be a lesson to all companies facing similar threats to their business. Instead of adopting the new way of playing the game, the Swiss responded by introducing the Swatch. This new watch did not pretend to be better than Seiko or Timex in price or features (the performance attributes the innovators at the time were emphasizing). Instead, the Swatch built its attack by emphasizing different product attributes – style and variety. Instead of responding to game B by embracing it, it went after it by creating game C. Since its launch in 1983, Swatch has become the world's most popular timepiece with more than 100 million sold in over 30 countries.

Two other companies that are currently responding in a manner similar to Swatch are Apple and British Airways. After its personal computer business came under attack from Dell and Compaq based on price and technology, Apple responded by emphasizing style and design as the performance attributes of its products – witness the Apple i-Mac. Similarly, after its airline market was attacked by easyJet and Ryanair on the basis of price and point-to-point flying, British Airways has responded by emphasizing comfort and luxury in its service offering with the introduction of seats that become flat beds and luxurious executive lounges around the world.

In summary, these examples demonstrate that established competitors can respond to a disruptive innovation not only by making their game better but also by actively trying to destroy the innovation. They can do this using the exact same strategy the disruptive innovators employ to destroy the established business – identify different product or service attributes than the ones the innovators are focusing on and make these the key purchasing criteria for the consumer. These different attributes will originally be attractive to only a small customer segment but continuous investments and innovation could improve other product attributes to such an extent that more and more consumers eventually switch.

Response 3: Embrace the Disruption but Scale It Up

The third response option available to established firms is to abandon their existing way of playing the game and embrace the disruptive innovation wholeheartedly. In doing so, their goal is not only to imitate the innovation but also to 'scale it up' and grow it into a mass market.

The first online bookstore was started *not* by Amazon.com but by Charles Stack, an Ohio-based bookseller, in 1991. He got his website up and running in January 1993. Amazon, popularly seen as the innovator in online bookselling, was actually third or fourth, opening its website in February 1995. The two first movers in the business – Charles Stack and Computer Literacy Bookstore – were eventually acquired by Barnes & Noble.

Similarly, the first online brokers were two Chicago firms, Howe Barnes Investments and Security APL Inc, which launched a joint venture called Net Investor in January 1995 to offer Internet-based stock trading. Six years later, they were dwarfed by the success of Charles Schwab, which took over Internet brokerage and made it its own.

A similar fate awaited CompuServe, which lost out to AOL in online services; Apple Computers, which lost the PDA market to Palm; Atari, which created the video game market in 1972 and then lost it to Sony and Nintendo; and Osborne Computers, which produced the first portable computer and then lost out to Apple and IBM.

All these examples highlight one key point: innovation involves two essentially different activities – coming up with a new product, technological, or strategic idea and then creating a market out of that idea. For an innovation to be successful both of these activities have to be effectively coupled – but there is no need for the same firm to do both. One firm may come up with the idea of a new and disruptive way of playing the game and another may take the idea and scale it up into a mass market.

In fact, the skills and competencies needed for scaling up are essentially different from those needed to come up with the new idea in the first place. This gives the established firm a window of opportunity. It can allow small or entrepreneurial firms to come up with a disruptive idea and then move in and adopt the idea as its own.

In the final analysis, this is the area where established firms have a competitive advantage over innovators: their skills and competencies are better suited to stealing others' ideas and growing them into big markets. All this means that established firms can respond to a disruptive innovation introduced by another firm by embracing the new way and growing it into a mass market.

To do this successfully, a firm needs to make serious investments in production so that it can produce a high-quality product very economically. It must also be able to help sway consumers and create the kind of consensus that would support the proposed dominant design. It needs to be able to identify and then reach out to the many potential consumers who are ready to purchase the new product or service but who are also unwilling to shoulder the risk of choosing between the many alternatives that first appear on the market. Creating an organization that can serve a large and rapidly growing market is also a requirement if the firm is to facilitate the growth of the market.

Established firms are, typically, slow movers – and they ought to be. Assembling this list of skills is a formidable undertaking. Most of the investments that are required involve substantial sunk costs and should not be undertaken lightly. Further, what starts the bandwagon rolling towards a particular dominant design is the substantive presence of a major league champion. This sends a clear signal to all concerned that the market is about to develop in new and very profitable ways. Only 'big-name' established competitors can send such a credible message.

In short, established competitors have the option of adopting someone else's disruptive innovation and growing it into a mass market. This idea is neither new nor novel. Other researchers have argued as much. What is amazing is how few of the established competitors that come under attack from disruptive innovations even consider this option.

In our own sample, many of the established companies that we interviewed talked about this option but none of them chose to implement it. Yet history suggests that companies that pursue this option successfully create for themselves the basis for tremendous growth for years to come. Established companies must not be so quick to discard this option.

Conclusion

We started out by posing a question: 'why are established companies so bad when it comes to strategic innovation?' Based on our discussion in this chapter, I believe the answer is simple: some firms – mainly start-up firms – have the skills and competencies needed for discovering new markets. Other firms – mainly established competitors – have the skills and competencies needed to take a newly created market and grow it into a mass market. The two sets of skills cannot co-exist – they conflict with each other. This explains why very few firms are successful at both creating and consolidating new markets.

What this implies is that the advice we should be giving to the big, established corporations is to forget all about trying to transform themselves into something that looks like a young, start-up firm in order to become a good strategic innovator. Instead, they ought to build on their existing strengths in order to take the innovations of others and scale them up into mass markets. *This is how mature firms innovate*.

17 Who Needs Multinationals? Lessons from Open-source Software

Robert M. Grant,[1] Andrea Lipparini,[2] Gianni Lorenzoni[3] and Elaine Romanelli[1]

[1]Georgetown University, [2]Catholic University of Milan, [3]University of Bologna

Since the late 1980s the focus of attention of strategy research has shifted from the external environment of the firm – competitive analysis and strategy–performance relationships under different environmental conditions – towards the internal environment of the firm, notably resources, capabilities, and internal organization.

This shift reflects two main factors. First, compared with the progress made in analysing competition, industry structure, and the external sources of competition advantage (drawing in particular on the tools of industrial organization economics), our understanding of the internal sources of competitive advantage is much more primitive.

Second, it is increasingly clear that the primary sources of profitability differences are internal rather than external. If only 4 to 19 % of profitability differences between companies can be attributed to the impact of industry and intra-industry profit differentials, then the quest for these profit differentials must address inter-firm differences with regard to resources, capabilities, structures, and systems.

Although we know about the characteristics of resources that confer sustainable competitive advantage, we remain largely ignorant of how these resources work together to create complex organizational capabilities. Individual expertise is developed through specialization but organizational capabilities require that individuals integrate their specialist know-how.

Such integration encounters two problems: cooperation and coordination. Organization theory has concentrated on the former to the neglect of the latter. Within the sociology tradition, the primary concerns have been goal alignment, power, and control. Within organizational economics, the dominant themes have been incentives, agency, and opportunism. Yet the problems of coordination are at least as important. Amid the flames of the New York's World Trade Center on the morning of September 11, 2001, there was no problem of cooperation. Police, firefighters, city officials, Port Authority employees, fellow workers, and passers-by were united in their desire to save the lives of as many office workers as possible. Even so, the problem of effective coordination was immense.

The Quest for New Organizational Forms and Alternative Organizational Principles

The limited ability of conventional organizational forms and existing organizational principles to solve the coordination problems of multi-product, multinational companies competing along multiple performance dimensions in turbulent environments has stimulated a quest for alternative approaches. Interest in non-hierarchical modes of coordination has directed interest at 'non-traditional' organizations such as jazz bands, string quartets, religious organizations, grass-roots political movements, and non-human organizations such as ant colonies, bee hives, and flocks of birds.

A common theme of these studies has been the observation that highly sophisticated forms of coordination can occur in the absence of hierarchical direction. In jazz bands, for example, basic coordination through the rhythm, mood, and storyline of the music is reconciled with a system of communication and mutual awareness that permits spontaneity and innovation in the form of improvisation.

Firms vs Networks

If complex adaptive systems are capable of co-evolving with their environments in an ordered fashion, why should the firm be seen as an optimally efficient institution for producing and distributing goods and services across national borders compared with more decentralized modes of ownership and control?

The superiority of integrated firms as institutions for the organization of production have not gone unchallenged. In a number of industries, inter-firm networks have emerged as alternative institutions for producing complex products with advantages over integrated firms in terms of speed, flexibility, and innovation. Prominent examples of such networks include the microelectronics and software clusters of California's Silicon Valley and packaging machinery and motorcycles in the industrial districts of northern Italy.

The extent to which such networks represent an alternative to the multinational firm is limited by two factors.

First, these networks are themselves composed of firms. Although in some industries, for example house construction, networks involve collaboration among self-employed individuals, most networks are composed of individual firms each specialized in the production of particular components or modules that are then assembled or integrated by a single firm that takes the role of the 'systems integrator'.

Second, such networks are characterized by localization. Although some networks may extend across national boundaries and some may even be global (for example, aerospace), most inter-firm networks are geographically concentrated. In the case of the Hollywood movie cluster, the Silicon Valley microelectronics cluster, the San

Diego biotech cluster, the Prato knitwear cluster, the telecom and Internet corridor of northen Virginia, or the reinsurance business in London, inter-firm networks are concentrated into a few square miles.

These limits suggest two conclusions. First, where production involves high levels of interdependence between individuals, then the firm provides the most suitable institutional context for coordination to occur. Only where some degree of loose coupling is possible can coordination extend across company boundaries.

Second, even with such loose coupling, coordination between firms is facilitated by proximity. Network arrangements that extend internationally are present in some sectors, for example in personal computers (notably Dell Computers' closely coordinated network) and the passenger aircraft networks of Boeing and EADS. However, in other sectors – notably airlines and telecommunication services – alliances have been unstable and short lived with many abandoned or displaced by full-blown mergers.

Hence, most of the available evidence suggests that inter-firm networks do not challenge in any fundamental way the dominant position of the multinational corporation (MNC) in organizing international production. The implied conclusion, therefore, is that coordination between independent firms is possible where proximity permits rich communication and where commonalities of language, culture, and social structure are present.

However, once these factors are absent, then the authority structure, incentive structure, and social structure of the international firm become necessary frameworks for achieving sophisticated modes of coordination between large numbers of individuals collaborating across substantial geographical distances.

There is, though, one clear anomaly to this general pattern of evidence – open-source software (OSS).

Open-source Software

The computer software sector offers a fascinating and contradictory case study for students of economic organization. Given the lack of national differentiation (except in relation to language), the extreme scale economies (almost all costs are sunk, marginal costs are very low), and the ease of distribution, computer software is the epitome of a global industry.

Given these observations, it is surprising to find that in several segments of the software industry multinational firms are being challenged by an extreme network form that is quite unlike the localized inter-firm networks that exist in many other industries.

OSS communities are networks of individuals rather than firms and they are global rather than local in their scope. These, of course, are only two of the unusual features of OSS communities. They are also distinguished by the fact that they give away their output free of charge and their software developers are unpaid volunteers. Putting these four characteristics together means that OSS communities are one of the most remarkable organizational innovations of the past quarter century.

The history of the OSS movement and the values and ideals that have driven it are well known. The organizational characteristics of OSS communities have also attracted attention. Interest has centred on the absence of direct financial incentives, which, at first view, contradicts the basic tenets of rational economic behaviour. Research shows that despite the absence of direct financial incentives, *indirect* economic incentives are important, especially in terms of individual reputation building and entrepreneurial incentives in complementary products and services. Comparatively little has been written about coordination within OSS communities, the extent to which such coordination is fundamentally different from that which occurs within integrated firms, and the circumstances under which such coordination may be superior.

Here we consider these issues and, in particular, seek answers to the following questions.

- How have OSS communities performed relative to MNCs in the markets for computer software?
- What are the mechanisms through which coordination occurs within OSS development?
- What circumstances need to be present for OSS communities to perform effectively?
- Does OSS development represent a model of an international collaborative network that could be applied in other sectors; and, more generally, what implications can be drawn about the feasibility of self-organization within decentralized business organizations?

Origins and Development of the Open-source Movement

The terms open-source software, free software, and community-based software refer to computer software that is produced largely by communities of volunteers and distributed under licences that make the source code freely available to users.

The free software movement was founded by Richard Stallman, who left MIT's Artificial Intelligence laboratory to establish the Free Software Foundation and the GNU project to develop a freely available operating system where the source code would be in the public domain.

The key factor determining the availability of free software was the GNU General Public License, which established the principles of 'copyleft' (in contrast to copyright). The licensing terms provide for free redistribution (and redistribution) of software and permit modifications of the software. However, all modifications and derivatives of the software are covered by the same licensing terms so that free software cannot be made proprietary.

The Free Software Foundation's efforts to develop a freely available Unix operating system were constrained by failure to develop a free, usable Unix 'kernel'. Meanwhile the Unix world became fragmented between the commercial AT&T version and Berkeley's BSD version (which formed the basis of Sun Microsystems' operating system). In 1991, the free software initiative was saved from oblivion when Linus Torvalds produced the first version of a free Unix kernel for 386-type machines. The ensuing boom in the Linux development community and the number of Linux users not only established Linux as the most widely used operating system after Windows but also spawned free software development communities across a wide range of computer software.

The free software movement has its roots in an ideology that rejects the commercialization of software and insists that software code is inherently a public good. However, the rejection of all commercial exploitation of community-based software limited its use to those with sufficient knowledge to be independent of usual commercial support services. The very success of Linux also encouraged modification of the uncompromising hacker ideology upon which Stallman had based his GNU General Public License.

The Open Source Initiative was founded to promote the wider use and more effective development of free software by allowing greater commercialization. 'Open-source' software is distinguished from 'free' software by embracing a wider range of licences than GNU GPL. The common dominator is that source code must be openly 'inspectable' but, subject to this, varying degrees of proprietary rights can be extended to developers and commercial partners. Here we use the term 'open-source software' to refer to all software where the source code is openly inspectable, where ownership is distributed, and where development is open to a wide community of volunteers.

The Performance of Open-source Software

The development of OSS has contributed to the emergence of an interesting and unusual distribution of institutional forms within the computer software industry. At one end of the industry is a group of large, integrated, multinational corporations. Preeminent among these is Microsoft together with software giants such as Oracle, SAP, and Computer Associates plus several combined hardware/software companies including IBM, Sun Microsystems, and Apple Computer.

At the other end of the distribution are a number of non-commercial OSS communities that are networks of individuals rather than firms and that distribute their software free. In a number of market segments, these two types of radically different organizations are in direct competition with one another. In many cases, the corporate representative is Microsoft, the company that most clearly epitomizes the corporate model of software development and distribution and which, for the hacker community, is the clearest manifestation of all things evil in cyberspace.

Yet despite the massive resources and concentrated economic power of the integrated multinational software corporations, open-source products have taken market share from their commercial rivals in several product areas. Although web servers, where Apache holds a dominant market position, is the only major product segment where OSS has established clear market leadership over rival proprietary products, there are others where OSS has a strong secondary market position (see Table 17.1).

Given that OSS is motivated by very different goals and values from commercial software, market share may be a less relevant performance measure for comparing OSS and proprietary software than product capabilities. Two principal advantages of OSS are apparent:

Table 17.1—Examples of market segments where open-source and proprietary software products compete.

Type of software	Open-source product	Proprietary product	Outcome by early 2002
Server software	Apache HTTP	Microsoft Internet Information Server	Apache has about 60 % of market
Internet browser software	Mozilla	Microsoft Internet Explorer	Microsoft IE dominant
Internet mail transfer	Sendmail	Microsoft Exchange	Microsoft Exchange leads
Operating systems for servers and workstations	Linux	Microsoft Windows Unix (e.g. Sun's Solaris)	Windows 47 %, Linux 32 %, Unix 10%
Graphic user interface for desktops	GNOME (GNU Network Object Model Environment)	Windows; MS Office	Windows dominates desktop/workstation market; GNOME leads in Unix segment (e.g. Sun's Solaris, HP-UX, Red Hat Linux). GNOME Office includes productivity applications such as spreadsheet, word processing, graphics, and project management and has tiny fraction of MS Office's market share
Programming languages for system administration	Perl	Java (Sun Microsystems); Microsoft's ActiveX	Unclear

- very rapid identification and fixing of bugs (this phenomenon – that 'many eyes make all bugs shallow' – has been dubbed 'Linus's law');
- new developments and extensions of the software develop very rapidly. For example, Linux has been adapted to the operating system needs not just of servers and workstations but almost the whole range of computing devices from mainframes to PDAs, including games machines and digital cameras. One of the key features of OSS has been the ability to produce differentiated versions to meet the needs of specific user segments.

The advantages of open-source communities in developing complex computer software lie not just in the numbers of developers involved but also the diversity and quality of their knowledge bases. Thus, leading members of open-source communities typically include university-based computer scientists, innovative designers from start-up IT companies, leading-edge developers from major computer companies such as HP, Sun, IBM, and Netscape, as well as the longstanding membership of individual hackers.

The Organization of Open-source Software Development

Given the size and dispersion of OSS communities, the absence of financial incentives, and the ineffectiveness of bureaucratic controls over unpaid volunteers, how does coordination occur?

In earlier research co-author Robert M. Grant argued that coordination within knowledge-based production requires mechanisms that are capable of integrating many different types of specialized knowledge while preserving the efficiencies in knowledge generation made possible by specialization.

Two mechanisms are of primary importance: instructions (in the form of rules and directives); and organizational routines. Knowledge-based explanations for the existence of firms and their advantages over alternative institutional forms emphasize the advantages of firms in supporting this coordination. Are these same mechanisms the basis for coordination within OSS projects or do these 'self-organizing communities' and 'dispersed social movements' rely upon quite different principles of coordination?

Rules and Directives

Instructions fall into two main categories. Repetitive activities are regulated by means of rules that take the form of standard operating procedures, prohibitions of certain actions, and guidelines, or 'policies'. Such rules are fundamental for allowing organizations to operate under normal circumstances through specifying the way in which one individual's work fits with another's. Directives relate to decisions over specific, irregular occurrences.

All OSS communities have created rules that govern almost every aspect of the interaction between community members and between community members and the software. These rules relate to the induction of new members into the community, the format of communication, the development tools used by community members, the protocols relating to the submission of code, the format for commenting on code, the storage of information on bugs, and procedures for reviewing and accepting patches.

Such rules govern regular, ongoing processes in software development. At the technical level, most of these rules form part of the software design tools that are utilized across the software sector as a whole. For example, the GNOME Project uses the GNU tool suite (gcc, make, emacs, gdb), CVS for software configuration management, and bugzilla for bug tracking.

More interesting as far as the organization of OSS communities is concerned are the ones that govern organizational processes, particularly the rules that govern individual responsibilities and decisions, product design, modes of work, decision procedures, and the norms of interaction between community members.

At GNOME, the 500 or so participating developers are organized into groups, each of which has its own mailing lists, and there are standard procedures for sending and reviewing patches and specific rights regarding who can directly access and modify particular modules.

For example, a new developer is expected to send patches to the maintainer of the module until the maintainer acknowledges that the new developer can directly apply his or her patches to the CVA repository. In some cases a patch may be rejected. The rejection can take two forms. At its simplest, the maintainer receives the patch from the developer and decides to reject it. A more complex situation arises when the developer applies his or her changes directly to the module and one of the maintainers does not like the patch and rolls back these changes. In either situation, the developer can appeal the decision of the maintainer to the community at large.

Conventionally, rules and directives have been viewed from a 'command and control' perspective. They ensure that the whole organization marches in the direction indicated by 'top management'. The knowledge-based view of the firm suggests an additional, equally important function. Rules and directives are efficient mechanisms for integrating knowledge. Sophisticated specialized knowledge that can only be transferred by means of costly training is converted into directives, rules, guidelines, and operating procedures. The efficiency of such rules and directives means that they can embody knowledge while those who simply follow the rules are relieved of the need to acquire that knowledge.

Whether their purpose is control or knowledge integration, rules and directives are dependent on authority. Rules need to be established and implemented by members of the organization empowered to regulate the behaviour and/or output of others. Directives are issued by organizational members who possess the supervisory decision-making authority over others in specified areas of activity.

These notions of authority and decision rights seem strange in organizations that are composed of unpaid volunteers. In the absence of financial incentives and employment contracts, the acquiescence of members of OSS communities is more about voluntary acceptance of rules and directives rather than direct incentives and penalties. Nevertheless, in common with boy scouts and churches, OSS communities' voluntarism does not mean an absence of authority. As with more formal organizations, in OSS communities authority is organized through hierarchical structures.

Hierarchy within OSS communities. Despite the image of open-source communities as loose, unstructured, egalitarian networks of volunteer contributors, all have clearly defined hierarchical structures.

In most organizations, two types of hierarchy are present. The structures depicted in most organizational charts are hierarchies of authority – they show who reports to whom and who gives orders to whom. In addition, system theory identifies hierarchies of integration. Most complex organizations are decomposed into modular structures that typically comprise several levels. Such modularity facilitates decentralized adaptation and innovation.

In most organizations, hierarchies of authority and integration tend to be related but far from identical. For example, product development may be closer to the top of the hierarchy of integration because of its need to integrate the knowledge and activities of almost every function within the firm but this does not imply that the heads of product development are members of the top management team.

Within OSS communities, the hierarchies of integration and authority tend to be closely related. The hierarchy of integration defines the structure for developing the software while the hierarchy of authority specifies the rights, responsibilities, and decision-making authority of individuals at each organizational level as well as the procedure for moving up the hierarchy.

As hierarchies of integration, modular structures were common to all the OSS projects we examined with organizational modules that replicated the modular structure of the code base. While most projects began with very little structure, modular structures were established at an early stage and these became increasingly elaborate. For example, the GNOME Project had four types of module: required libraries (19 modules); the core (four modules); applications (16 modules); and 'other' (over 30 modules). Similar patterns of product and organizational modularity are apparent in other OSS projects (see Figure 17.1). In large projects, individual modules may be subdivided into sub-modules.

The hierarchies of integration corresponded closely to the hierarchies of decision-making authority in the OSS communities that we observed. Three main hierarchical levels can be identified.

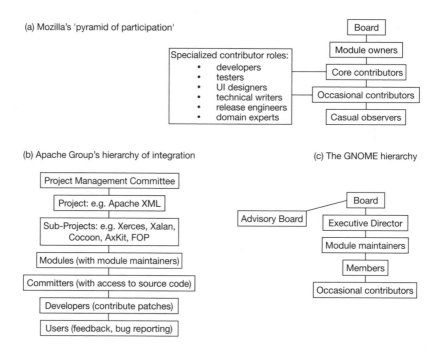

Figure 17.1—The hierarchical structure of OSS communities.

- *Members*. At the bottom are the individual members. These members are users who are also developers and, with the exception of a growing number of corporate employees, are self-selecting volunteers. In their early development, most projects experienced a debate over 'democracy versus meritocracy'. This debate was typically resolved by means of establishing different levels of community membership (for example, 'occasional contributors' and 'regular' or 'core contributors') with an established means for moving from one level to another. In most OSS communities, functional specialization was apparent among members. Such specialization of roles tended to emerge based on the interests and expertise of individual members. In others such roles became more formalized.

- *Middle management*. Modules and sub-modules were typically headed by a 'coordinator' or 'maintainer' or 'module owner'. These module managers were responsible for integrating the contributions from different community members, exercising quality control, and liaising with 'upper management' and other module managers over cross-module integration. On some projects there might be divided module leadership with coordination shared between several module maintainers. The process of appointing individuals to positions of module leadership varies between the different communities; in most projects they were voted by members.

- *Top management*. Overall coordination involves elements of autocratic leadership (by the founders of OSS projects), democracy, and representative governance. The tendency has been towards greater formalization over time. Thus, on the GNOME project, architectural decisions were taken democratically (through the gnome-dev-list mailing list) but in August 2000 a GNOME Foundation with an elected board of directors was created to coordinate and plan the entire project. The board comprises 11 directors formed into committees for specific activities. The executive work of the GNOME board is conducted by corporate officers that comprise a board chairman, a president (who acts as chief executive), a secretary, a treasurer, and additional vice-presidents. This tendency for OSS communities to incorporate – typically as non-profit corporations – has been a general feature of the organizational evolution of OSS communities.

Voluntary organizations differ from shareholder-owned corporations in relation to the sources of decision-making authority. In a shareholder-owned corporation, authority lies with the shareholders, who vest decision-making power in a board of directors. Executive power is then devolved downward from the board to salaried managers. In the case of voluntary, non-profit organizations, 'sovereignty' lies with the members. OSS communities are, in principle, democratic organizations where decision-making power moves bottom-up from the individual developers to the board and executive positions.

In practice, the situation is not so simple. As we shall see, an important feature of OSS communities is the role of charismatic leaders whose legitimacy arises from their role as founders and who continue to exert powerful informal (and sometimes formal) influence over strategy and specific decisions.

Finally, the increasing role of business corporations within OSS communities also represents the incursion of traditional company hierarchies into many aspects of OSS development. For example, the 2,000 IBM software engineers who are involved in various Linux projects participate as individual members. However, IBM's development work within the Linux operating environment is coordinated and directed within IBM. Similar corporate influence is exerted by the employees of Red Hat and Sun Microsystems within the GNOME project.

Organizational Routines

Organizational routines are regular, repetitive patterns of coordination that permit different specialists to input their distinctive skills while minimizing the need for communication and cross-learning between them. They provide the primary mechanism for different individuals to integrate their knowledge into the production of goods and services while preserving the efficiencies of knowledge specialization. Organizational routines tend to be closely complementary to rules in achieving coordination.

While most processes have rules in the form of standard operating procedures, such rules are rarely consulted by the individuals involved once coordination is made routine. In the case of OSS development, organizational routines are characterized by two main features.

First, they are relatively simple in terms of the sophistication of inter-personal coordination. The extent of modularization of software development is such that each individual can produce (report bugs, write code) individually. Hence, routines relate the sequencing of activities and patterns of interface between different members as compared to the more complex interdependency that occurs with simultaneous, synchronized production in a restaurant or a steel plant.

Second, routines tend to be sector-wide rather than specific to particular organizations. Thus, in the same way that routines for bricklaying are similar throughout the construction industry and routines for carrying out an appendectomy are similar among abdominal surgeons, so there tends to be considerable standardization of processes and procedures across the software sector. Hence, the organizational routines present in OSS communities tend to be independent of the two factors that are most closely associated with the superiority of firms as institutions for organizing production: co-location and continuity of association of organizational members.

Conditions Facilitating Coordination

The effectiveness of rules, directives, and routines in organizing production depends on the organizational conditions that facilitate cooperation and coordination among individuals. Several factors are involved.

Coordination between organizational members with differentiated knowledge sets requires the presence of common knowledge. The fact that almost all members of OSS communities are software engineers with common technical skills sets, common programming languages, and widely used development tools establishes a common platform of understanding at a high threshold. Technical competence engenders a high level of mutual respect that results from membership of an elite technical community. One of the contrasts made between commercial software produced by integrated companies and open-source software is that the latter is geared to the needs of leading-edge users. The direct involvement of customers as developers provides the key to exceptionally rapid development of improvements and new features.

The high level of common knowledge among community members is supported by a relatively low heterogeneity of knowledge. In contrast to most software multi-nationals that span a full range of business functions from research to product development and marketing and customer support, OSS communities are almost exclusively software development organizations. Marketing, sales, and customer support is provided by for-profit companies, many of which were founded by community members.

Coordination is supported by a cheap and highly effective communication medium. The take-off point of the OSS movement coincided closely with the emergence of the Internet. Not only does the Internet provide the framework for email communication, the distribution of tools and finished software, and integrating software contributions, it offers some of the fastest-growing and most successful applications of OSS (notably the Apache web server).

While common knowledge and a common communication network facilitate coordination, the effectiveness of coordination depends ultimately upon the will to cooperate. Two factors are critical: culture and leadership.

Culture

At the core of the culture of OSS communities is the ideology represented by Stallman and his Free Software Foundation. The basic tenet is that access to software code is a fundamental human freedom. This ideology has been defined by the opposition to commercial software. The OSS movement has adsorbed the mythology of J. R. R. Tolkien, *Star Wars,* and Camelot in identifying itself as a crusade for freedom against the forces of darkness represented by Microsoft. Yet the values and social norms of OSS communities predate the Free Software Foundation, tracing their roots to the hacker culture that emerged in the 1970s from the fusion of IT and hippydom. These values of individuality, anarchy, anti-corporatism, initiative, and fun create a global unity within OSS communities. They are found as much in Hamburg, London, and Mexico City as they are in Berkeley.

Leadership

In most of the OSS communities we examined, the founders continued to play a leading role. Despite their apparent absence of formal authority, most successful OSS projects featured a charismatic leader whose vision and technical prowess created credibility, trust, and direction. These leaders have included Linus Torvalds (Linux), Brian Behlendorf (Apache), Larry Wall (Perl), and Eric Allman (Sendmail).

The status of these individuals was enhanced by their leading roles in developing prototype versions of the software. Thus, in addition to the charismatic leadership conferred by their actions and values, they also derive legitimacy from the *de facto* ownership rights arising from their authorship of the founding contributions to the software.

Despite the democratic constitutions and ethos of most OSS communities, the founder-leaders demonstrate ongoing decision-making power. For example, Linus Torvalds continues to exercise a tight autocratic control over the Linux kernel.

Lessons Learned

The remarkable success of OSS in several types of computer software has generated considerable excitement over the prospects for community-based software development to transform the computer software industry.

Among the predictions are that the growing adoption of collaborative software development will change the global software industry by altering its economics of scale, location, and price; the growth of non-proprietary code will depress prices in the proprietary sector; the possession of source code will enable the growth of more software industrial centres around the world and their emergence will threaten the business of current leaders.

The purpose of this chapter is to explore some of these further implications, in particular the extent to which decentralized networks represent a viable alternative to the MNC for organizing international production. If one of the world's largest and most profitable multinationals, Microsoft, can lose out to an international community of hackers in web server software and is ceding market share to Linux in operating systems, this raises the question of whether there are other sectors where networked communities might substitute for multinational corporations.

In particular, if we regard economic organizations as complex adaptive systems they may have the potential to evolve to an area between static decay and chaos where self-organized adaptive change occurs. The management implications are considerable: if organizations with distributed intelligence and the capacity for self-organization can adapt more effectively to change than traditional command-and-control, top-down organizations, new approaches to leadership, strategy, and organization design are possible.

The performance of the more successful OSS projects – particularly in terms of the speed at which errors are corrected, new functions added, and customization for specific user needs is added – supports arguments for the adaptive efficiency of self-managed systems.

But are OSS projects really examples of decentralized, self-managed networks?

Despite speculation about the superiority of decentralized network organizations in business, empirical evidence is limited. Closer inspection of the co-evolutionary dynamics of self-organization often reveals the 'visible hand' of management. Such is the case with OSS communities. Claims that such organizations are exemplars of self-organizing complex adaptive systems conflict with much of our evidence regarding the structure and operation of OSS communities.

Our findings regarding the structures and processes through which coordination occurs in OSS communities suggest that rather than manifestations of 'self-organization', coordination occurs through the same kinds of structures and processes present in conventional business firms. Rules, directives, and routines provide the basic mechanisms for coordination. OSS communities are hierarchically organized modular structures and within these hierarchies authority is exercised both through the appointment of officers with specific decision-making powers and through the presence of founders who provide charismatic (and often autocratic) leadership.

Thus, while most aspects of the organizational context of OSS communities are very different from the MNCs that dominate the commercial segment of the industry, the mechanisms that permit coordination between the hundreds, even thousands, of developers are very similar.

Our second major finding concerned the potential for networked communities to be applied in other economic sectors. It is clear that OSS communities are a unique and novel organizational form. It is also apparent that they are the outcome of an unusual set of circumstances.

Networked communities have been successful in software development because:

- the key production workers are also the leading-edge consumers of the product;
- the projects have strong organizational cultures that facilitate cooperation and coordination because they draw their values and behavioural norms from the hacker community in which they have their origins;
- the nature of the product, namely its existence as programmed instructions written in code and accessible electronically from anywhere on the globe, greatly facilitates its geographically dispersed development.

Thus, OSS communities are very different from firms from the perspective of legal, contractual or ownership approaches to the theory of the firm.

Conclusion

OSS communities are one of the most interesting organizational innovations of the past two decades. In an era when production has become increasingly dominated by corporations committed to the maximization of shareholder value and deploying management techniques based on the provision of individual incentives, it is remarkable that organizations based upon such radically different principles could have achieved such widespread market success.

Yet, in terms of offering a new paradigm of the organization of international production, it would appear that decentralized, community-based networks offer only a modest threat to the dominant position of MNCs in the organization of international production. Despite all the enthusiasm with which management scholars have greeted ideas of self-management and distributed leadership, the basic fact is that, for all their novelty and radical ideology, OSS communities are organized along similar lines of hierarchy and adopt similar mechanisms of coordination as giant corporations.

Despite the evidence of democratic decision making, there is not much evidence of 'self-management' within OSS projects. The ability of OSS communities to utilize these conventional modes of coordination appears to be closely related to the specific technical features of software development and to the strong, unifying cultures that have provided the bedrock for OSS development. Establishing international decentralized networks in sectors that do not possess the common technical tools and languages of software engineering or well-established cultural links between community members are unlikely to provide such fertile ground for supporting such effective coordination.

Section 4

FINAL THOUGHTS

18 Management Research: Reprise and Prologue

John Stopford

London Business School

Strategy is often visible only after the event. Though I have always been curious about how managers add value to their organizations, that was not where I started. The three main strands of my research – which also form the organizing logic for this book – emerged only slowly as I asked questions at each step along the way. As a newly arrived foreign doctoral student at Harvard, I had the enormous good fortune to fall under the spell of Lawrence (later Dean) Fouraker, who was a fine empirical economist and later my first co-author. He introduced me to Raymond Vernon, another economist, who was initiating his mammoth research into the then-novel 'multinational enterprise'. I was hired to look at the organizational issues. I had no idea what would be involved but I was intrigued to find out.

That initial work focused on the formal organization structures of the 187 largest US-based multinationals of the mid-1960s. I had noticed that there were many patterns in the choices of structure and many common sequences of change. Looking back, it seems clear to me now that I was acting more as an engineer than an economist or managerial student: I was back in my MIT laboratory searching for regularities and causal linkages. I was searching for clues about how managers were solving one of the major problems of the day, namely how to design effective means of control and coordination of these far-flung empires and defeat the problems of geographical and cultural distance.

I was lucky. I found some strong patterns that could be labelled a 'model'. Structure was clearly linked to corporate strategy, though the causality of choice and timing of change could only be inferred. I was also fortunate that my thesis committee defended me against strong attack from the business policy faculty. In those days it was conventional for Harvard doctoral theses to examine in great detail the managerial behaviour of a few (usually no more than four) firms and to draw practical, general inferences from the observations. Large-sample work was regarded as heretical by many of my colleagues.

The act of examining a large sample of firms left me with more questions than I had at the outset. I had become conscious of the need to look closely at the role of individual managers, though I was not sure how to do this. Such words as experimentation, innovation, and entrepreneurship hardly appeared in my thesis but I sensed they would become important if I were to continue to examine these complex organizations. I also knew that the context within which mangers operated had an effect on their choices. In particular, Vernon's 1971 book *Sovereignty at Bay* made it inevitable that I would need to look at the political role of these enterprises if I were to take the initial arguments much further.

In effect, I had started a journey that has taken me down three distinct, though linked, paths. Each provides a context for asking questions about how outcomes are created. The first is the context of government and public policy. Here we have to conjure with major questions of *qui bono?* Who benefits in the globalizing economy? Can we rely on governments to be wise? How best can managers engage constructively in the debate?

The second context is the firm and its organizational architecture. How to determine and manage an appropriate level of complexity in multinational operations? How has the advent of both new technologies and new 'rules' of competition affected those choices? Are the dilemmas increasing as more design options become available?

The third context is about renewal. Sometimes organizational change cannot be accomplished merely by altering structures. A much more profound set of human changes is needed. Here personal leadership and the energy of a few exceptional individuals must be included in the inquiry. Structure and strategy are not determined primarily by external circumstance; they are the products of human imagination. We know there is no one best way to organize an activity, but what is best for a particular enterprise at a particular time?

This book moves from the very broad context of international policy to the context for the individual leader. It has many pieces from co-authors. To them and many others I owe a great intellectual debt. They have all helped to educate me in what is needed both in specialized areas and in making links across disciplines. In this short chapter, my purpose is to reflect on the changes in each of these three strands over the past few decades. Retrospection can then be turned into a prospective review of the research agenda today – the journey continues.

Rival States, Rival Firms

The late Susan Strange and I wrote a book with the above title as a way to link the field of international business to international relations. From our different perspectives, we shared a concern that all too often the contracts struck between multinationals and host states proved to be insufficiently robust to withstand the pressures of changing circumstance. In large part, we argued, this fragility of relationship came from the adversarial nature of the initial bargaining. Mutual ignorance allied with mutual distrust led to outcomes that satisfied no one and that were far short of what might be achieved in alternative forms of collaboration.

The wider context for our exploration of how collaboration might be achieved was our conviction that the very basis of competition among states was shifting from a competition over the control of more territory to a contest for *the means to create wealth* within their own territories. International relations was moving out of the Foreign Office and into commerce. All the recent trends of globalization and the social backlash suggest we were right in our diagnosis that the contest for wealth was central to the current debate. But we were right only in part, for we ignored the role of society in general and non-governmental organizations in particular. There are more players directly involved with a legitimate 'voice' to complicate the issues even more.

Equally salient is the contest for regulation and control. On the 'demand' side, some markets, as for many financial services, have become near boundary-less. Yet, on the 'supply' side, politics, regulation, and taxation remain nationally grounded. Consider the activity involved in the following transaction. An Indian computer engineer working for a Japanese multinational in Bangalore uses a satellite uplink to deploy machines located in New York and London to fix a client's computer system problem in Brazil.

In what currency is this work priced? Who gets to tax the transaction? Where does the profit from the work reside? (I am indebted to Steve Kobrin for this type of example of unclear regulations in the global economy.) The World Trade Organization cannot by itself devise systems and institutions capable of resolving the implied dilemmas of choice and regulation: many others must be involved.

In such a setting, the role of managers in multinationals takes on a new importance. How best can they enter the dialogue that is needed? A starting point is to think, as John Dunning does in an early chapter (page 14), about the moral nature of capitalism. Firms cannot survive without being sanctioned by society. If society considers that the recent scandals in Enron and some other major firms are indicative of a wider malaise, then the foundations of capitalism as we know it today will be attacked. Managers must, perforce, enter into the social dialogue. But how best to do this when they are not elected representatives remains an open research question, as Louis Turner knows well (page 3).

Though these issues are central in the debate about international wealth creation, few managers seem well equipped to be part of the dialogue. Moreover, few business schools pay much attention to them, preferring to concentrate on the familiar ground of product and market analyses. There is now a case to be made that management education should become less myopic and more attuned to the thought that senior managers in multinationals will become part of the new diplomacy.

Further complication arises from the fact that the structure of many markets remains far from global. As Alan Rugman and Alain Verbeke point out (page 45), the regional multinational is nearer the norm despite all the growth of cross-border transactions. The political and diplomatic interests of managers are not therefore uniform. Their plurality of interests can provide a cacophony of noise in societal negotiation. And yet, just as in the environmental debate, where large firms are both the major polluters and the owners of the resources needed for the clean-up, so multinationals are well positioned to be a central part of the movement towards wise and equitable regulation. Governance issues are moving centre stage, both inside the firm and between firms and society. The simple assumptions of good order can no longer be taken for granted.

Confronting Complexity

Thirty years ago, the multinational was distinct from national organizations both in its geographical 'reach' and in the managerial complexity it confronted. Over time, the barriers to internationalization have fallen and the population of multinationals has mushroomed. Today there are few, if any, large commercial organizations that are entirely national in the scope of their operations – from supply chains to customers. Consequently, the distinction between multinational enterprise and 'big business' has effectively disappeared. And many new firms are 'born global', especially in digital markets. For the purposes of organizational studies, the interest has shifted into what can more generally be called corporate strategy.

How can one satisfactorily explain the causes of firms' long-run performance? My original proposition was that a clear 'fit' between strategy and the organizational structure would produce superior returns. In the event, I could find no correlation at all. Instead of being curious about the absence of support for what seemed to be an entirely reasonable proposition, I left it to others to ask why. Their emerging answers are discussed elsewhere in this book and so do not need to be repeated here. They all share the common theme that it is not structure *per se* that shapes performance but rather the informal structures – the underlying processes and the people.

The field of strategy has moved a long way beyond the tenets of industrial economics. It is no longer held that industry structure is the prime determinant of firm performance: the variance of performance around the industry mean is simply too great. Besides, it is much less clear today than 30 years ago where the 'boundaries' to an industry lie. US banks now channel less than 20 % of the nation's money flow, having given way to new competitors like supermarkets and pension fund managers. Similarly, competitors with similar strategies, structures, and resources will experience quite different outcomes. One has to look at the 'dominant logic' a management team has adopted to determine its business mode to gain some clues as to how resources are both created and allocated.

My early work was done at a time when just a few multinationals were beginning to experiment with some form of a matrix organization. They were the multinationals at the extremes of complexity in the array of products, technologies, geographies, and cultures assembled to deliver returns to shareholders. They faced the most severe managerial challenges. Since then many others have joined those pioneers. Indeed, Christopher Bartlett and Sumantra Ghoshal's 1989 'transnational' organization – a development of my early 'grid' model – was presumed to be the ideal goal for multi-industry players. More recent evidence, however, has shown that the ensuing complexities for firms like ABB acted to reduce margins and erode competitiveness over time.

Even attempts to create a 'mental matrix' rather than a structural solution have lacked conviction. Yet, human ingenuity is unrestrained in the face of this challenge of complexity. In organizations that have been dubbed 'metanational', new approaches are visible to the old problem of managing the core asset of the firm – knowledge. Better ways to create and meld knowledge across internal boundaries may in turn inspire a whole new generation of organizational 'solutions' to the management of complexity. If the limits of both scale and complexity are pushed back, then perhaps we really will see the trillion-dollar corporation become a reality.

In addition to these internal process developments, complexity is also being addressed as managers choose different ways to draw a 'boundary' around the assets they plan to own. This is an age of outsourcing, indirect supply chain management, and, most notably, strategic alliances. One does not need to own an asset in order to control it, or at least gain benefit from its existence under someone else's ownership. Whereas the earlier debates about organization were to do with markets versus hierarchies, today we have to add the role of contracts. It is becoming commonplace for managers to talk about their 'asset ecologies' – those assets that help create value for them. Microsoft, it has been estimated, owns a mere four per cent of the assets that create its value. The rest of the value comes from contracts, such as those with IBM.

The consulting firm Accenture has recently estimated that strategic alliances of all types could contribute more than $25 trillion to the revenues of US firms by 2004. It also estimated that a substantial number of the Fortune 500 firms will have 40 % of their revenues and profits from alliances. Should this occur, many firms would have to modify quite seriously their approaches to organization. The dominant logic of organizing a hierarchy, albeit a flattening one, is quite different from that required to manage collaborative arrangements. Whereas many firms currently regard their alliances as exotic options at the periphery of their empires, tomorrow they will have to create alliance management capabilities as a central plank of their strategies.

All these options may serve to add back new complexity for management until the governance provisions and 'logic' are sorted out clearly. How managers go about the task will provide a fruitful and challenging domain for future research.

Rejuvenation

The third strand of the research is closely tied to the second. All the organizational options now available will no doubt spawn a new generation of competitors and force many incumbents dramatically to rethink their approaches if they are to survive. Old firms will have to find new ways to rejuvenate their operations. As they do, issues of leadership, entrepreneurship, and innovation will come centre stage in the puzzle about what really determines the performance of firms.

It is in this strand of work that the role of individual managers comes most clearly into focus. Do they really make a difference? If so, how? Charles Baden-Fuller and I have written on the role of individuals' ability to 'sense' opportunity before it can be proven in a separate chapter in this book (page 171). But that is only one small part of the puzzle.

Sumantra Ghoshal and Heike Bruch (page 179) emphasize the central importance of 'purposeful action taking by individuals'. This is not another 'great leader' explanation of superior performance. Rather it is a reflection on one of the central roles of leadership – to be able to induce in others the desire to reach for ambitious goals and get up and do something about getting there. Relatively few CEOs, it would seem, command this capability; for the *knowing–doing gap*, as Jeffrey Pfeffer and Robert Sutton call it, is pervasive. Managers all too seldom confront the inertia that can paralyse them and actively create their own futures.

In a curious way, one can see in the behaviour of senior managers leading their organization along the path of rejuvenation and discontinuous change the same effects that Dunning has raised in his work on moral capitalism. To be effective, one has to be fair. Moreover, one must be capable of inducing self-reliance and similar values into others. Neither firms' internal processes nor the wider system of capitalism can be effective in wealth creation without these and similar properties.

My colleagues have extensively covered the related dimensions of entrepreneurship and innovation. Costas Markides (pages 115 and 211) make the point that it is the rare incumbent competitor that can innovate strategically in its industry and create a 'climate' of entrepreneurship among units within a geographically dispersed hierarchy. Much easier to imitate or follow orders from the centre.

It is for this reason if no other that Charles and I were right when we observed that David (the small new entrant) could frequently defeat Goliath. We argued that competition was not merely a resource contest but also a contest among competing strategies. We now need to add that it is also a contest of the energetic and action-oriented teams versus the inert. And, as Markides observes, if Goliath were capable of learning rapidly from David he would use his bulk to win with the new competitive weapons.

Future Directions

Each of the three strands of the research that underpins the logic of this book is being drastically twisted and transformed by developments in the market place of ideas and actions. Where I could start with some very simple models and propositions to create a publishable piece, today a researcher needs to be much more adequately equipped to capture the nuances of those small differences that can, over time, add up to major discrepancies in performance.

Though I was indeed fortunate to start early in these strands of research, I find it tempting to think about starting all over again. There is a current of excitement as the pace of change seems to accelerate and the scope available to researchers widens. We can now ask new questions using quite different units of analysis. How best should research capture the nuances of effective behaviour? If we look only at exceptional individual managers we may lose sight of the impact of global structures or shifts in social expectations. But if we look only at industry structures or systems of capitalism, we risk falling into the old trap of inferring that structure is the dominant determinant of performance.

Generating a new sense of balance and linkage across disciplines, types of questions, and scope of analysis is a formidable task. Yet that is the challenge ahead if the field is to preserve its ability to turn research into signals that have an impact on practice. If we are to hold on to the sense of managerial relevance and not give in to the temptations to look solely at one of the many available options, we must retain an ability to ask 'big' questions and make real the old adage that 'there is nothing so practical as good theory'.

References

Ancona, Deborah, Kochan, Thomas B., Scully, Maureen, Van Maanen, John and Westney, D. Eleanor (1999). *Managing for the Future: Organizational Behavior and Processes* (second edition). Southwestern Press.

Anderson, P. (1999). Complexity theory and organizational science. *Organization Science,* **10**, 216–232.

Ante, S. E. (2001). Big Blue's big bet on free software. *Business Week*, December 7, pp. 56–57.

Argyris, C. and Schön, D. (1978). *Organizational Learning*. Reading, MA: Addison-Wesley.

Asakawa, K. and Doz, Y. L. (2001). Shiseido France 1998. INSEAD Case Study, Fontainebleau.

Ashby, W. R. (1952). *Design for a Brain*. London: Chapman & Hall.

Baden-Fuller, C. and Stopford, J. (1990). Corporate Rejuvenation. *Journal of Management Studies*, **4**, 21–33.

Baden-Fuller, C. W. and Stopford, J. (1991). Globalization frustrated: The case of white goods. *Strategic Management Journal*, **12**, 493–507.

Baden-Fuller, C. and Stopford, J. (1992). *Rejuvenating the Mature Business: The Competitive Challenge*. London: Routledge.

Baden-Fuller, C. and Stopford, J. M. (1994). *Rejuvenating the Mature Business*. Boston, MA: HBS Press.

Barney, J. B. (1991). Firm resources and sustained competitive advantage. *Journal of Management*, **17**, 99–120.

Barr, P. S. (1998). Adapting to unfamiliar environmental events: A look at the evolution of interpretation and its role in strategic change. *Organization Science,* **9**(6), 644–669.

Barr, P. S., Stimpert, J. L. and Huff, A. S. (1992). Cognitive change, strategic action, and organizational renewal. *Strategic Management Journal*, **13**, 15–36.

Bartlett, C. A. (1979). Multinational structural evolution: The changing decision environment in international division. Unpublished doctoral dissertation, Harvard University.

Bartlett, C. (1983). Procter & Gamble Europe: Vizir Launch. Harvard Business School case no. 9–384–139. Boston: Harvard Business School.

Bartlett, C. and Ghoshal, S. (1997). *The Individualized Corporation*. Harper Business.

Bartlett, C. and Ghoshal, S. (1989). *Managing Across Borders: The Transnational Solution*. Boston: HBS Press.

Bartlett, C., De Koning, A. and Verdin, P. (1999). Procter and Gamble Europe: Ariel Ultra's Eurobrand Strategy. INSEAD-HBS Case Study. Fontainebleau, France: INSEAD.

Baum, J. A. C. (1996). Organizational ecology. In: S. R. Clegg, C. Hardy and W. R. Nord (eds), *Handbook of Organisation Studies,* pp. 77–114. London: SAGE.

Beamish, P., Rosenzweig, P. M. and Inkpen, A. (1999). *International Management*. Boston: McGraw-Hill.

Berle, A. and Means, G. (1932). *The Modern Corporation and Private Property.* New York: Macmillan.

Berlin, I. (1991). *The Crooked Timber of Humanity.* London: Fontana.

Berstein, M. D. (ed.) (1966). *Foreign Investment in Latin America.* New York: Alfred A. Knopf.

Bettis, R. A. and Prahalad, C. K. (1995). The dominant logic: Retrospective and extension. *Strategic Management Journal,* **16**(1), 5–14.

Bilefshy, D. (2002). Philips sees 2002 as a turnaround year. *Wall Street Journal,* January 8.

Birkinshaw, J. (1996). How multinational subsidiary mandates are gained and lost. *Journal of International Business Studies,* **27**(3), 467–495.

Birkinshaw, J. (1997). Entrepreneurship in multinational corporations: the characteristics of subsidiary initiatives. *Strategic Management Journal,* **18**, 207–230.

Birkinshaw, J. (1998). Corporate entrepreneurship in network organizations: How initiatives drive internal market efficiency. *European Management Journal,* May.

Birkinshaw, J. (2000). *Entrepreneuship in the Global Firm.* London: Sage.

Birkinshaw, J. and Hood, N. (2001). Unleash innovation in foreign subsidiaries. *Harvard Business Review,* **79**(3), 131–137.

Birkinshaw, J., Hood, N. and Jonsson, S. (1998). Building firm-specific advantages in multinational corporations: The role of subsidiary initiative. *Strategic Management Journal,* **19**(3), 221–241.

Birkinshaw, J., Morrison, A. and Hulland, J. (1995). Structural and competitive determinants of a global integration strategy. *Strategic Management Journal,* **16**, 637–655.

Birkinshaw, J. M., Toulan, O. and Arnold, D. (2001). Global account management in multinational corporations: Theory and evidence. *Journal of International Business Studies,* **32**(2), 321–348.

Bodner, G. M., Gordon, M., Tang, C. and Weintrop, J. Both sides of corporate diversification: the value impacts of geographical and industrial diversification, NBER Working Paper No.6224. Cambridge, MA: National Bureau of Economic Research.

Bower, J. L. (1972). *Managing the Resource Allocation Process: A Study of Corporate Planning and Investment.* USA, Irwin.

Bower, J. L. and Christensen, C. M. (1995). Disruptive technologies: Catching the wave. *Harvard Business Review,* January–February, 43–53.

Brannen, M. Y. and Wilson III, J. M. (1996). Recontextualization and internationalization: Lessons in transcultural materialism from the Walt Disney Company. *CEMS Business Review,* **1**(1,2), 97–110.

Brown, G. (2003). Governments and supranational agencies: a new consensus? In: J. H. Dunning (ed.), *The Moral Imperatives of Global Capitalism.* Oxford: Oxford University Press.

Brown, S. L. and Eisenhardt, K. M. (1998). *Competing on the Edge: Strategy as Structured Chaos.* Boston: Harvard Business School Press.

Brunsson, N. (1982). The irrationality of action and action rationality: Decisions, ideologies and organizational actions. *Journal of Management Studies,* **19**, 29–34.

Brusco, S. (1982). The Emelian model: Productive decentralization and social integration. *Cambridge Journal of Economics,* **6**, 167–184.

Buckley, P. and Casson, M. (1976). *The Future of Multinational Enterprise.* London: Macmillan and Co.

Burgelman, R. A. (1994). Fading memories: A process theory of strategic business exit in dynamic environments. *Administrative Science Quarterly,* **39**(1), 24–56.

Butler, B., Sproull, L., Keisler, S. and Kraut, R. (2002). Community effort in online groups: Who does the work and why? In: S. Weisband and L. Atwater (eds), *Leadership at a Distance,* New Jersey: Erlbaum.

Calori, R., Baden-Fuller, C. and Hunt, B. (2000). Managing change at Novotel: Back to the future. *Long Range Planning,* **33**(6), 779–804.

Caves, R. E. (1971). International corporations: The industrial economics of foreign investment. *Economica,* **38**, 1–27.

Chandler, Alfred P. (1962). *Strategy and Structure: Chapters in the History of the American Industrial Enterprise*. Cambridge, MA: MIT Press.

Charitou, C. and Markides, C. (2002). Winning by standing still? How to respond to disruptive strategic innovation. LBS Working Paper, August 2002.

Christensen, C. M. (1997). *The Innovator's Dilemma: When New Technologies Cause Great Firms to Fail*. Boston, MA: Harvard Business School Press.

Clayton, L. A. and Conniff, M. L. (1999). *A History of Modern Latin America*. Fort Worth, TX: Harcourt Brace.

Conger, J. A., Spreitzer G. M. and Lawler E. E. (eds) (1999). *The Leader's Change Handbook*. San Francisco: Jossey-Bass.

Costin, H. and Vanolli, H. (eds) (1998). *Economic Reform in Latin America*. Fort Worth, TX: The Dryden Press.

Court, D., Leiter, M. and Loch, M. (1999). Brand leverage. *The McKinsey Quarterly*, **2**.

Cowan, G. A. (1994). Opening remarks. In: G.A. Cowan, D. Pines and D. Meltzer (eds), *Complexity, Metaphors, Models, and Reality*. Reading, MA: Santa Fe Institute, Addison-Wesley.

Dalai Lama (1999). *Ethics for the New Millennium*. New York: Riverhead Books.

Daniels, J. D. and Bracker, J. (1989). Profit performance: Do foreign operations make a difference? *Management International Review*, **29**(1), 46–56.

Daniels, J. D., Pitts, R. A. and Tretter, M. J. (1984). Strategy and structure of U.S. multinationals: An exploratory study. *Academy of Management Journal*, **27**(2), 292–307.

Daniels, J. D., Pitts, R. A. and Tretter, M. J. (1985). Organizing for dual strategies of product diversity and international expansion. *Strategic Management Journal*, **6**, 223.

Dasu, S. and de la Torre, J. (1997). Optimizing an international network of partially owned plants under conditions of trade liberalization. *Management Science*, **43**(3), 313–333.

Davidson, W. H. and Haspeslagh, P. (1982). Shaping a global product organization. *Harvard Business Review*, July–August, 125–132.

Davis, E. P. (1999). Institutionalization and EMU: Implications for European financial markets. *International Finance*, **2**(1), April, **33**.

Deal, T. E. and Kennedy, A. A. (1982). *Corporate Cultures*. Reading, MA: Addison-Wesley.

De Koning, A., Verdin, P. and Williamson, P. (1997). So you want to integrate Europe: How do you manage the process? *European Management Journal*, **15**, 252–265.

De Koning, A., Subraminian, V. and Verdin, P. (1999). Regionalization: Is it *the* way for the multinational? Euro-Asia Centre working paper number 60. Fontainebleau, France: INSEAD.

de la Torre, J. (1997a). Trade liberalization: The dilemma for multinationals. *Transformation*, **11**.

de la Torre, J. (1997b). Multinacionales en Latinoamérica: Estructuras organizacionales para el nuevo entorno. *Transformación estratégica: Una exigencia de hoy*, pp. 31–48. Lima, Peru: ESAN.

de la Torre, J., Esperança, J. P. and Martínez, J. (2002). Multinational corporate reaction to market liberalization: Strategy and structure in Latin American operations, 1990–2000. CIBER Working Paper, The Anderson School at UCLA, June.

De Tocqueville, A (1981). *Democracy in America* (abbreviated with an introduction by Thomas Bender). New York: The Modern Library.

Dibona, C. (1999). *Open Sources: Voices from the Open Source Revolution*. Sebastapol, CA: O'Reilly.

Dierickx, I. and Cool, K. (1989). Asset stock accumulation and sustainability of competitive advantage. *Management Science*, **35**, 1504–1513.

DiMaggio, P. J. and Powell, W. W. (1983). The iron cage revisited: Institutional isomorphism and collective rationality in organizational fields. *American Sociological Review*, **48**(2), 147–160.

Djankov, S., La Porta, R., Lopez de Silanes, F. and Shleifer, A. (2000). The regulation of entry. NBER working paper No. 7892.

Doz, Y. (1976). National policies and multinational management. Doctoral dissertation, Harvard University.

Doz, Y. and Prahalad, C. K. (1981). Headquarters influence and strategic control in MNCs. *Sloan Management Review*, **23**(1), 15–29.

Doz, Y. L. and Prahalad, C. K. (1987). Quality of management: An emerging source of global competitve advantage? In: N. Hood and J. E. Vahlne (eds), *Strategies in Global Competition*. London: John Wiley & Sons.

Doz, Y. and Prahalad, C. K. (1991). Managing DMNCs: A search for a new paradigm. *Strategic Management Journal*, **12**, 145–164.

Doz, Y., Santos, J. and Williamson, P. (2001). *From Global to Metanational: How Companies Win in the Knowledge Economy*. Boston: Harvard Business School Press.

Dunning, J. (1958). *American Investment in British Manufacturing Industry*. London: Allen and Unwin.

Dunning, J. H. (1981). *International Production and the Multinational Enterprise*. London: Allen & Unwin.

Dunning, J. H. (2001). Regions, globalization and the knowledge economy. *Global Capitalism at Bay*, pp. 195, 220. London: Routledge.

Dunning, J. H. (2003). *Making Globalization Good: The Moral Challenges of Global Capitalism*. Oxford: Oxford University Press.

Dunning, John H. and Mucchielli, Jean-Louis (2002). *Multinational Firms: The Global-Local Dilemma*. London: Routledge.

Dunning, J. H. and Pearce, R. D. (1981). *The World's Largest Industrial Enterprises*. UK: Westmead.

Dunning, J. H. and Rugman, A. M. (1985). The influence of Hymer's dissertation on the theory of foreign direct investment. *American Economic Review*, **75**(2), 228–232.

Dyas, G. P. and Thanheiser, H. T. (1976). *The Emerging European Enterprise: Strategy and Structure in French and German Industry*. London: Macmillan.

Dyer, G. (2002). GSK considers spinning off its research units. *Financial Times*, January 25, p. 15.

Eccles, R. (1981). The quasi firm in the construction industry. *Journal of Economic Behavior and Organization*, **2**, 335–357.

Eccles, R. G. and Nohria, N. (1999). *Beyond the Hype*. Boston, MA: HBS Press.

Economist, (2001). A great leap, preferably forward. January 20.

Edwards, S. (1995). *Crisis and Reform in Latin America: From Despair to Hope*. New York: Oxford University Press.

Egelhoff, W. G. (1982). Strategy and structure in multinational corporations: An information-processing view. *Administrative Science Quarterly*, **27**, 435–458.

Egelhoff, W. G. (1988). Strategy and structure in multinational corporations: A revision of the Stopford and Wells model. *Strategic Management Journal*, **9** (1), 1–14.

Egelhoff, W. G. (1991). Information processing theory and the multinational enterprise. *Journal of International Business Studies*, **22**(3), 341–368.

Egelhoff, William G. (1993). Information processing theory and the multinational corporation. In: Sumantra Ghoshal and D. Eleanor Westney (eds), *Organization Theory and the Multinational Corporation*, pp. 184–210. London: Macmillan.

Eisenstat, R. A., Foote, N., Galbraith, J. and Miller, D. (2001). Beyond the business unit. *McKinsey Quarterly*, **1**, 54–63,.

Enright, M. J. (2002). The globalization of competition and the localization of enterprises, 1970–79. *Management International Review*, **23**(2), 4–14.

Fielding, R. T. (1998). The Apache HTTP server project: Lessons learned from collaborative software development. Irvine, CA: University of California (http://www.ics,uci.edu/~fielding/talks/apache).

Fiol, C. M. and Lyles, M. A. (1985). Organizational learning. *Academy of Management Review*, **10**(4), 803–813.

Foote, N. W., Galbraith, J., Hope, Q. and Miller, D. (2001). Making solutions the answer. *McKinsey Quarterly*, **3**, 84–93.

Foreign Policy (2002). Globalization's last hurrah? *Foreign Policy*, January–February: 38–51.

Fortune (1992). A tough Swede invades the U.S. June 29.

Fouraker, L. E. and Stopford, J. M. (1968). Organizational structure and the multinational strategy. *Administrative Science Quarterly*, **11**(2), 47–64.

Franke, E. and von Hippel, E. (2002). Satisfying heterogeneous user needs via innovation toolkits: the case of Apache security software. MIT, Sloan School Working Paper, 4143–02.

Franko, L. G. (1976). *The European Multinationals*. London: Harper and Row; Stamford, CT: Greylock Press.

Franko, L. G. (1983). *The Threat of Japanese Multinationals – How the West Can Respond*. Chichester, UK: John Wiley & Sons; Geneva, Switzerland: IRM.

Franko, L. 1991. Global Corporate Competition II: Is the Large American Firm in decline? Business Horizons, **34**(6), 14–23.

Frost, T. S., Birkinshaw, J. and Ensign, P.C. (2002). Centers of excellence in multinational corporations: The characteristics of subsidiary initiatives. *Strategic Management Journal*, **23**, 997–1018.

Galbraith, J. K. (1967). *The New Industrial State*. Boston, MA: Houghton Mifflen.

Galbraith, J. (1973). *Designing Complex Organizations*. Reading, MA: Addison-Wesley.

Galbraith, J. (1977). *Organization Design*. Reading, MA: Addison-Wesley.

Galbraith, J. (1997). Managing the new complexity. IMD Working Paper.

Galbraith, J. R. (2000). *Designing the Global Corporation*. San Francisco: Jossey-Bass.

Galbraith, J. and Edstrom, A. (1976). International transfer of managers: Some important policy considerations. *Columbia Journal of World Business*, summer, 100–112.

Galbraith, J., Downey, D. and Kates, A. (2002). *Designing Dynamic Organizations*. New York: American Management Association.

Garten, Jeffrey E. (2002). *The Mind of the CEO*. New York: Perseus Publishing.

Gell-Mann, M. (1994). *The Quark and the Jaguar: Adventures in the Simple and the Complex*. New York: W. H. Freeman.

German, D. M. (2002). *The Evolution of the GNOME Project*. Victoria, BC: Department of Computer Science, University of Victoria, BC.

Gestrin, M., Knight, R. and Rugman, A. (1998). *The Templeton Global Performance Index*. Oxford: Templeton College.

Ghoshal, S. and Bartlett, C. (1990). The multinational and interorganizational network. *Academy of Management Review*, **15**, 626–646.

Ghoshal, S. and Nohria, N. (1993). Horses for courses: Organizational forms for multinational corporations. *Sloan Management Review*, Winter, 23–35.

GNOME Foundation (2002). Bylaws (http://foundation.gnome.org/bylaws.pdf).

Grant, R. M. (1996a). Toward a knowledge based theory of the firm. *Strategic Management Journal*, **17** (Winter special issue), 109–122.

Grant, R. M. (1996b). Prospering in dynamically competitive environments. *Organization Science*, **7**, 375–387.

Green, T. H. (1941). (1st Edition, 1882). *Lectures on the Principles of Political Obligation*. London.

Gupta, A. K. and Govindarajan, V. (2000). Knowledge flows within multinational corporations. *Strategic Management Journal*, **21**(4), 473–496.

Guth, W. D. and Ginsburg, A. (1990). Guest editors' introduction: Corporate entrepreneurship. *Strategic Management Journal*, **11**, 5–15.

Hall, W. (2001). Swiss electrical giant ABB launches sweeping revamp. *Financial Times*, January 12, p. 25.

Hamel, G. (1996). Strategy as revolution. *Harvard Business Review*, July–August, pp. 69–82.

Hamel, G. (1999). Bringing Silicon Valley inside. *Harvard Business Review*, September–October, pp. 71–84.

Hamel, G. (2000). *Leading the Revolution*. Boston, MA: Harvard Business School Press.

Hannan, M. T. and Freeman, J. H. (1984). Structural inertia and organizational change. *American Sociological Review*, **49**, 149–164.

Harrison, L. E. and Huntington, S. P. (eds.) (2000). *Culture Matters: How Values Shape Human Progress*. New York: Basic Books.

Hatch, M. J. (1998). Jazz as a metaphor for organizing in the 21st century. *Organization Science*.

Hawley, J. P. and Williams, Andrew T. (2000). *The Rise of Fiduciary Capitalism*. Philadelphia, PA: University of Pennsylvania Press.

Hayek, F. A. (1988). *The Fatal Conceit: The Errors of Socialism*. London: Routledge.

Heckhausen, H. (1991). *Motivation and Action* (2nd edn). Berlin: Springer.

Hedberg, B. and Jönsson, S. (1978). Designing semi-confusing information systems for organizations in changing environments. *Accounting, Organizations and Society*, **3**(1), 47–64.

Hedlund, G. (1981). Autonomy of subsidiaries and formalization of headquarters–subsidiary relations in Swedish MNCs. In: L. Otterbeck (ed.), *The Management of HQ–Subsidiary Relations in Multinational Corporations*, pp. 25–78. Aldershot, UK: Gower.

Hedlund, G. (1986). The hypermodern MNC – A heterarchy? *Human Resources Management*, **25**(1), 9–35.

Hedlund, G. (1994). A model of knowledge management and the N-form corporation. *Strategic Management Journal*, **15**, 73–90.

Himmelfarb, G. (1995). *The Demoralization of Society: From Victorian Virtues to Modern Values*. London Institute of Economic Affairs, Health and Welfare Unit.

HMSO (2000). *Eliminating World Poverty: Making Globalisation Work for the Poor*. London. HMSO: Cmd. 5006.

H. M. Treasury (2002). *The Case for Aid for the Poorest Countries*. London: H.M. Treasury.

Howard, Ann (ed.) (1995). *The Changing Nature of Work*. San Francisco: Jossey-Bass.

Hughes, T. P. (1983). *Networks of Power: Electrification in Western Society, 1880–1930*. Baltimore: The Johns Hopkins University Press.

Ietto-Gilles, G. (1998). Different conceptual frameworks for the assessment of the degree of internationalization: An empirical analysis of various indices for the top 100 transnational corporations. *Transnational Corporations*, **7**(1), 17–39.

Jarillo, J. C. and Martínez, J. I. (1990). Different roles for subsidiaries: The case of multinational corporations in Spain. *Strategic Management Journal*, **11**, 501–512.

Johnson, G. (1988). Rethinking incrementalism. *Strategic Management Journal*, **9**, 75–91.

Kanter, R. M. (1983). *The Change Masters: Innovation and Entrepreneurship in the American Corporation*. New York: Simon and Schuster.

Kauffman, S. A. (1995). Technology and evolution: Escaping the Red Queen effect. *The McKinsey Quarterly*, **1**, 118–129.

Kaufman, S. A. (1995). *At Home in the Universe: The Search for Laws of Self-Organization and Complexity*. New York: Oxford University Press.

Kim, W. C. and Mauborgne, R. (1997). Value innovation: The strategic logic of high growth. *Harvard Business Review*, January–February, 103–112.

Kogut, B. and Zander, U. (1992). Knowledge of the firm, combinative capabilities, and the replication of technology. *Organization Science*, **3**, 381–396.

Kogut, B. and Zander, U. (1996). What firms do: Coordination, identity, and learning. *Organization Science*, **7**, 502–518.

Kogut, B. and Zander, U. (1993). Knowledge of the firm and the evolutionary theory of the multinational corporation. *Journal of International Business Studies*, fourth quarter, 625–645.

Kotabie, M (1998). Efficiency versus effectiveness orientation of global sourcing strategy: A comparison of U.S. and Japanese multinational companies. *Academy of Management Review*, **12**(4), 109–119.

Kotter, J. P. and Heskett, J. L. (1992). *Corporate Culture and Performance*. New York: Free Press.

Kwong, K.-S. (1997). *Technology and Industry*. The Hong Kong Policy Studies Service, City University of Hong Kong Press.

Lal, D. (2003). Private morality and capitalism: Learning from the past. In Dunning, J. H. (ed.). *The Moral Challenges of Global Capitalism*. Oxford: Oxford University Press (forthcoming).

Lawrence, P. R. and Lorsch, J. (1967). *Organization and Environment: Managing Differentiation and Integration*. Boston, MA: Harvard University Press.

Lerner, J. and Tirole, J. (2000). The simple economics of open source. NBER Working Paper, Cambridge, MA.

Lessard, D. (1986). Finance and global competition. In: M. C. Porter (ed.), *Competition in Global Industries*. Boston, MA: Harvard Business School Press.

Lessard, D. (1989). Country risk and the structure of international financial intermediation. In: C. C. Stone (ed.), *Financial Risk: Theory, Evidence, and Implications*. Boston: Kluwer Academic Publishers.

Lessard, D. (1996). Incorporating country risk in project evaluation. *Journal of Applied Corporate Finance*, Autumn.

Lessard, D. and Nohria, N. (1990). Rediscovering functions in the MNC: The role of expertise in firms' responses to shifting exchange rates. In: Y. Doz, C. Bartlett and G. Hedlund (eds), *Managing Global Firms*. New York: Routledge.

Lester, R. and Berger, S. (eds) (1997). *Made by Hong Kong*. Oxford: Oxford University Press.

Levinthal, D. A. and March, J. G. (1993). The myopia of learning. *Strategic Management Journal*, **14**, 95–112.

Levinthal, D. A. and Warglien, M. (1999). Landscape design: Designing for local action in complex worlds. *Organization Science*, **10**, 342–357.

Lewin, A. Y. and Volberda, H. W. (1999). Prolegomena on co-evolution: A framework for research on strategy and new organizational forms. *Organization Science,* **10**(5), 519–534.

Lorenzoni, G. and Lipparini, A. (1999). The leveraging of interfirm relationships as a distinctive organizational capability: A longitudinal study. *Strategic Management Journal*, **20**, 317–338.

Lorenzoni, G. and Lipparini, A. (2001). The Honda effect, part 3: Network specific advantage in the Italian motorcycle industry. Paper presented at the Strategic Management Society Conference, Berlin.

Maljers, F., Baden-Fuller, C. and Van den Bosch, F. (1996). Maintaining strategic momentum: The CEO's agenda. *European Management Journal,* **14**(6), 555–561.

Malnight, T. (1995). Globalization of an ethnocentric firm: An evolutionary perspective. *Strategic Management Journal*, **16**, 119–142.

Malnight, T. (1996). The transition from decentralized to network-based MNC structures: An evolutionary perspective. *Journal of International Business Studies*, **27**, 43–66.

March, J. G. (1991). Exploration and exploitation in organizational learning. *Organization Science,* **2**(1), 71–87.

March, J. G. (1995). The future, disposable organizations, and the rigidities of imagination. *Organization,* **2**(3/4), 427–440.

Markides, C. C. (1997). Strategic innovation. *Sloan Management Review*, **38**(3), 9–23.

Markides, C. C. (1998). Strategic innovation in established companies. *Sloan Management Review*, **39**(3), 31–42.

Markides, C. C. and Stopford, J. (1995). From ugly ducklings to elegant swans: Transforming parochial firms into world leaders. *Business Strategy Review*, **6**(2), 1–24.

Marquand, M. and Reynolds, A. (1996). *The Global Learning Organization*. New York: Irwin Professional Publishing.

Marsh, P. (2002). Learning to live with downturn after the boom. *Financial Times*, pp. 10–11.

Martinez, J. I. and Jarillo, J. C. (1989). The evolution of research on coordination mechanisms in multinational corporations. *Journal of International Business Studies*, **20**(3), 489–514.

Martinez, J. I. and Jarillo, J. C. (1991). Coordination demands of international strategies. *Journal of International Business Studies*, **22**(3), 429–444.

McGahnan, A. M. and Porter, M. E. (1997). How much does industry matter, really? *Strategic Management Journal*, **18**, summer special issue.

McMillan, R. (2002). Interview: Linus's latest lieutenant. *Linus Magazine*, March.

McKelvey, W. (1999). Leading distributed intelligence: Strategy, microevolution, and complexity. UCLA working paper.

Medcof, J. W. (2001). Resource-based strategy and managerial power in networks of internationally dispersed technology units. *Strategic Management Journal*, **21**(11), 999–1012.

Miles, R. E. and Snow, C. (1994). *Fit, Failure, and the Hall of Fame: How Companies Succeed or Fail*. New York: Free Press.

Miller, R. and Lessard, D. (2000). *Strategic Management of Large Engineering Projects: Shaping Institutions, Risks, and Governance*. Cambridge, MA: The MIT Press.

Mintzberg, H. (1973). *The Nature of Managerial Work*. New York: Harper Collins.

Mintzberg, H. and Westley, F. (1992). Cycles of organizational change. *Strategic Management Journal*, **13**, 39–59.

Mitchell, Will, Shaver, J. M. and Yeung, B. (1992). Getting there in a global industry: Impacts on performance of changing international presence. *Strategic Management Journal*, **13**, 419–432.

Montgomery, D., Yip, G. and Villalonga, B. (2002). An industry explanation of global account management. Working paper.

Morrison, A., Ricks, D. and Roth, K. (1991). Globalization versus regionalization: Which way for the multinational? *Organizational Dynamics*, **19**, 17–29.

Murray, J. Y., Wildt, A. R. and Kotabe, M. (1995). Global sourcing strategies of US subsidiaries of foreign multinationals. *Management International Review*, **35**(4), 307–317.

Nadeau, Tom (2001). Learning from Linux, www.os2hq.com/archives/linmemo1.htm.

Nadler, D. A. and Tushman, M. L. (1997). *Competing by Design: The Power of Organizational Architecture*. New York: Oxford University Press.

Nelson, R. R. and Winter, S. G. (1982). *An Evolutionary Theory of Economic Change*. Cambridge, MA: Harvard University Press.

Nohria, N. and Ghoshal, S. (1997). *The Differentiated Network: Organizing Multinational Corporations for Value Creation*. San Francisco: Jossey-Bass Inc.

Nonaka, I. and Takeuchi, H. (1995). *The Knowledge-Creating Company*. New York: Oxford University Press.

Nonaka, I., Toyama, R. and Konno, N. (2000). SECI, Ba and leadership: A unified model of dynamic knowledge creation. *Long Range Planning*, **33**, 5–34.

Novak, M. (1991). *The Spirit of Democratic Capitalism*. Lanham, Maryland: Madison Books.

O'Donnell, S. W. (2000). Managing foreign subsidiaries: Agents of headquarters, or an independent network? *Strategic Management Journal*, **21**, 525–548.

O'Mahony, S. (2001). Adapting to a new commercial actor: Community managed software projects. Department of Management Science and Engineering, Stanford University, October 30.

Ouchi, W. G. and Johnson, J. B. (1978). Types of organizational control and their relationships to emotional well being. *Administrative Science Quarterly*, **23**, 293–317.

Pantzalis, C. (2001). Does location matter? An empirical analysis of geographic scope and MNC market valuation. *Journal of International Business Studies*, **31**(1).

Perlmutter, H. V. (1969). The tortuous evolution of the multinational corporation. *Columbia Journal of World Business*, **4**, 9–18.

Pfeffer, Jeffrey and Sutton, Robert I. (2000). *The Knowing–Doing Gap: How Smart Companies Turn Knowledge into Action*. Harvard Business School Press.

Poole, M. S. and Van de Ven, A. H. (1989). Using paradox to build management and organization theories. *Academy of Management Review*, **14**(4), 562–578.

Porter, M. E. (1990). *The Competitive Advantage of Nations*. London: Macmillan.

Porter, M. E. (1996). What is strategy? *Harvard Business Review*, November–December, 61–78.

Porter, M. E. (1986). Changing patterns of international competition. *California Management Review*, **27**, 9–40.

Prahalad, C. K. (1976). The strategic process in a multinational corporation. Unpublished doctoral dissertation. School of Business Administration, Harvard University.

Prahalad, C. K. and Bettis, R. A. (1986). The dominant logic: A new linkage between diversity and performance. *Strategic Management Journal*, **7**(6), 485–501.

Prahalad, C. K. and Doz, Y. (1987). *The Multinational Mission: Balancing Local Demands and Global Vision*. New York: The Free Press.

Prebisch, R. (1964). *Towards a Dynamic Development Policy for Latin America*. New York: United Nations.

Raymond, E. S. (2001). *The Cathedral and the Bazaar* (2nd edn). Sebastopol, CA: O'Reilly.

Redwood, S., Goldwasser, C. and Street, S. (1999). *Action Management*. New York: John Wiley & Sons.

Reed, R. and deFillippi, R. (1990). Causal ambiguity, barriers of imitation and sustainable competitive advantage. *Academy of Management Review*, **15**(1), 88–102.

Root, Franklin R. (1994). *Entry Strategies for International Markets*. New York: Lexington Books.

Rosenberg, D. K. (2001). *The Coming Software Revolution*. Stromian Technologies.

Ross, S. A., Westerfield, R. W. and Jordan, B. (1991). *Fundamentals of Corporate Finance*. Homewood, IL: Irwin.

Roth, K. (1992). International configuration and coordination archetypes for medium-sized firms in global industries. *Journal of International Business Studies*, **23**(3), 533–549.

Roth, K., Schweiger, D. and Morrison, A. J. (1991). Global strategy implementation at the business unit level: Operational capabilities and administrative mechanisms, *Journal of International Business Studies*, **22**(3): 361–94.

Rugman, A. M. (1979). *International Diversification and the Multinational Enterprise*. Lexington, MA: Lexington Books.

Rugman, A. M. (1985). The comparative performance of U.S. and European multinational enterprises, 1970–79. *Management International Review*, **23**(2), 4–14.

Rugman, A. M. (1987). Multinationals and trade in services: A Transaction cost approach. *Weltwirtschaftliches Archiv*, **123**(4), 651–667.

Rugman, A. M. (2000). *The End of Globalization*. London: Random House; New York: Amacom.

Rugman, A. M. and D'Cruz, J. R. (2000). *Multinationals as Flagship Firms: Regional Business Networks*. Oxford: Oxford University Press.

Rugman, A. M. and Verbeke, A. (1990). *Global Corporate Strategy and Trade Policy*. London: Routledge.

Rugman, A. M. and Verbeke, A. (1993) *Research in Global Strategic Managment (4): Global Competition beyond the Three Generics*. Greenwich, CT: JAI Press.

Rugman, A. M. and Verbeke, A. (2001). Location, competitiveness and the multinationaal enterprise. In: A. M. Rugman and T. Brewer (eds), *The Oxford Handbook of International Business*, pp. 150–180. Oxford: Oxford University Press.

Rumelt, R. P. (1974). *Strategy, Structure and Economic Performance*. Cambridge, MA: Harvard Business School Division of Research.

Rumelt, R. P. (1984). Toward a strategic theory of the firm. In: R. B. Lamb (ed.), *Competitive Strategic Management*, pp. 566–570. Englewood Cliffs, NJ: Prentice-Hall.

Rumelt, R. P. (1991). How much does industry matter? *Strategic Management Journal*, **12**, 167–185.

Sadtler, D., Campbell, A. and Koch, R. (1997). *Breakup! Why Large Companies Are Worth More Dead Than Alive*. Capstone.

Safarian, A. E. (1966). *Foreign Ownership of Canadian Industry*. Toronto: McGraw-Hill.

Santos, J. (in press). STMicroelectronics. INSEAD Case Study. Fontainebleau, France: INSEAD.

Schlie, E. H. and Yip, G. (2000). Regional follows global: Strategy mixes in the world automotive industry. *European Management Journal*, **18**(4), 343–356.

Schnaars, S. P. (1994). *Managing Imitation Strategies*. New York: The Free Press.

Schumpeter, J. A. (1934). *The Theory of Economic Development*. Cambridge, MA: Harvard University Press.

Schutte, H. (1998). Between headquarters and subsidiaries: The RHQ solution. In: J. Birkinshaw and N. Hood (eds), *Multinational Corporate Evolution and Subsidiary Development*, pp. 268–298. Basingstoke: Macmillan.

Scott, W. R. (1992). *Organizations: Rational, Natural, and Open Systems*. Englewood Cliffs, NJ: Prentice-Hall.

Searle, G. R. (1998) *Morality and the Market in Victorian Britain*. New York: Clarendon Press, Oxford University.

Seligman, M. (1975). *Learned Optimism*. New York: Knopf.

Selznick, P. (1957). *Leadership in Administration: A Sociological Interpretation.* New York: Harper & Row.

Shapiro, A. (1999). *Multinational Financial Management*, sixth edn. Upper Saddle River, NJ: Prentice-Hall.

Skidmore, T. E. and Smith, P. H. (1989). *Modern Latin America* (2nd edn). New York: Oxford University Press.

Skoknic, E. S. (1993, revised 1999). Endesa. Institutor Adolfo Ibanez. Reprinted in J. de la Torre *et al.*

Slywotzky, A. J. (1996). *Value migration: How to Think Several Moves Ahead of the Competition.* Boston, MA: Harvard Business School Press.

Smircich, L. and Stubbart, C. (1985). Strategic management in an enacted world. *Academy of Management Review,* **10**(4), 724–736.

Spender, J.-C. (1980). Strategy making in business. University of Manchester, Doctoral dissertation.

Stopford, J. (1982). *The World Directory of Multinational Enterprises 1982–83.* London: Macmillan.

Stopford, J. (1995). Competing globally for resources. *Transnational Corporations,* **4**(2), 34–57.

Stopford, J. M. and Baden-Fuller, C. (1988). Why global manufacturing. *Multinational Business,* 15–25.

Stopford, J. and Baden-Fuller, C. (1994). Creating corporate entrepreneurship. *Strategic Management Journal,* **15**, 521–536.

Stopford, J. and Dunning, J. (1982). *Multinationals: Company Performance and Global Trends.* London: Macmillan.

Stopford, J. and Strange, S. (1991). *Rival States, Rival Firms: Competition for World Market Shares.* Cambridge: Cambridge University Press.

Stopford, J. and Turner, L. (1985). *Britain and the Multinationals.* Chichester, UK: John Wiley & Sons; Geneva, Switzerland: IRM.

Stopford, J. M. and Wells, L. T. (1972). *Managing the Multinational Enterprise: Organization of the Firm and Ownership of the Subsidiaries.* New York: Basic Books.

Stout, Lynn (2001). Review of the Rise of Fiduciary Capitalism by James Hawley and Andrew Williams. *The Journal of Economic Literature.* XXIX(4) December: 1248–1249.

Sull, D. (1999). Why good companies go bad. *Harvard Business Review.* July–August. **77**(4), 42–51.

Sullivan, Daniel (1994). Measuring the degree of internationalization of a firm. *Journal of International Business Studies,* **25**(2), 325–342.

Tellis, G. J. and., Golder, P. N. (2002). *Will and Vision: How Latecomers Grow to Dominate Markets.* New York: McGraw-Hill.

Thompson, J. D. (1967). *Organizations in Action: Social Science Bases of Administrative Theory.* New York: McGraw Hill.

Tushman, M. (1979). Managing communication networks in R&D laboratories. *Sloan Management Review,* **20**(Winter), 37–49.

UNCTAD (1995). *World Investment Report, 1995: Transnational Corporations and Competitiveness.* New York and Geneva: United Nations.

Ushijima, T. (2002). Multinationality, over-extension, and the value of the firm. Working paper, The Anderson School at UCLA, May.

Vaill, P. (1982). The purposing of high performing systems. *Organization Dynamics,* Autumn, 23–40.

Van der Haas, H. (1967). *The Enterprise in Transition.* London: Tavistock.

Van Heck, N. and Verdin, P. (1996). *The European Temporary Work Services Industry in 1994.* Leuven: K.U. Leuven.

Van Heck, N. and Verdin, P. (1996). 3M Europe Case. Adaptation of Muzyka, D. and Ackenhusen, M., INSEAD and K.U. Leuven.

Verdin, P. and Van Heck, N. (2001). *From Local Champions to Global Masters: A Strategic Perspective on Managing Internationalisation.* London: Palgrave.

Vernon, R. (1966). International investment and international trade in the product life-cycle. *Quarterly Journal of Economics*, **80**, 190–207.

Vernon, R. (1971). *Sovereignty at Bay.* New York: Basic Books.

Vernon, R. (1979). The product cycle hypothesis in a new international environment. *Oxford Bulletin of Economic and Statistics*, **41**(4), 255–267.

Volberda, H. W. (1996). Towards the flexible firm: How to remain vital in hypercompetitive environments. *Organization Science*, **7**(4), 359–374.

Volberda, H. W. (1998). *Building the Flexible Firm: How to Remain Competitive.* Oxford: Oxford University Press.

Volberda, H., Baden-Fuller, C. and Van den Bosch, F. (2001). Mastering strategic renewal. *Long Range Planning*, **34**, 159–178.

Weick, K. E. (1979). *The Social Psychology of Organizing.* Reading, MA: Addison-Wesley.

Wells, L. T. and Gleason, E. S. (1995). Is foreign infrastructure investment still risky. *Harvard Business Review* (September–October).

Westney, D., Westney, E. and Zaheer, S. (2001). The multinational corporation as an organization. In: Alan Rugman and Tom Brewer (eds), *The Oxford Handbook of International Business*, pp. 349–379. Oxford: Oxford University Press.

White, R. E. and Poynter, T. E. (1990). Organizing for worldwide advantage. In: C. A. Bartlett, Y. L. Doz and G. Hedlund (eds), *Managing the Global Firm.* London: Routledge Press.

Wiechmann, U. (1974). Integrating multinational marketing activities. *Columbia Journal of World Business*, Winter, 7–16.

Williamson, P. (1997). Asia's new competitive game. *Harvard Business Review*, September–October.

Williamson. P. (1999). Strategy as options on the future. *Sloan Management Review*, **40**(3), 117–126.

Williamson, P. (2002). ARM Holdings Plc. INSEAD Case Study, Fontainebleau.

Wolff, J. and Egelhoff, W. (2002). A reexamination and extension of international strategy-structure theory. *Strategic Management Journal*, **23**, 181–189.

World Bank. (1999). *Attacking Poverty. World Development Report 2000–2001.*

Yip, G. S. (2000). *Asian Advantage.* Cambridge, MA: Perseus Publishing.

Yip, G. S. (2001). Global strategy in the 21st century. In: Crainer, S. and Dearlove, D. (eds), *Financial Times Handbook of Management*, 2nd edn, pp. 150–163. London: Financial Times/Prentice Hall.

List of Contributors

Charles Baden-Fuller is Professor of Strategy at the Cass Business School, City University London and Research Professor at the Rotterdam School of Management, Erasmus University. He has published extensively with John Stopford on the subject of rejuvenation of firms and on globalisation. He has also done much work on cognition (with Joseph Porac) and on renewal (with Henk Volberda) and is currently working on biotechnology. He is the editor-in-chief of *Long Range Planning*.

Julian Birkinshaw is Associate Professor and co-chair of Strategic and International Management at the London Business School. He is a graduate of the Richard Ivey School of Business, and a former faculty member of the Stockholm School of Economics. He is the author of five books, including *Entrepreneurship in the Global Firm* and *Inventuring: Why big companies must think small* (with W. Buckland and A. Hatcher). He has published extensively on issues of strategy, entrepreneurship and knowledge management in large multinational firms.

Heike Bruch is Professor and Director at the Institute for Leadership and HRM of the University of St. Gallen (Switzerland). Her research interests include managers' emotion, volition and action as well as leadership in change processes and organizational energy. She is a consultant to several large European and U.S. companies.

Yves L. Doz is the Timken Professor of Global Technology and Innovation at INSEAD, in Fontainebleau, France. Between 1990 and 1995, he was associate dean for R&D, and between 1999 and 2002 he was dean of Executive Education at INSEAD. He has also served in the faculty of the Harvard Business School and held visiting appointments at Stanford University and at Aoyama Gakuin University in Japan. Yves has consulted for many multinational corporations. He has published five books on the strategy and organization of multinational companies – the most recent, *From Global to Metanational*, co-authored with José Santos and Peter Williamson, was published in 2001 by Harvard Business School Press.

John Dunning is Emeritus Professor of International Business at the University of Reading, U.K., and State of New Jersey Emeritus Professor of International Business at Rutgers University, New Jersey, U.S.A. He is also Senior Economic Adviser to the Director of the Division on Transnational corporations and Investment of UNCTAD in Geneva. He has been researching into the economics of international direct investment and the multinational enterprise since the 1950s. He has authored, co-authored, or edited 40 books on this subject and on industrial and regional economics.

José Paulo Esperança is Professor of International Financial Management at ISCTE, in Lisbon, Portugal, where he directs the management PhD program. He has written and consulted on service industries, the internationalization of small firms, governance issues, and questions of international financing and venture capital. His publications have appeared in *Portuguese Review of Financial Markets, Journal of Multinational Financial Management* and *Journal of Applied Financial Economics.*

Lawrence G. Franko is a Professor of Finance and Strategic Management in the College of Management of the University of Massachusetts, Boston. He is also Senior Investment Advisor with Thomas Weisel Partners Asset Management. He has a DBA from the Harvard Business School, and degrees from The Fletcher School of Law and Diplomacy and Harvard College. He is the author of many articles and books, notably *The European Multinationals, The Threat of Japanese Multinationals*, and *Joint Venture Survival in Multinational Corporations.*

Sumantra Ghoshal is Professor of Strategic and International Management at the London Business School. He is a graduate of both the Harvard Business School (DBA) and MIT (PhD), and held prior faculty positions at INSEAD and MIT. He is a leading authority on issues of strategy, organisation and management in large multinational firms. He has written 9 books, including *Managing Across Borders: The Transnational Solution, The Individualized Corporation* (both with C.A. Bartlett), *The Differentiated Network* (with N. Nohria) and *Organization Theory and the Multinational Corporation* (With D.E. Westney).

Robert Grant is Professor of Management at Georgetown University where he teaches strategic management. His current interests are knowledge management and the knowledge-based view of the firm, the nature and sources of organizational capability, and strategic planning processes in large companies.

Alice de Koning (Ph.D., INSEAD) is Assistant Professor in Management and Entrepreneurship at J. Mack Robinson College of Business, Georgia State University (USA).

Donald R. Lessard is the Epoch Foundation Professor of International Management and Deputy Dean at the MIT Sloan School of Management. He has published extensively on risk management, global strategy, international corporate finance, and emerging markets finance. He has been consultant to banks, firms and government agencies throughout the world and is a senior advisor to the Brattle Group. His latest book, *Strategic Management of Large Engineering Projects; Shaping Institutions, Risks, and Governance* (with Roger Miller) was published by The MIT Press in February 2001.

Anthony Leung holds a Ph.D. in Marketing from the Manchester School of Management, UMIST, and completed a post-doctorate at Cambridge. He is an independent researcher, consultant and adviser to private family businesses. He is currently conducting research on global aspects of the Chinese herbal medicine industry. Member of the Hong Kong Management Association.

Andrea Lipparini is Professor of Management at the Catholic University of Milan. His research focuses upon strategy and organizational capability within inter-firm networks. He is the author of *La Gestione Strategica del Capitale Intellettuale e del Capitale Sociale* (Mulino, Milan, 2002).

Gianni Lorenzoni is Professor of Management at the University of Bologna and chairman of the AlmaCube, an incubator for start-up companies. He is known for his research into Italian regional clusters and his analysis of the efficiency and innovation benefits arising from inter-firm collaboration.

Constantinos Markides holds the Robert P. Bauman Chair in Strategic Leadership at the London Business School where he teaches strategic management. A native of Cyprus, he received his MBA and DBA from the Harvard Business School. He is the author of three books, *Diversification, Refocusing and Economic Performance* (1995), *All the Right Moves: A Guide to Crafting Breakthrough Strategy* (1999), and *Strategic Thinking for the Next Economy* (2001, with M. Cusumano), and numerous articles in such leading journals as Harvard Business Review, Sloan Management Review, Strategic Management Journal and the Academy of Management Journal.

Jon I. Martínez is Professor of International Strategy and Management and holds the Jorge Yarur B. Chair on Families in Business at ESE, Universidad de los Andes in Santiago, Chile. He has done research and consulted on the internationalization process of small-to-medium size firms, multinational strategies and coordination mechanisms, and the strategy of subsidiaries of multinational companies. He has published a book on these topics, *Estrategia Internacional* (McGraw-Hill, 1991), and articles in *Journal of International Business Studies, Strategic Management Journal, Sloan Management Review, International Marketing Review,* and *Journal of Business Research*.

Elaine Romanelli is Associate Professor of Management at Georgetown University where she teaches strategic management and directs the Global Entrepreneurship Studies Program. Her research examines the development of regional industry clusters and the role of such clusters on organizational strategy and survival.

Alan M. Rugman is L. Leslie Waters Chair of International Business at the Kelley School of Business, Indiana University, where he is also Professor of International Business and Professor of Business Economics and Public Policy. Dr Rugman has published over 200 articles and is the author of over thirty books including *The End of Globalization*. He was Thames Water Fellow in Strategic Management at Templeton College, University of Oxford from 1998–2001, where he remains a Fellow.

José F. P. dos Santos is a professor of International Management at INSEAD, in Fontainebleau, France. He is also a guest professor at the Catholic University at Porto, Portugal, and has held visiting appointments at Bocconi University, Italy, Bled School of Management, Slovenia, and Fundação Dom Cabral, Brazil. José has an extensive experience as an executive: When he returned to the academic world in 1995, he had held for ten years the position of member of the board of directors and Managing Director of Segafredo Zanetti, an Italian multinational. He has also served as non-executive director of various corporations. His research area is naturally the management of multinational firms, and in particular on innovation and global customer management.

Örjan Sölvell is a Professor of International Business and has been active at the Institute of International Business, IIB, in Stockholm, for over 20 years. He was Director of IIB between 1994–2002. Professor Sölvell has done extensive research in the areas of international competitiveness, and competition and strategy. Since 2000 he has also been a fellow at the Institute for Strategy and Competitiveness, ISC, at Harvard Business School, under leadership of Professor Michael E. Porter.

John Stopford has recently retired from the London Business School, where he was Professor of International Business and chairman of the world-class strategy department. His publications include 20 books and monographs and over 80 scholarly articles. He is an engineer by original training and has held many posts in industry and government. He is now active as a consultant to multinational corporations and studies managerial processes both for managing strategic alliances and for organizational learning.

Venkat Subramanian is a Doctoral Research Fellow in Strategy and Finance at Solvay Business School. He has worked extensively on international strategy, value-based management, performance drivers and country importance to shareholder value creation.

Siri Terjesen is a doctoral candidate at London Business School. She holds degrees from the Norwegian School of Economics and Business, and the University of Richmond, Virginia. Her current research interests are in International Management, and corporate and divisional headquarter location.

José R. de la Torre is Dean of the Alvah H. Chapman Graduate School of Business and holds the Byron Harless Eminent Scholar Chair at Florida International University. He was previously Professor of International Business at the Anderson School at UCLA, and INSEAD. He is co-author of *Managing the Global Corporation* (McGraw-Hill, 2000) and serves as a director of several international companies. His recent research deals with the impact of e-commerce on global business, multinational corporate reaction to regional market liberalization, and the management of international collaborative agreements, which has appeared in the *Journal of International Business Studies*, *Management Science*, *Organization Science*, and the *California Management Review*.

Louis Turner is the Chief Executive of the Asia-Pacific Technology Network. In 1970, he published *Invisible Empires*, an early attack on Multinational Companies. Since then he has written another ten books on various aspects of the International Political Economy , including *Britain and the Multinationals,* written with John Stopford. Since 1986, he has focused on running high-level conferences, increasingly on Asian Technology.

Alain Verbeke holds the McCaig Chair in Management at the Haskayne School of Business, University of Calgary and is an Associate Fellow of Templeton College, University of Oxford. He has authored or edited 15 books and more than 160 refereed publications, including several recent articles in Strategic Management Journal and Journal of International Business Studies. His present research focuses on key governance challenges faced by many large MNEs, especially the internal limits to global strategies.

Paul Verdin (Ph.D. Econ., Harvard) is Professor and Chair in Strategy and Organization at Solvay Business School (Université Libre de Bruxelles). He is also Professor of Strategy and International Management at K.U.Leuven (Belgium) and at INSEAD (France). His most recent book, *From Local Champions to Global Masters: A Strategic Perspective on Managing Internationalisation* (with N. Van Heck) is a guide to the many pitfalls and real opportunities in the management of internationalisation.

Eline Van Poeck (M.A.in Economics and International Relations), is a Research Associate in International Management at K.U.Leuven.

D. Eleanor Westney is the Society of Sloan Fellows Professor in the Strategy and International Management group at the M.I.T. Sloan School of Management. Her research has focused on the cross-societal transfer and adaptation of organizational patterns. With Sumantra Ghoshal she edited *Organization Theory and the Multinational Corporation* and she is one of the authors of *Managing for the Future,* a text on organization processes written with Sloan School colleagues.

Peter Williamson is Professor of International Management and Asian Business at the INSEAD in Fontainebleau, France and Singapore. He was formerly Dean of MBA Programmes at London Business School and Visiting Professor of Global Strategy and Management at Harvard Business School. Professor Williamson's research and publications span globalisation, strategy innovation, joint ventures and alliances, and competitive dynamics. His books include *The Economics of Financial Markets (1995)*; *Managing the Global Frontier* (1994); and *The Strategy Handbook (1992)*. Peter has acted as consultant on business strategy and international expansion to numerous multinational companies in Asia/Pacific, Europe and North America. He is a non-executive director of several listed companies.

George Yip is Professor of Strategic and International Management at the London Business School where he is also Associate Dean, MBA program and Andersen Research Fellow. He held prior faculty positions at Cambridge University, UCLA, Georgetown University, and Harvard Business School. He is the author of 9 books, including *Total Global Strategy II, Asian Advantage: Key strategies for winning in the Asia-Pacific region* and *Strategies for central and Eastern Europe* (with A. Kozminski). He is the author of more than 50 articles in such journals as Harvard Business Review, Sloan Management Review and Strategic Management Journal.

Index

Note: Page references in *italics* refer to Figures; those in **bold** refer to Tables